Theta Theory

Studies in Generative Grammar 78

Editors

Henk van Riemsdijk
Harry van der Hulst
Jan Koster

Mouton de Gruyter
Berlin · New York

Theta Theory

by

Martin Haiden

Mouton de Gruyter
Berlin · New York

Mouton de Gruyter (formerly Mouton, The Hague)
is a Division of Walter de Gruyter GmbH & Co. KG, Berlin.

The series Studies in Generative Grammar was formerly published by
Foris Publications Holland.

♾ Printed on acid-free paper which falls within the guidelines
of the ANSI to ensure permanence and durability.

Library of Congress Cataloging-in-Publication Data

Haiden, Martin, 1969–
Theta theory / by Martin Haiden.
p. cm. – (Studies in generative grammar ; 78)
Includes bibliographical references and index.
ISBN 3-11-018285-8 (cloth : alk. paper)
1. Lexicology. 2. Cognition. 3. Semantics. 4. Grammar, Comparative and general – Syntax. 5. German language – Verb. I. Title. II. Series.
P326.H347 2005
413.028–dc22

2005011293

ISBN 3-11-018285-8

Bibliographic information published by Die Deutsche Bibliothek

Die Deutsche Bibliothek lists this publication in the Deutsche Nationalbibliografie;
detailed bibliographic data is available in the Internet at <http://dnb.ddb.de>.

Cover design: Christopher Schneider, Berlin.
Printed in Germany.

Preface

Well beyond the framework of generative grammar, a central question of linguistic research is whether, or how, certain aspects of meaning influence the form of a sentence. This question is addressed from a lexical perspective in this book. It is assumed that a verb is lexically associated with information that determines, at least in part, the predicate-argument structures it can appear in. The lexical approach raises a set of basic questions. First, there is a *properties problem*: which kind of lexical information enters into the determination of argument structure? Second, there is an *interface problem*: how are the relevant chunks of information encoded, such that they are accessible to both general cognition, and the derivation of syntactic predicate-argument structures? Third, there is a *mapping problem*: how exactly are lexical-semantic properties translated into grammatical functions?

The first two questions are addressed in chapter one, which concludes with an introduction to the *Theta System* of Reinhart (2000) and subsequent work. Rather than decomposing verb-meanings into complex lexical event structures, the Theta System analyses thematic roles like *Agent*, *Theme*, *Experiencer* into clusters of two binary features, which are labeled *c* (for *cause change*) and *m* (for *mental contribution*). Chapter one explores the psychological basis of these features and identifies them as expressing agency in two domains of a modular mind: a *commonsense theory of body movements* (*folk physics*), and a *commonsense theory of mind mechanisms* (*folk psychology*). Every verb classifies the participants in the event, state, or process it denotes with respect to the cognitive domain in which it is to be interpreted, and it specifies whether the event participant is an agent or a patient in that domain. The Theta System thus derives exactly eight thematic roles as (possibly underspecified) clusters [αc, βm].

This notation answers the first two questions posed above, the *properties problem*, and the *interface problem*. The grammatically relevant property of verb meaning is agency in two crucial domains of cognitive event interpretation, *folk physics* and *folk psychology*. Encoded as clusters of binary features, this information is accessible in grammatical derivations by hypothesis. The third question regarding the mapping of lexical semantic information on syntactic functions is addressed on the basis of German data in chapters two, three and four.

Chapter two lays the empirical basis with a detailed description of a set of German verbs. The chapter first develops the routines that allow us to postulate specific role-clusters for a given verb, and then establishes generalizations about the relation between role configurations and corresponding predicate-argument structures, including diathesis alternations. The overall conclusion is that Reinhart's (2000, 2002) theory is accurate in most cases.

Although the generalizations of the Theta System are robust and most probably universal, they are by no means exhaustive. A number of non-semantic factors enter into the determination of syntactic structures, in particular morpho-phonology, and purely syntactic requirements like structural case. These issues are addressed in chapter three.

Starting with a discussion of morphological conditions on argument structure, the chapter develops a theory of parallel grammatical derivation, in which the notion *interpretation at the interface* is formalized as a homomorphic mapping. Objects of prosodic structure are interpreted by a mapping into syntax, and objects of syntactic structure are interpreted by a mapping into semantics.

The relation between lexicon and grammar is not an interface in this technical sense. It is assumed with Chomsky (1995) that a lexical item enters a grammatical derivation together with all of its features by being selected into an initial array. Empirical problems relating to the mapping of lexical semantic structure into syntactic structure simply do not arise in this theory, because there is no syntactic structure in the lexicon.

Once a lexical item has been selected into an initial array, its features no longer form an un-analyzable unit. Generalizations over argument-linking are formulated in terms of merging instructions for thematic role-clusters. In general, the thematic roles provided by a lexical verb-entry merge with syntactic heads of category [/-N], and they are assigned to [/-V]. In particular, a [+] cluster must merge with the head v (which introduces external arguments), and the fully specified cluster [-c-m] must merge with V. No reference to arguments needs to be made in these merging instructions. The argument-interpretation of a given noun phrase arises exclusively in configuration with a thematic role-assigning head. This is an important feature of the present theory, which distinguishes it sharply from the event decomposition framework. It is possible to make explicit generalizations on how the perception of predicate-argument relations determines the projection of syntactic argument structure, but no recursive, pre-syntactic system of event-representation is needed to do that. With the constructional approach, the present theory shares the assumption that a noun phrase can only receive an argument-interpretation, if it appears in a specific syntactic configuration. It sharply differs from the constructional approach in that it explains why and how the thematic role-assigning potential of any given construction depends on the lexical entries, from which it is projected.

Chapter four extends this approach, pursuing the interaction between lexical specification, morphological markedness, syntactic structure, and semantic interpretation. It discusses the present participle, modal infinitival complements to the auxiliaries *haben* 'have' and *sein* 'be', the erratic auxiliary selection of intransitive manner of motion verbs, verbal and adjectival properties of the second participle, *un*-prefixation, verb-particle constructions, the verbal passive, and auxiliary selection in perfect, passive and future constructions.

This book contributes to the larger research project of the Theta System in three areas. First, it supplies a cognitive-psychological foundation for the coding system, the features *c* (cause change), and *m* (mental contribution). Second, it extends the Theta System into a general theory of argument projection by formalizing the relation between lexical access, morphological markedness, and syntactic argument structure. Third, it explores a wide range of data from German, which have not been discussed in this framework before.

Acknowledgements

Für Sabrina.

This book is a revised and extended version of my Tilburg University PhD thesis directed by Henk van Riemsdijk and Martin Prinzhorn, whose support is gratefully acknowledged. Many improvements to the original version were prompted by written comments I have received from Hans Broekhuis, Lázló Molnárfi, and Susi Wurmbrand.

I am especially grateful to Henk van Riemsdijk for his unwavering support of this and other projects, and to Tanya Reinhart for many pages of extremely helpful comments.

Thanks to Josef Bayer for inviting me to present a part of this material in Konstanz, and to the audience there, in particular to Ellen Brandner.

Last, but not least, I would like to thank my new colleagues in Lille, especially Philip Miller, Danièle Monseur, and Edouard Neidenberger, and acknowledge logistical support by the *UMR 8528 Silex* (CNRS, Lille 3).

Contents

Chapter 1
From lexical semantics to cognitive psychology, and back again

Let us assume as a working hypothesis that s-selection can determine the projection of syntactic structure. Projection from lexical semantics presupposes the existence of a theory that predicts syntactic structure from lexical meaning without circularity. Finding such a theory was the initial goal of the research reported in this book. Section 1 documents this search, summarizing a state-of-the-art article by Levin and Rappaport-Hovav, where they show how the mapping of lexical semantics into syntax is plagued with inconsistencies and empirical problems. The conclusion drawn from these problems will be that a theory of lexical semantics must be firmly embedded in theories on adjacent domains, the hypothesis being that a proper delineation of domains can eliminate most of the problems.

Section 2 undertakes an excursion into cognitive psychology. The conclusion of section 2 will be that the powerful compositional apparatus assumed in much work on the lexicon is neither necessary, nor desirable. Linguistic complexity is a product of syntax, and event representations are computed by central sub-systems of a modular mind, a *commonsense theory of body movements* (*folk physics*), and a *commonsense theory of mind mechanisms* (*folk psychology*) (Leslie 1994). Each of these components delivers a fundamental distinction, the one between agents and patients. Thus, the lexical entry of a verb must specify for each of its arguments: (i) whether it should be assigned to *folk psychology*, to *folk physics*, or to both for interpretation, and (ii) whether it is an agent, or a patient in the respective domain.

The remainder of section 2, and section 3 are dedicated to the feature-notation developed in Reinhart (2000), which matches the demands just outlined.

1. Lexical semantics: an overview

An important question in lexical semantics is figuring out which aspects of word meaning are relevant for argument expression. Pesetsky (1995:13) for example observes that, "though there are doubtless relevant and identifiable distinctions between *shout* and *whisper* [...], these distinctions probably play no role at all in syntax/semantics interactions." Other semantic distinctions do play such a role. I will refer to the question of identifying relevant distinctions as the *properties problem.*

Another, equally important question is how these distinctions are encoded such that both the computational system and the semantic component can read them. This question will be referred to as the *interface problem.*

A third question is how lexical relations are represented in syntax: the *mapping problem.*

This section gives an overview of some major approaches to these topics. Unless otherwise indicated, I will follow a manuscript by Levin and Rappaport Hovav (1996), henceforth L&R (1996).

1.1. Thematic role lists

An assumption that is common in both the semantic and the syntactic literature is that the meaning of a verb specifies the nature of the arguments it requires in the form of a list of role-predicates. In semantics, this assumption was pioneered by Castañeda (1967) in what has come to be known as the neo-Davidsonian view. On this view, arguments and adjuncts are introduced by independent predicates, as illustrated in Kratzer's (1996:109) example:

(1) a. *We bought your slippers in Marrakesh.*
b. *∃e [buying(e) & Agent(we)(e) & Theme(your slippers)(e) & in (Marrakesh)(e)]*

In syntax, most uses of the term *theta-role*, especially the widely shared formulation of the *Theta-Criterion* in (2), presuppose a role-list approach.[1]

(2) Theta Criterion (Chomsky 1981:36)
Each argument bears one and only one Θ-role, and each Θ-role is assigned to one and only one argument.

Theta role lists thus appear to supply a straightforward answer to the *interface problem.* They are selected into a syntactic derivation in conjunction with the verb they are part of, and then handed over to semantics. The question, of course, is whether such lists are empirically adequate.

Thematic role list approaches share the assumption that natural classes of verbs can be established on the basis of the number and kind of arguments a given verb takes. To illustrate this point, Levin and Rappaport Hovav (1996) sketch Fillmore's discussion of *break*- and *hit*-type verbs (Fillmore 1970).

Both *hit* and *break* verbs have agentive and non-agentive transitive alternants:

(3) a. *John broke the window with a rock.*
    b. *John hit the fence with a stick.*
(4) a. *A rock broke the window.*
    b. *A stick hit the fence.*

However, only *break* verbs have an unaccusative alternant. *Hit* verbs lack such a use:

(5) a. *The window broke.*
    b. **The fence hit.*

This difference is related, according to Fillmore (1970), to a difference in the thematic (case-) roles the respective verbs have to assign. The *break* class selects an *Object*, which can appear as (unaccusative) subject. The *hit* class selects a *Place*, which cannot.

In striking contrast to its ubiquitous use outside lexical semantics, the thematic role list approach faces severe criticism in lexical semantics. Its problem is its arbitrariness, and it surfaces in three facets.

First, and this is reflected by the vast differences in roles assumed, there are no reliable tests for identifying a universally valid list of roles. Second, any given role list is just that. It cannot express relations among different roles that might be part of equivalence classes. Finally, we do not always find a clear correspondence between roles and argument positions: Some arguments appear to bear more than one role, and some roles appear to be assigned to more than one argument.

The universal list problem was discussed in great detail by Dowty (1991), who states that

> [t]he dilemma is, if we adopt the finer characterization of roles to achieve certain distinctions, do we not thereby miss generalizations by not being able to refer to the grosser [...] category as well? (Dowty 1991:554)

Levin and Rappaport Hovav (1996) exemplify the dilemma with their notion of *immediate cause*, which figures in their lexicon-syntax mapping rules. *Immediate cause* is a very broad concept, including *agents*, *causes*, and even *emitters* in verbs of sound and light emission, but it does have consistent meaning, and its syntactic realization is likewise predictable. Immediate causes are always realized as subjects. The notion therefore qualifies as an excellent candidate for a thematic role.

On the other hand, some constructions require finer grained distinctions. For example, *emitters* appear in the locative inversion construction, *agents* usually do not (examples from Levin and Rappaport Hovav 1995:255).

(6) a. **In the factory worked young boys at the age of 7.*
b. *And in their wake rumbled trucks to haul off the remains.*

A thematic role list approach has no way to state both the subject- and the locative inversion-generalization without contradiction.

This leads to the second aspect of the problem. It might be suggested that *agents*, *causes* and *emitters* are thematic roles, and that they form a natural class of *immediate causes*. *Immediate cause* might thus be a super-role that can itself feature in generalizations. However, such a move is excluded under the thematic role list approach: "there is nothing in a semantic role list which tells us that there is anything which unifies" (L&R 1996:14) the members of whichever super-role we might want to postulate.

The *proto-roles* in Dowty (1991) are designed to avoid this problem, however at a cost. First, the entailments related to *proto-agents* and *proto-patients* are arbitrary lists again. While they might be doing a fair job describing natural classes of verbs, Dowty (1991) offers no clue as to how those entailments derive from the meaning of a given verb. And second, *proto-roles* give rise to the grosser generalizations, mainly subject-object asymmetries, while offering no tool to handle finer grained distinctions among smaller classes. We will return to this proposal in the discussion of mapping theories.

Simple thematic role lists are motivated to a large extent by their behavior in the lexicon-syntax mapping. Roughly, we would find a similar behavior of a class of verbs with respect to an argument and a construction, and we conclude from this similarity that the verbs in question share a thematic role.

Such a reasoning is called into question if it turns out that the lexicon-syntax mapping is not unique. Indeed it has been argued that the mapping is many-to-many. L&R (1996) quote Gruber (1965) and Jackendoff (1972) with the assumption that verbs of motion may assign both the *agent* and the *theme* role to their subject, and they give *resemble* as an example of a verb that assigns the same role to both the subject and the object.

I thus conclude with L&R (1996) that simple thematic role lists are not appropriate tools for the description of syntactically relevant lexical information.

1.2. Roles and events

According to a wide consensus among lexical semanticists, many of the above mentioned problems can be avoided, if the mental representation of events is taken into account. The properties of individual thematic roles should thus follow from a more general theory of event representation, which would also have to determine natural classes of roles.

Nevertheless, such an approach will still have to answer to the *properties problem*. Event representations have been suggested from various perspectives, and it is not a necessary truth that any one of them is most relevant for syntactic structure. In addition, this approach introduces the *interface problem*. In contrast to Θ-roles, there is no agreement as to how structured events are represented in syntax, and how exactly they are transferred into semantics. The event-representation approach introduces yet another manifestation of the *interface problem*, to be discussed in section 3: is a given lexical verb meaning a representation of, derived from, or identical with the mental representation of an event?

Let us first turn to the *properties* problem. In the literature on lexical semantics, we find three perspectives on how events are conceptualized, the *localist*, the *aspectual*, and the *causal* approach.

1.2.1. The localist approach

On the localist approach, which was pioneered by Gruber (1965), there are two basic event types, *motion* and *location*, from which all other event types are derived. In other words, it is assumed that we conceptualize all events as spatial metaphors. Jackendoff (1983) summarizes this approach in his *Thematic Relations Hypothesis*.

(7) Thematic Relations Hypothesis (Jackendoff 1983:188)
In any semantic field of events and states, the principal event, state, path, and place functions are a subset of those used for the analysis of spatial motion and location.
Fields differ in only 3 possible ways:
- what sorts of entities may appear as theme
- what sorts of entities may appear as reference objects (i.e., locations)
- what kind of relation assumes the role played by location in the field of spatial expressions.

An advantage of this approach is that it can account for cases of systematic polysemy, as in the following example, where the object NP of a single verb receives quite different thematic interpretations (L&R 1996:21):

(8) a. *John kept the car in the garage.*
b. *John kept the book.*
c. *John kept Andy happy.*

(9) [CAUSE (x, (STAY y,z))]

On the localist approach, all of these interpretations can be derived from a single representation (9) of the verb *keep*, which is realized in different semantic fields: the positional field in (8a), the possessional field in (8b), and the identificational field in (8c).

The main problem of the localist approach is that local relations do not seem to be directly relevant for the realization of lexical-semantic roles in syntactic argument positions. Acknowledging this fact, Jackendoff (1990) introduces an *action tier* that takes precedence over the *thematic tier* in the selection of subjects and objects. While the *thematic tier* encodes local relations, the *action tier* encodes causal relations like *agent* vs. *patient*. The precedence of the action tier with respect to grammatical functions indicates that the causal approach is more adequate in the investigation of the lexicon-syntax interaction than the localist approach.

1.2.2. The aspectual approach

The aspectual approach to argument realization has received a lot of attention recently because of its prima facie plausibility. First, the notions it introduces, *measuring out* and *delimitation* are much smaller in scope than traditional listed Θ-roles. Second, the event participants designated by these notions largely correspond to internal arguments, which makes them a good tool to describe the lexicon-syntax interaction.

Tenny (1994) summarizes the foundations of the aspectual approach in her *aspectual interface hypothesis*:

(10) Aspectual Interface Hypothesis (Tenny 1994:2)
The universal principles of mapping between thematic structure and syntactic structure are governed by aspectual properties. Constraints on the aspectual properties associated with direct internal arguments, and external arguments in syntactic structure constrain the kinds of event participants that can occupy these positions. Only the aspectual part of thematic structure is visible to the universal linking principles.

Unfortunately, the aspectual approach suffers from a number of loose ends. Take first the generalization that telic intransitives are unaccusative (Dowty 1991; Hoekstra 1984; van Valin 1990). Borer (1994) extends this generalization to derive unaccusativity from telicity.

However, Levin and Rappaport Hovav (1995:172ff). show that certain verbs of directed motion like *descend, rise*, and degree achievement verbs like *cool, lengthen*, are both unaccusative and atelic. Atelicity is shown by the compatibility with durative *for* phrases and punctual *at* phrases:

(11) a. *The temperature rose steadily for three hours.*
b. *The temperature rose at one o'clock.*

(12) a. *The soup cooled for half an hour.*
b. *The soup cooled at three o'clock.*

Unaccusativity is shown for the motion verbs by their incompatibility with the *X's way* construction, and by the absence of cognate objects. For degree achievements, unaccusativity is shown by the fact that they have causative alternants, and by their incompatibility with the *X's way* construction:

(13) a. **She rose her way to the presidency.*
b. **She rose a wobbly rise.*
(14) a. *The soup cooled.*
b. *I cooled the soup.*
c. **The soup cooled its way to room temperature.*

We can conclude from this evidence that telicity does not derive unaccusativity. This takes out a forceful argument in support of the aspectual approach.

Second, Jackendoff (1996) argues that *measuring out* and *delimitation* are sometimes determined by pragmatic, rather than lexical-semantic factors. Take as an example a predicate like *draw*. The object of *draw* is normally interpreted as an *event-measure*, or *incremental theme*: the fraction of the object drawn measures, so to say, the completeness of the drawing event. This is not the case, however, if an object is not drawn in the normal way, but, for example, sprayed on a piece of paper in one swoop by a printer.

The same holds for many other examples. When we eat an apple, the size of the remaining portion of the apple measures the completion of the event. But when we eat a grape, or even more so a raisin, it usually disappears at once, and therefore cannot measure the event.

On the aspectual approach, we would expect different argument realization patterns caused by an altered measuring behavior. This expectation is not borne out.

Third, Jackendoff (1996) argues that the aspectual approach fails to predict that certain affected objects, which do not necessarily measure out or delimit an event, are nevertheless realized as objects (15). Thus, affectedness (a causal notion), rather than delimitation, determines objecthood here.

(15) *What John did to the bread was chew/ knead/ jiggle/ spin it.*

Forth, Tenny (1994) and Dowty (1991) claim that locative inversion excludes an agentivity reading, because NP must be generated as an object in this construction, and objects must measure (Tenny), or have proto-patient properties (Dowty). However, an agentive reading is possible, at least in some cases:

(16) *Across my windowsill walked a whole army of ants.*

Finally, Reinhart (2000) argues against the very notions of *measurement* and *delimitation*. The intuitive nature of these notions, she claims, is responsible for much of their initial appeal, which evaporates, once they are semantically formalized. According to Reinhart (2000), the only aspectually relevant notion is *homogeneity*, which classifies both states vs. events, and mass vs. count nouns: states and mass nouns are homogeneous, events and count nouns are not.

Notice that homogeneity does not face Jackendoff's problem of duration above. If an event is homogeneous, it does not matter how much (or little) time it consumes on a given occasion: it can always be split in half, and is still the same event. In a non-homogeneous event, a part is never equal to the whole, no matter how short it might actually be on a given occasion.

In sum, the aspectual approach to argument realization does not stand up to closer scrutiny mainly for the same reason that underlies its initial appeal: the intuitive nature of the notions applied. Once pinned down to a falsifiable core, they lend themselves to fragmentary generalizations regarding argument structure, at the best.

1.2.3. The causal approach

Dealing with the localist approach, it has been shown that causal relations play a more important role in the realization of arguments than local relations. Within the causal approach, this intuition is taken as a starting point. Croft (1991, 1998), building on work by Talmy (1976, 1988), argues that causation is conceptualized as a transmission of force between event participants, and that "certain non-causal relationships are conceptualized as if they were asymmetric force-dynamic relationships" (Croft 1998:31).

Verbs, on this approach, name segments of a causal chain. In such a chain, "[o]ne participant outranks another if it is antecedent to the other on the causal chain" (Croft 1998:23). In this way, Croft derives a partial ordering of arguments that can be used in the mapping from lexical semantics to syntax.

An example of such an ordering is the distinction between antecedent and subsequent oblique roles. Antecedent roles are ranked high on the causal chain, and include instrumental, manner, means, comitative, cause. Subsequent roles are ranked low, and include benefactive, recipient, result.

Croft (1991) supports the distinction between antecedent and subsequent roles with case syncretisms, which appear inside a class, but not across classes. In Croft (1998), he extends this generalization to acquisition, reporting a study by Clark and Carpenter (1989):

According to that study, when English children mistakenly use prepositions, they never substitute an antecedent preposition for a subsequent one, or vice versa, while they regularly mix up prepositions within a class. For example, they would substitute *by* for *with* in instrumentals, or *with* for *by* for passive agents (Croft 1998:40):

(17) a. *I just eat it by my spoon.*
b. *Sometimes Eva needs to be feeded with you because she doesn't eat.*

The causal approach seems to fare better than the local, or the aspectual approach in several respects. Take for one example causative change of state verbs. On the aspectual approach, such verbs are analyzed into two sub-events, an activity and a result state, which are connected by a causal relation. Nothing in the aspectual approach requires that the activity-phase and the result state must always share an argument (the affected object). The force-dynamic approach predicts this (L&R 1996:34).

L&R offer several more examples, where the causative approach seems superior to the aspectual one. The objects of activity verbs like *wipe, rub*, and another class: *jiggle, chew*, do not measure-out or delimit, so the aspectual approach does not predict that they must be realized as direct objects. The causal approach does, because force is applied to them.

The same holds for the locative alternation: (18a) means that Pat did something to, or with the paint, while (18b) is more readily read as Pat doing something to the wall.

(18) a. *Pat sprayed paint on the wall.*
b. *Pat sprayed the wall with paint.*

It seems to me, however, that the causal approach as it stands faces challenges too. As long as it is not embedded in, and derived from, a proper theory of mind mechanisms, the notion *force* remains intuitive. Its application to syntactic argument structure is vague, and hard to falsify. As an illustration, take psychological verbs of the *fear* class:

(19) *Jörg feared a short blonde bloke with thin hair.*

In (19), it is well conceivable that force is emitted by the individual that triggers the fear, and that it is transferred to the individual denoted by the subject. In other words, there is a force-differential that places the direct object above the subject. If force-differentials were the only factor to determine syntactic argument structure, *fear* should behave like *frighten*, with the stimulus in subject- and the experiencer in object position.

(20) *A short blonde bloke with thin hair frightened Jörg.*

The force-dynamic approach offers an account of such problems, for example in terms of Croft's *verbal profiles*, which specify exactly which segment of the causal chain is denoted by a given verb. *Fear*-verbs might thus be taken to denote the emission of cognitive energy by the experiencer towards a representation of the stimulus. Another option would be to distinguish the roles *cause* and *subject matter of emotion* (Pesetsky 1995). However, since the cause of an emotion can also be its subject matter, it remains unclear, in which way force-dynamic relations have the potential to order thematic roles with respect to each other, rather than describing the dynamics of particular events.

Nevertheless, the causal approach seems to be the most promising strategy with respect to the *properties problem*: causal relations are robustly involved in the determination of grammatical functions. Where the causal approach faces problems, primarily with respect to psychological predicates, the rivaling approaches do not fare better.

As it stands, the causal approach does not supply an answer to the *interface problem*. It does not deliver a formalization of relevant properties that is both accurate and legible by the computational system. Neither is it embedded in an explicit theory about the relation between mental and linguistic representations. Before turning to that in section 3, let us take a quick look at how the *mapping problem* has been dealt with in the literature.

2. The mapping procedure

According to a widely held conjecture, compositional lexical semantic structure is preserved under the mapping of lexical items into syntax. This conjecture has been expressed in several different ways, the most general of which is the *Universal Alignment Hypothesis* (UAH) of Perlmutter and Postal (1984):

(21) Universal Alignment Hypothesis (Perlmutter and Postal 1984:97 - from L&R 1996:37)
There exist principles of UG which predict the initial [grammatical] relation borne by each nominal in a given clause from the meaning of the clause.

The UAH states that there are unique grammatical realizations of thematic relations. This is not an innocent assumption, and indeed weaker formulations of the lexicon-syntax mapping can be found. One of them is Rosen's (1984) *Little Alignment Hypothesis* (LAH), which comes quite close to Chomsky's *Projection Principle* in one respect.

While the UAH assumes there are general properties of clauses from which lexical relations can be read off, both the LAH and the Projection Principle assume that individual lexical items have constant properties, which are not altered by the computational system, and indeed determine the way in which the item projects syntactically. The Projection Principle fundamentally differs from the LAH with respect to the properties it describes. The LAH talks about semantic roles, the Projection Principle about formal features, i.e. subcategorization. Chapters 2-4 will rely on the importance of this distinction.

(22) The Little Alignment Hypothesis (Rosen 1984:53(45) - from L&R 1996:37)
For any one predicate in any one language, there is a fixed mapping which aligns each semantic role with an initial GR. The alignment remains invariant for all clauses with that predicate.

(23) Projection Principle (Chomsky 1981:29)
Representations at each syntactic level (i.e., LF, and D- and S-structure) are projected from the lexicon, in that they observe the subcategorization properties of lexical items.

In spite its weakness, disallowing generalizations across predicate classes and languages, the LAH might still be too strong. It is not a given truth that the semantic roles assigned by a given predicate are always realized in an identical way. Therefore, lexical semanticists usually favor (some version of) the UAH. The discussion is more on the type of mapping, than on the question whether it is universal or not.

Turn first to *direct mapping* accounts. *Direct Mapping* means that lexical properties are translated into grammatical relations directly, without any mediating level of representation. Probably the most influential such account is given in Levin and Rappaport Hovav (1995), exemplified here with their *immediate cause linking rule*:

(24) Immediate Cause Linking Rule (Levin and Rappaport Hovav 1995:135)
The argument of a verb that denotes the immediate cause of the eventuality described by that verb is its external argument.

As noted by Levin and Rappaport Hovav (1996), a disadvantage of direct mapping rules of this kind is that they are arbitrary. There is nothing in a direct mapping account that would tell us, for example, why an instrument (which is an immediate cause) is not linked to an external argument position, when an agent is present.

Mediated mapping approaches seek to deal with exactly this problem. Thematic role hierarchies are probably the best-known devices of mediated mapping. There is some agreement to the assumption that linking rules map the highest ranked argument to the subject position, and the lowest one to the object.

Thematic role hierarchies inherit several problems from the roles they order. Without clear criteria to distinguish particular roles, such roles are hard to rank with respect to each other. Worse still, it is extremely difficult to compare hierarchies based on different definitions of roles.

> Over and above this, the proposed mapping rules make reference to the hierarchies in strikingly different ways, and these divergences also need to be factored into any comparison of the hierarchies. Unfortunately, we are unaware of thorough comparative assessments [...] (L&R 1996:44).

To illustrate this problem, consider the presentation of hierarchies in L&R (1996:43-44):

No mention of goal and location
Belletti and Rizzi (1988): Agt > Exp > Th
Fillmore (1968): Agt > Inst > Obj

Goal and location ranked above theme/patient
Grimshaw (1990): Agt > Exp > G/S/L > Th
Jackendoff (1972): Agt > G/S/L > Th
van Valin (1990): Agt > Eff > Exp > L > Th > Pat

Goal and location ranked below theme/patient

Speas (1990):	Agt > Exp > Th > G/S/L > Manner/Time
Carrier-Duncan (1985):	Agt > Th > G/S/L
Jackendoff (1990):	Agt > Pat/Ben > Th > G/S/L
Larson (1988):	Agt > Th > G > Obl
Baker (1989):	Agt > Inst > Th/Pat > G/L

Goal above patient/theme; location ranked below theme/patient

Bresnan and Kanerva (1989):	Agt > Ben > Rec/Exp > Inst > Th/Pat > L
Kiparsky (1985):	Agt > S > G > Inst > Th/Pat > L
Givón (1984):	Agt > Dat/Ben > Pat > L > Inst

Another approach to mediated mapping makes use of intermediate roles. The most influential proposal involving intermediate roles is developed in Dowty (1991). His *thematic proto roles* are lists of entailments. If a given argument gives rise to more proto-agent entailments than proto-patient entailments, it is realized as a subject. If the proto-patient entailments predominate, it is realized as an object.

Contributing properties for the Agent Proto-Role:
a. volitional involvement in the event or state
b. sentience (and/or perception)
c. causing an event or change of state in another participant
d. movement (relative to the position of another participant)
(e. exists independently of the event named by the verb)

Contributing properties for the Patient Proto-Role:
a. undergoes change of state
b. incremental theme
c. causally affected by another participant
d. stationary relative to movement of another participant
(e. does not exist independently of the event, or not at all)
(Dowty 1991:572)

Dowty (1991:572) gives these lists "without implying that [they] are necessarily exhaustive or that they could perhaps eventually be better partitioned in some other way". In this sense, they just postpone the initial problem of explaining why particular roles are mapped on specific grammatical functions. They describe generalizations that we would want to follow from either the conceptualization of events, or from other factors. In this sense, they only re-state the well-known problem that grammatical functions are loosely related to the thematic properties of event descriptions.

2.1. Beyond the UAH

It is not unreasonable to suspect, based on the problems with direct and mediated mapping proposals, that such problems stem from too loose a conception of the lexicon-syntax mapping. Several authors adopt this strategy, and suggest mapping procedures that are more restricted than the UAH would predict them to be.

A first class of theories strengthens the UAH by adding the assumption that the lexicon-syntax mapping is isomorphic. The advantage of this move is the transparency of the operation. However, the abundance of lexical semantic distinctions necessitates substantial adjustments in the generation of syntactic structure, in order to maintain the isomorphism hypothesis. An example is the introduction of an entirely new level of representation, *lexical syntactic structure*, which is subject to slightly different wellformedness conditions than syntax proper, in the work of Hale and Keyser (1993, 1999).

More often than isomorphism, we find the assumption of a homomorphism between lexical and syntactic structure. A homomorphic mapping allows the realization of multiple lexical properties by a single grammatical function. An example of a homomorphic mapping approach is the *Uniformity of Theta Assignment Hypothesis* (UTAH) of Baker (1988):

(25) The Uniformity of Theta Assignment Hypothesis (UTAH) (Baker 1988:46)
Identical thematic relationships between items are represented by identical structural relationships between those items at the level of d-structure.

Provided a given syntactic relationship can be identical to more than one thematic relationship, Baker's version of the UTAH allows the desired one-to-many mapping. One way to accomplish this is by formulating the lexicon-syntax mapping as structure preserving for relative prominence. The UTAH then roughly translates into the requirement that a prominence relation between two roles in the lexicon must be conserved in syntax. Several relativized versions of the UTAH make comparable assumptions (Belletti and Rizzi 1988; Larson 1988, 1990; Jackendoff 1990).

2.2. Problems with diathesis alternations

Theories based on homomorphic mapping can account for many-to-one relations between lexical and syntactic configurations, but diathesis alternations seem to require a relation from one lexical role to a variety of different syntactic functions. The mapping therefore must be many-to-many. A homomorphism does not allow many-to-many relations.

Such problems have been tackled from two perspectives. Either, lexical entries are viewed as constant in meaning, with diathesis alternations arising from grammatical transformations. This is the *projectional* approach. Or, lexical entries are viewed as massively ambiguous, with syntactic realization coercing constructional meaning on it, the *constructional* approach.

An example of where the first strategy has successfully been adopted is the passive alternation, which crucially does not affect the thematic relations of the arguments of a predicate.

(26) a. *John ate the grape.*
     b. *The grape was eaten by John.*

The locative alternation is more problematic in this respect:

(27) a. *The farmer loaded the hay on the truck.*
     b. *The farmer loaded the truck with hay.*

L&R (1996:60) point out that the two alternants exhibit a difference in meaning that can be accounted for in terms of lexical semantics: (27a) expresses a causative change of location. (27b) expresses a causative change of state.

If a theory based on the projectional approach maintains a single lexical entry for such verbs, it cannot account for the difference in meaning, unless it doubles lexical semantic structure in syntax. Generative Semantics did just that; see Fodor (1970) for why this approach is problematic: it forces the introduction of otherwise unattested, and largely arbitrary transformations.

This leaves us with the constructional approach, which is recently enjoying great attention (Borer 1994, 1998, 2000; Erteshik-Shir and Rapoport 1995; Ghomeshi and Massam 1995; Goldberg 1995; Hoekstra 1992; Ritter and Rosen 1996). On the constructional approach, the lexical content of a predicate is reduced to a minimum, which indeed remains constant across different constructions, and thematic meaning is attributed to specific constructions.

As an illustration, take the lexical items *boat, dog, sink*. According to Borer (2000, 2003) (cf. Chapter 3 for details and discussion), these lexical items have a conceptual core meaning that is, kind of loosely, related to what we think of dogs, boats, and sinking. This conceptual meaning helps us interpreting utterances like those in (28):

(28) a. The dog sank the boat.
     b. The boat dogged the sink.
     c. The sink boated the dog.

(28b) might be a rare utterance to come about, and (28c) seems even less likely to be ever produced. However, such unlikely sentences are interpretable. In (28b), we understand that a boat did something to a sink, and this event reminds us of the *dog*-concept. Similarly in (28c). A sink does something to a dog, and the event is reminiscent of boats.

On the constructional approach, syntactic structure is much more than a projection of lexical items. It supplies an event-structural template that forces thematic roles upon the lexical items inserted into them. Thus, the answer to the *mapping problem* offered by the constructional approach is trivial. There is no mapping of thematic information from the lexicon into syntax. What the constructional approach fails to give is a principled explanation of why particular syntactic configurations should have the assumed thematic properties. Borer (1994) and subsequent work attribute most of the explanatory burden to aspect. The limitations of this approach were discussed in section 1.2.2 above.

2.3. Summary

In sum, the three problems stated at the outset have been dealt with in the literature in rather inconsistent ways. A solution to the *properties problem* seems to call for a causal approach to lexical semantics, while the *interface problem* clearly favors thematic role lists, which are problematic on independent grounds. Given this disparity of requirements, it is hard to even start to answer the *mapping problem*. It might just as well turn out that there is a way of formalizing lexical knowledge and syntactic projection such that the mapping problem must be addressed from a different perspective than the one taken in lexical semantics.

In the following subsection, I will evaluate the object of research, lexical semantic representation, in the light of recent developments in cognitive psychology. Building on a strictly modular theory of the mind, I will argue that thematic relations encode two fundamental concepts of a commonsense representation of events: mechanical and psychological agency. These concepts can be encoded as binary features (Reinhart 2000), which makes it possible to dispense with recursive mechanisms in the lexicon, and to answer the *interface problem*: by hypothesis, Reinhart's features are legible by the computational system, and they can be interpreted in semantics as neo-Davidsonian role predicates. Chapter 2 is dedicated to an empirical re-examination of the mapping problem with data from German.

3. The architecture of the mind, and the lexicon

In *Modularity of Mind*, Fodor (1983) defends the thesis that the mind can be analyzed into a central system of thought and highly specialized interface systems, by which the central system interacts with the outside world. One of these interface systems is the language faculty. Embedded in Fodor's model, language interfaces with the central system of thought on one end, and with the shallower systems of motor control and sensual input on the other end. So if we want to find out about the interface of language with thought, i.e., with the manipulation of concepts, as lexical semantics attempts to do, we need to find out which conditions the central system of thought imposes on the representation and manipulation of concepts.

However, in Fodor's theory, "conceptual processes [...] are presented as a big holistic lump lacking joints at which to carve", as Sperber (1994:39) puts it. If this approach is correct, then the most basic question of lexical semantics, what I called the *properties problem* above, cannot reasonably be addressed at all. The reason is that, on the view described by Sperber (1994), there is no single set of properties that characterizes the handling of concepts in the mind. If constraints on the lexical representation of concepts exist at all, then they must be specific to the language faculty. Research in lexical semantics indeed seems to be based on this assumption. A powerful lexicon shoulders the heavy burden of event representation. However, there is a much more elegant, and successful way to approach the problem.

3.1. The lexicon is a list: Fodor & Lepore

The existence of recursive mechanisms in the lexicon has been called into question by Fodor and Lepore (1998), henceforth F&L. According to F&L,

> lexical entries are typically atomic [...]. [T]he only thing a lexical entry specifies is the denotation of the item it describes (Fodor and Lepore 1998:270).

They immediately relativize this strong position, granting that

> lexical *entries* are typically complex. But we claim that they are complex in a way that does not jeopardize the thesis that lexical *meaning* is atomistic, or the identification of lexical meaning with denotation (Fodor and Lepore 1998:270; italics by F&L).

It is interesting to see exactly which aspects of lexical complexity F&L reject, and why they do so.

F&L consider inter-lexical relations, ambiguity, semantic wellformedness, and (apparent) syntactic effects of lexical complexity, and argue that none of these issues calls for lexical complexity in the sense that real-world relations among objects be represented by similar relations in the lexicon, or that the lexicon had recursive, generative, capacities like syntax.

First, words are related to other words in a way that can be captured by analytic inference. A *dog*, for example, is also an animal, and one might want to represent this fact as part of the meaning of *dog*. However, F&L argue, such facts are related to what a speaker knows (or believes, pretends, etc. to know) about the world, and not to structural properties of the lexicon. For example, the question whether a *tomato* is a *vegetable* or not, is answered in biology, not in the lexicon. The fact that a *dog* is an animal can be stated as part of its (arbitrary) denotation, like *has four legs*, *barks and bites*, *carries flees*, and a few other contingent truths about dogs. Any of these properties can be changed, and indeed reversed, without serious effect on the use of the word (Lewis 1981). In sum, inter-lexical relations do not support recursive procedures in the lexicon.

Second, lexical generativity is required, in the theories F&L attack, by the varying meanings a given lexical item may assume. They consider as an example the meaning of *bake* in *bake a cake* (creation) versus *bake a potato* (cook). The generalization here would be that *bake* assumes the meaning of creation when combined with an artifact, and that of cooking otherwise. The question is whether the lexicon should have the power to explicitly derive these two meanings.

Both conceptual economy and empirical fact militate against this. Different uses of a given lexical item are just as well compatible with lexical ambiguity and (partial) pragmatic disambiguation. Such an approach actually fares much better than the complex lexicon approach, once we consider the availability of half-baked bread in every supermarket (an artifact that is being cooked, not created).

> [...] in fact, even assuming that the lexicon distinguishes artifacts from natural kinds is not enough. Notice that although *knives* and *trolley cars* are artifacts, *bake a knife* and *bake a trolley car* resist a creative reading quite as much as *bake a potato* does. But if *bake a cake* is heard as creative because *cake* is marked as denoting an artifact, then *bake a trolley car* should be heard as creative too. Clearly, something has gone wrong. (Fodor and Lepore 1998:12)

A third piece of evidence is the capacity of a lexical semantic theory to state conditions on semantic wellformedness. Again, it is doubtful whether the lexicon should have that power. F&L call into question the very existence of wellformedness conditions "distinct from ungrammaticality, necessary falsity, and any of a variety of kinds of pragmatic malfeasance" (Fodor and Lepore 1998:275). All such conditions efficiently apply in domains other than the lexicon. The null hypothesis would thus appear to be the attribution of a given illformedness to syntax, semantics or pragmatics. Since the primary function of the lexicon is stipulating the atoms of linguistic operations, and systems of linguistic operations exist outside the lexicon, the very concept of lexical-semantic wellformedness is questionable.

In conclusion, neither inter-lexical relations, nor ambiguity or semantic wellformedness call for recursive mechanisms in the lexicon. I therefore follow F&L and conclude that the lexicon is an arbitrary list.

F&L endorse a forth argument that is very closely related to our *properties problem* above. In this argument, F&L try to refute the claim that the semantic properties of a lexical item determine (some of) its syntactic properties. The argument is based on the difficulty to formalize "the semantic end of the putative semantics/syntax correlations [...] with sufficient clarity to permit the claims to be evaluated" (Fodor and Lepore 1998:276).

Notice that this kind of reasoning is substantially different from the arguments presented above. Instead of calling into question the desirability of a theoretical goal, it simply states the difficulty of getting there. What is more, F&L capitalize on the notoriously vague notions of *affectedness*, and the *boundedness* of events in their argument (cf. section 1.2.2). Surely, the absence of an adequate theory on how lexical knowledge is represented in syntactic structure at this moment in history does not imply that such a theory could not, eventually, exist. Far from refuting lexical semantics, F&L have identified its object of inquiry.

In the following sections, we will turn to a modular analysis of central thought processes, trying to extract an answer to the *properties problem*, which is compatible with the conclusion that the lexicon is a list.

3.2. Domain specific thought: ToBy, ToMM, and agency

A strong version of the modular hypothesis holds that even central, conceptual processes are domain-specific operations. Fodor (1987:27) disqualifies such an assumption as "modularity theory gone mad". Nevertheless, a substantial field of research has since grown, producing significant insights, especially for the development of cognitive mechanisms from infancy onwards.

An implementation of this hypothesis is the *theory* theory that considers "everyday knowledge as falling into folk or commonsense theories" (Hirschfeld and Gelman 1994:12). A commonsense theory can be viewed as a set of beliefs that allows an individual to interpret and explain the behavior of an object of a given domain, as well as predict its future behavior (Gopnik and Wellmann 1994).

Specified knowledge systems of this kind presuppose mechanisms that allow a categorization of objects into domains, a system of *domain-specific perception*. Once an object is categorized as belonging to a particular domain, its future behavior can be predicted in line with the principles governing that domain.

The perception and interpretation of events appears to depend on two major systems of cognition. One of them is responsible for the individuation of physical objects as distinct from others, with their mechanical properties, and with the prediction of their behavior in three-dimensional space. Another system is responsible for the recognition of volitional agents as opposed to dead objects. In addition to movement and interaction in three-dimensional space, volitional agents are capable of internalized, mental behavior and interaction at a distance. The latter system is responsible for the prediction of such behavior.

3.2.1. Physical objects and ToBy

According to Carey and Spelke (1994), physical objects are perceived "in accordance with the principles of cohesion, contact, and continuity" (p.175). The principle of *cohesion* predicts that an object maintains its integrity under movement. As a consequence of this principle, two adjacent objects lacking clear boundaries are perceived as one object if they appear stationary, but they are perceived as two distinct objects, if there is movement of one with respect to the other. The principle of *contact* predicts that objects move together only if they are in contact. Reaction at a distance is not interpreted as a property of physical (inanimate) objects. *Continuity* finally predicts that an object moves on exactly one, continuous path. If an object vanishes, and then reappears in a different position, moving in a different direction, the two occurrences are perceived as distinct objects.

Once a physical object has been individuated as a single entity, its central property is inertia. When it moves, it is predicted to continue moving on its path, and when it is stationary, it is predicted to stay where it is. However, physical objects can be pushed or pulled by other physical objects, and individuals can predict the resulting movements. Leslie (1994) argues that there is a cognitive domain responsible for just that. A *Theory of Body mechanism* (ToBy) is

> concerned with Agents in a mechanical sense [...]. Distinguishing agents from other physical bodies that are not Agents and describing their mechanical interactions are important functions of **ToBy** (Leslie 1994:122).

According to Leslie, human individuals have adapted to the physical world in which "object motions are invariably the result of energy distribution" (Leslie 1994:125) by ascribing *force* to objects:

> ToBy is concerned with three-dimensional objects as the principal bearers, transmitters, and recipients of FORCE (Leslie 1994:126).

The concept of *force* is the psychological interpretation of physical energy, and although it is extremely shallow from a scientific point of view, it is useful as a psychological postulate, because it allows wide-spread commonsensical force-ascriptions, where physical energy is actually absent.

In sum, a commonsense theory of mechanical action (labeled *ToBy*) is responsible for the recognition of physical objects, and for the interpretation and prediction of their behavior in three-dimensional space, as caused by *force*. This notion corresponds to the one used in lexical semantics by Talmy (2000), Croft (1990, 1991, 1998) and others.

3.2.2. Intentional agents and ToMM

A commonsense theory of physics cannot predict the behavior of volitional agents. Predicting such behavior requires a *theory of mind* that specifies how (possibly counterfactual) representations of states of affairs are related to each other, and how such mental representations can trigger actions. In Leslie (1994), the folk theory of mind is called **ToMM** (Theory of Mind Mechanism).

The distinguishing property of living and sentient kinds is autonomous, goal-directed movement.[2] Goal-directed movement must be distinguished from superficially similar kinds of movement: being pushed (Montgomery 1996) or pulled (White and Milne 1997) towards a goal by another object:

> [...] if Michael Jordan consistently hits his baskets, we would say that the movements of Michael Jordan were goal-directed, but we would not say that the movement of the basketball itself was goal-directed. Indeed, 3- and 5-year-olds reliably see the difference between being pushed toward a goal and moving there autonomously [...] (Opfer 2002:100)

White and Milne (1997) argue that an impression of pulling is decreased by a delay before movement, and a change in direction. Furthermore, goal-directed movement typically ends upon reaching the goal (*satisfaction*), and it is characterized by a *direct trajectory* towards the goal (Gergely et al. 1995; Premack and Premack 1997). When these factors are taken into account, then goal-directed motion consistently elicits animacy judgments in adults (Opfer 2002).

A subsequent question is of course whether goal-directed movement indicates merely life, or also sentience. In other words, is it a necessary condition of goal-directedness that the agent possesses a mental representation of the goal?

Indeed, this domain is subject to fundamental changes during development. Opfer and Gelman (2001) observe that children at age 10 and adults are capable of attributing goal-directed action to insentient plants. Like adults, 10 year-olds possess the relevant knowledge about biological objects, which allows them to make such judgments. By contrast, preschoolers do not. In explaining goal-directed action, they "referred to psychological states more often than any other factor" (Opfer 2002:103).

At an even earlier stage, when children do not yet ascribe psychological states to individuals, they can nevertheless identify and predict goal-direction motion. Gergely and colleagues (Csibra et al. 1999; Gergely et al. 1995; Gergely and Csibra 1997; cf. also Perner and Davies 1991; Perner

1995) argue that children as young as 12 months can interpret goal-directed movement as a rational means action. They do so by taking a *teleological stance*. "[W]hen interpreting behavior as goal-directed" at this stage, "rationality is attributed as a property of the *action*, and not of the agent (or the agent's mind)." (Gergely and Csibra 1997:233).

> Developmentally, teleological interpretations are transformed into causal mentalistic ones by 'mentalizing' the explanatory constructs of the teleological stance: i.e., by turning representations of actual reality constraints into 'beliefs' (which mentally represent such constraints), and representations of future goal states of reality into 'desires' (which mentally represent goal-states) (Gergely and Csibra 1997:232).

As Opfer and Gelman (2001) have shown, this *mentalization* is fully developed in preschoolers at the age of 5 years, who predict autonomous goal-directed motion with reference to mental states like beliefs and desires. The developmentally later distinction between non-sentient plants and sentient animals/humans only restricts the set of volitional agents in response to growing knowledge of the biological world. Such developments no longer affect the way in which volitional action is identified, interpreted and predicted.

The central explanatory construct employed by the adult folk-theory of mind is what the philosophical literature knows by the name of a *propositional attitude* (Frege 1879, 1892; Schiffer 1987). Like *force* in the domain of mechanical interaction, a *propositional attitude* is a relation between an agent and an object. In contrast to *force*, the agent of a propositional attitude must be sentient, and its object can be fictional, or far removed in space and time. Most importantly, the object of a propositional attitude may have the power to teleologically cause mechanical action.

3.3. Crossing the interface: cognition, syntax, and the lexicon

Turning back to the representation of verb meanings, recall the conclusion of Fodor and Lepore (1998) that recursive mechanisms in the lexicon are both redundant and undesirable. On the assumption of domain specificity in the central system, the situation becomes even worse for event composition in the lexicon. There are highly specialized subsystems of the mind, which are responsible for the computation of event representation. Conceptual parsimony dictates that such mechanisms should not be duplicated in the lexicon.

What the lexicon does need to encode is the information necessary for the central system to interpret the meaning of a verb, and it must do so in a way that is legible to the computational system. In this sense, the lexicon is indeed an interface. The question is now whether the complexity of representation we find at both sides of the lexicon, in the central systems of thought, and in the computational system of language, is sufficiently similar in order to justify the hypothesis of a structure preserving mapping from the mind into language. This question has been at the core of linguistic theorizing for a long time, and indeed there is mounting evidence to the effect that the mechanisms involved in the generation of linguistic complexity are fundamentally different from those involved in thought.

First, linguistic competence and general intelligence are functionally dissociated. Various forms of *specific language impairment* (Wexler 2003), both in acquisition and loss of linguistic competence, can occur without repercussions for the central system of thought. On the other hand, linguistic competence can be fully developed in spite of a severe cognitive impairment, as in *Williams syndrome* (Pinker 1999).

Second, linguistic expressions exhibit a number of peculiarities we do not find outside the language faculty. Chomsky (2001) recently calls such peculiarities *imperfections*, because they cannot be reduced to general cognitive or biological mechanisms. One of these is the *displacement* property. Constituents of a linguistic expression often appear in a position we would not expect, if language were a direct expression of thought. This second aspect, one of the cornerstones of the universalist hypothesis, is particularly relevant for the present discussion, and what we have called the *mapping problem* above. Recall from section 2 that theories on the mapping from lexical semantic structure into syntax face a severe problem. The problem was that lexicon-syntax relations cannot be formalized as a morphism: they are *many-to-many*.

On the assumption of a modular theory of the mind, such arbitrariness is expected. If the language faculty is a module, it operates encapsulated and blind. If we were to find a morphic mapping from event representation (i.e., cognition) into syntactic structure, such a finding would seriously challenge the encapsulated status of the language faculty, and support a more holistic view. As a matter of fact, it turned out throughout section 1 above that the relation between event representation (i.e., cognition) and syntax is notoriously vague. While some core notions like *agent* and *af-*

fected object tend to have regular realizations in grammar, the more complex an event representation becomes, the less likely it is that we find all event participants realized in a canonical grammatical environment, or that they are realized at all. Furthermore, the picture is blurred by the possible interaction of distinct sub-systems of cognition in the computation of a given event, especially when it comes to psychological predicates. If there is a morphic mapping from cognition into syntax, which module of cognition should take precedence over the other?

None of these problems arises if we assume that the lexicon is a list. When we speak of a verb as naming a section in the representation of an event in this sense, we can only mean that the lexical entry of the verb classifies its arguments as agents and patients with respect to the respective sub-system of cognition. Rather than representing complex event structures, a listed lexicon makes reference to a finite set of analyzable thematic roles. Consider as an illustration the contrast between *fear* and *frighten*:

(29) a. *John feared Helen/a renewed outbreak of cholera.*
b. *Helen/The renewed outbreak of cholera frightened John.*

Both verbs clearly name a psychological event. In the case of *fear*, the subject exhibits cognitive activity. It is therefore an agent for ToMM. The object, even if it denotes a sentient individual, corresponds to the content of the emotion. Therefore, it is a patient for ToMM. As far as the physical world is concerned, the verb *fear* does not constrain interpretation of its object (cf. the distinction between *cause* and *subject matter of emotion* in Pesetsky (1995).

The verb *frighten* behaves differently. Here it is the object, not the subject, which refers to a sentient, mentally active individual, i.e., an agent for ToMM. At the same time, the object of *frighten* is understood as the target of an external agent (the cause of its emotion). This state of affairs is accounted for, if *frighten* selects one argument (the subject), which is an agent for ToBy, and underspecified for ToMM, and another argument (the direct object), which is both an agent for ToMM and a patient for ToBy.

Specifications of this sort do not require lexical semantic *structure*. They can be spelled out as a simple list of features associated with any given lexical entry. A proposal along these lines has been made by Reinhart (2000), who argues that thematic information should be modeled in the form of feature clusters. Each cluster describes properties of one event participant. Although Reinhart (2000) motivates her features from a completely different perspective, the structure of narrative discourse (Miller and Johnson-Laird 1976; Rumelhart 1975; Shen 1985), they are ideal for the present purpose, because they refer to the domains of physical and mental activity, respectively. The feature referring to mental activity is called *m*, the one referring to physical activity is called *c*.

Coming back to the examples in (29), we may want to say that the lexical entry of *fear* incorporates two feature clusters (or Θ-roles). The cluster assigned to the direct object is specified as [-m], because the object must be the content of an emotion, and it is underspecified with respect to the physical domain. The cluster assigned to the subject is specified as [αc +m], because the subject of *fear* must engage in a mental activity. Whether this cluster is specified for the feature *c* is irrelevant for the present purpose of illustration.

(30) *fear*: {[αc +m], [-m], ...}

Likewise, the lexical entry of *frighten* must make reference to an argument, which is both an agent for ToMM, and a target of *force*. These properties are encoded as [-c+m]. In addition, *frighten* requires an argument that is an agent for ToBy, but underspecified with respect to the mental domain, which is encoded as [+c]. This gives us the following partial entry for *frighten*:

(31) *frighten*: {[+c], [-c+m], ...}

4. Reinhart's feature theory

> There is no syntactic structure in the lexicon; this would be a superfluous reduplication of the syntactic component. [...] Furthermore, we believe that lexical arity operations apply to the verb entry itself, which is a collection of properties/features, and not to an abstract event semantics representation (e.g., *λyλxλe(wash(e) & Agent(e, x) & Theme(e, y))*. More specifically, we assume that the event semantics representation is associated with the verb only during the derivation, and it is built compositionally on the basis of syntactic structure (Reinhart and Siloni 2005:12).

The following section is a brief sketch of the most important assumptions, exemplified with mostly English data.

4.1. The lexicon uniformity principle

At the basis of Reinhart (2000), we find a principle of economy, the *Lexicon Uniformity Principle.* This principle substantiates the status of the lexicon as a kind of "bottle-neck" between the domains of cognition and grammar.

(32) Lexicon Uniformity Principle (Reinhart 2000:4)
Each verb-concept corresponds to one lexical entry with one thematic structure. → The various thematic forms of a given verb are derived by lexicon-operations from one thematic structure.

In line with the Lexicon Uniformity Principle, Reinhart assumes that lexical entries encode the sum of information that can be realized in different diatheses. Correspondingly, the syntactic realization of a verb is often less complex thematically than its lexical representation would allow it to be. In this respect, Reinhart's approach differs from many others, e.g., Kratzer (1996), Pesetsky (1995), who assume argument-roles can be introduced in syntax, by means of adding an appropriate head. In Reinhart (2000), complex thematic configurations can be created in syntax, but they require the merger of distinct lexical items. A single lexical item cannot be causativized in syntax.

Therefore, if one diathesis of a verb indicates the presence of a given thematic feature-cluster, then it is assumed that this cluster is part of the verb's lexical entry. If this very role is absent in another diathesis, Reinhart assumes with Chierchia (1989) it has been eliminated by one of a small set of lexicon-operations, to which we turn in section 4.5.

Take as an example the contrast between causative and inchoative *melt*:

(33) a. *The sun melted the ice-cube.*
b. *The ice-cube melted.*

On Reinhart's assumptions, the causative use of the verb represents the basic lexical entry: both the cause ([+c]), and the theme-role ([-c-m]) are assigned to an argument. The inchoative use of *melt* in (33b) is derived from its lexical representation by a reduction-operation that eliminates [+c] (sect. 4.5).

4.2. Notational conventions

If we want to state generalizations for natural classes of thematic roles, we need notational conventions to refer to specific features. Reinhart (2001:3) adopts the following conventions:

(34) Notation (Reinhart 2001:3)
[α] = Feature cluster α.
/α = Feature (and value) α. (E.g. the feature /+m occurs in the clusters [+c+m], [-c+m] and [+m])
[/α] = A cluster one of whose features is /α. (E.g. [/-c] clusters are [-c+m], [-c-m] and [-c].)
[+] = A cluster ALL of whose features have the value +. (E.g. [-] clusters are [-c-m], [-c], [-m].)

These conventions are adopted here without modification. We might want to add the possibility to refer to a feature irrespectively of its value:

(35) α = Feature α. (E.g. the feature m designates an argument for interpretation in *folk psychology* (ToMM))

4.3. Feature clusters and verb classes

The two binary features c and m define natural classes of verbs that often cut across the correspondence classes defined by traditional listed roles, or those that follow from specific assumptions about basic predicates in event decomposition frameworks. For example, Reinhart's notation allows the statement of generalizations affecting agents, causes, emitters (i.e., *immediate causes* in Levin and Rappaport Hovav (1995): all of these roles are [/+c] clusters. They differ with respect to the presence and value of m. Agents are specified as [+c+m], causes as [+c], and emitters (like instruments and some others) are specified as [+c-m]. Likewise, the notation allows generalizations over agents and experiencers. Both are [/+m] roles. Agents are specified as [+c+m], experiencers as [-c+m]. A third possibility, underspecified [+m], is mentioned, but not discussed in Reinhart's work. It will become important from chapter 2 onwards.

Generalizations of this sort are exemplified in the following subsections, with examples from Reinhart (2001).

4.3.1. Underspecified causes: [+c]

An underspecified [+c] cluster is compatible with agents, causes and instruments. It is postulated for verbs allowing a range of subjects, like the following:

(36) V([+c], [-c-m]) – *break, open, roll...*
  a. *The wind/Max/the key opened the door.*
  b. *The storm/Max/the stone broke the window.*
  c. *The earthquake/Max the stick rolled the stone.*

(37) V ([+c], [-c+m] – *worry, amuse, scare, surprise...*
  a. *Max/the noise/the gun scared Lucie.*
  b. *Fred/Fred's behavior/the discussion surprised Lucie.*

A typical property of the theme-object verbs in (36) is that they tend to alternate with unaccusatives, while the experiencer-object verbs in (37) tend to alternate with unergatives (38a) or reflexives (38b) in many languages, like for instance German (38b).

(38) a. *Max worries.*
  b. *Max wundert sich.*
  Max surprises refl.
  'Max is surprised.'

We can formulate these observations in terms of feature specifications:

- Underspecified [+c] can be reduced.
- The resulting intransitive is realized as an unaccusative, if it selects [-c-m].
- The resulting intransitive is realized as an unergative or reflexive, if it selects [/+m].

4.3.2. Agents: [+c+m]

Fully specified [+c+m] is postulated, if the subject selected by a verb must be an agent in volitional control over the event:

(39) V ([+c+m], [-c-m]/[-c+m]) - *eat, shave, dress...*
a. *The baby/ *the spoon/ * hunger ate the soup.*
b. *Lucie/ *The razor/ *the heat shaved Max.*
c. *Lucie/ *the snow/ *the desire to feel warm dressed Max.*
d. *Max shaved/dressed.*

Members of the agent-subject class tend to have reflexive (39d), but no unaccusative alternate. Reinhart (2000) generalizes from this (and other) facts that a [/+m] cluster cannot be reduced.

4.3.3. Manner verbs and indirect causation: [/+c], [+c-m]

An interesting class of verbs allows either a volitional agent, or an instrument, but excludes a cause in subject position (40a/b vs. c). Reinhart (2001) refers to the verbs in this class as *manner verbs*, because they specify a specific way in which an agent performs an action. This property is represented by the selection of two [/+c] clusters. When the agent is realized in subject position, the [+c-m] cluster can be realized as an instrumental PP (40a). The instrument may also be realized in subject position. In that case, the agent cannot be realized at all (40b).

(40) a. *Max peeled the apple (with the knife).*
b. *The knife peeled the apple.*
c. **The heat peeled the apple.*

(41) *drill/peel* ([+c+m], [-c-m], [+c-m])

A comparable class of verbs is discussed in Grimshaw (1990) and Rapp (1997): *verbs of indirect causation.* Verbs of this kind name events that are typically composed of two sub-events: an activity and a resultant state. Unlike the event decomposition framework employed by Rapp (1997), Reinhart's notation does not require a lexical stipulation of the fact that the mediating activity must be identical with the cause of the resultant state. It is merely encoded in the form of a [+c-m] cluster. By /-m, it is an object of the agent's intention, and by /+c, it physically acts upon the argument specified as /-c.

Like *manner verbs*, *verbs of indirect causation* have two transitive alternants, an agentive and an instrumental one:

(42) a. *Hans enttäuschte uns mit seiner Leistung.*
Hans disappointed us with his performance
b. *Seine Leistung enttäuschte uns.*
his performance disappointed us

We can generalize that alternations of this sort occur whenever a verb selects two [/+c] clusters. Other example verb classes are cause-substance verbs like *fill* (notice that *fill* selects [+c] rather than [+c+m], and that German *füllen* behaves differently):

(43) a) *Max/ the hose/ the storm filled the pool with water.*
b) *The water filled the pool.*

(44) *fill* ([+c], [-c-m], [+c-m])

In line with the generalization that [+c] can be reduced, verbs like *fill* have unaccusative alternants:

(45) *The pool filled (with water).*

4.4. The realization of thematic feature clusters

The thematic feature specifications associated with a given verb determine the merging order of its arguments. This is accomplished by two interacting mechanisms.

First, a marking procedure designates thematic features for internal and external realization, respectively. In addition to this indexation, some verbs are marked with a subcategorization feature, accusative case. Verbs that are marked in this way must merge an argument DP in the position of a direct object.

In a second step, merging instructions guide the introduction of NP-arguments in accordance with the thematic features they are to realize.

4.4.1. Marking

The marking procedure is intended to serve several functions in Reinhart's work. First, it introduces a fundamental distinction between transitive and intransitive verbs. Only transitive verbs are marked, intransitives are left unmarked.

Second, the marking procedure distinguishes three classes of thematic role clusters: [+] clusters are marked with index 1, [-] clusters are marked with index 2. The mixed value clusters remain unmarked, as does the single cluster selected by underlyingly monadic verbs.

Finally, the marking procedure assigns an accusative subcategorization feature to prototypical transitives, which select both a [+] cluster, and a fully specified [/-c] cluster.

(46) Lexicon marking (Reinhart 2001:16)
Given an n-place verb-entry, n>1,
a. Mark a [-] cluster with index 2.
b. Mark a [+] cluster with index 1.
c. If the entry includes both a [+] cluster and a fully specified cluster [/α,/-c], mark the verb with the ACC feature.

(46) effectively derives much of the predictions Talmy (2000), Croft (1991, 1998) arrive at on the basis of their force-dynamic theory. The most important departure from Croft's proposal is the distinction between mental and physical activity. The effect of this distinction is that psychological verbs are no longer exceptional, and no separate system of verb-frames is needed to account for them. Their behavior is fully expected on the basis of the mixed value specification of experiencers, and their interaction with other clusters at the moment they are realized in a syntactic derivation.

4.4.2. Merging

Reinhart's *merging instructions* distinguish three scenarios. (i) The assignment of marked clusters is governed by their index (47b). (ii) If no cluster is marked with index 1, then the default rule (47a) applies. (iii) In the presence of two unmarked clusters, their realization is free.[3]

(47) CS merging instructions (Reinhart 2001:16)
  a. When nothing rules this out, merge externally.
  b. An argument realizing a cluster marked 2 merges internally; an argument with a cluster marked 1 merges externally.

This system derives the prototypical transitive sentence as one with two marked clusters assigned, a [+] cluster in external position, and fully specified [/-c] cluster in internal position.

The system also derives unergatives as prototypical intransitives. This follows from the default merging rule (47a), and the exemption of genuinely monadic verbs from the marking procedure (46).

Most unaccusatives, and reflexives are analyzed as derived forms.

4.5. Arity operations and the like

There are two major classes of verbs that show a systematic alternation between transitive and intransitive uses cross-linguistically: unaccusatives and reflexives. Several authors take the intransitive use as basic, and derive the transitive variant with the help of a transitivizing syntactic head (Kratzer 1996; Pesetsky 1995).

In Reinhart's framework (cf. also Chierchia 1989), the transitive entries are basic, and the intransitive ones are derived. An operation of reduction derives intransitive from marked transitive entries.

Reduction can apply to an internal, or to an external cluster. Consequently, Reinhart distinguishes between internal and external role reduction: *expletivization* deletes an external cluster; *reflexivization* an internal cluster with an external one.

Turn first to external role reduction, the one that derives unaccusatives. This kind of operation targets only transitive entries with a [+c] external cluster. It deletes the external Θ-role and the ACC feature of the verb. If the remaining cluster is marked *2* (i.e., [-c-m], [-c], or [-m]), it must be realized internally, and the result is an unaccusative verb, as in (49).

(48) Decausativization: Reduction of an external [+c] role ((67a) in Reinhart and Siloni 2005)
$V_{acc}(\Theta_{1[+c]}, \Theta_2) \rightarrow V(\Theta_2)$

(49) *open*$_{ACC}$ ([+c], [-c-m] → *open* ([-c-m])

On the other hand, if the remaining cluster is not marked, it must be realized externally by the default rule (47a). This is most notably the case with psychological predicates like *worry* in (50).

(50) *worry*$_{ACC}$ ([+c], [-c+m] → *worry* ([-c+m])

A second major operation bundles an internal and an external role and forms a single, conjoined role cluster. Reflexivization eliminates the ACC feature in some, but not in all languages.

(51) Reflexivization ((24) in Reinhart and Siloni 2005)
$[\Theta_i]$ $[\Theta_j] \rightarrow [\Theta_i - \Theta_j]$, where Θ_i is an external role

(52) *Max shaved.*

Third, saturation can apply to implicit arguments. Saturation is typically involved in the derivation of passives and middles (Marelj 2004).

(53) a. *wash* (Θ1, Θ2)
b. Saturation: ∃x (*wash* (x, Θ2)
c. *Max was washed t ≡ ∃x (x washed Max).*

There is one more lexicon operation in Reinhart's system: *causativization.* Rather than eliminating or saturating a role cluster, causativization manipulates the feature specification of existing roles, and adds an agent cluster.

(54) a. *John walked.*
b. *John walked the dog.*

(55) Causativization ((21) in Reinhart 2002)
a. *Decausativize:* Change a /+c feature to a /-c feature.
walk([+c+m]) → *walk*([-c+m])
b. *Agentivize:* Add an agent role.
walk([-c+m]) → *walk*([+c+m],[-c+m])

Causativization is necessary, because the alternation it describes affects a [/+m] cluster, and [/+m] cannot be eliminated by hypothesis.

The only thing that can happen to a lexical [/+m] cluster is to remain unrealized, as it is the case in the alternation described for *manner verbs* and *verbs of indirect causation* above:

(56) a. *Max peeled the apple (with the knife).*
b. *The knife peeled the apple.*
c. **The heat peeled the apple.*

(57) *drill/peel* ([+c+m], [-c-m], [+c-m])

Remaining unrealized is an option not only for *manner* verbs. It is made use of in the context of the *subject matter* problem (Pesetsky 1995; Reinhart 2002). Consider the following paradigm:

(58) a. *The article angered Bill.*
b. *The government angered Bill.*
c. **The article angered Bill at the government.*

(59) *The article made Bill angry at the government.*

Pesetsky (1995) shows that verbs like *anger* select two cause-like thematic roles, a *cause* ([+c] in the present notation), and a *target/subject matter of emotion* ([-m] here):

(60) *anger* [+c], [-c+m], [-m]

Although they are logically compatible as shown in (59), the two roles cannot co-occur in a single predicate (58c). Reinhart (2001) argues that this observation must be blamed on a condition of cluster distinctness:

(61) Cluster distinctness (Reinhart 2001:14)
a) Two indistinct Θ-clusters cannot be both realized on the same predicate.
b) Distinctness: Two feature-clusters α, β are distinct iff a. they share at least one feature, and b. there is at least one feature or value which they do not share.

Since [+c] and [-m] do not share a feature by which they could be distinguished, one of them must remain unrealized.

5. Conclusion

This chapter undertook to delimit the demands on a theory of lexical semantics, stating three questions: a *properties problem*, an *interface problem*, and a *mapping problem*. After a brief summary of the literature, it was argued that the theoretical status of lexical semantics must be determined by explicit assumptions about adjacent domains of the mind, namely cognition and language. With respect to cognition, a modular theory of central thought processes was adopted. It was claimed that two modules are of primary importance for the interpretation of events, a *commonsense theory of physics*, and a *commonsense theory of mind mechanisms*. Since these modules are powerful enough to create complex event representations, complexity in lexical representation was rejected as unnecessary. It was argued, however, that lexical verb meanings should encode information about (i) domain-specific categorization, and (ii) agentive status of its arguments. This was the answer to the *properties problem*.

The feature notation in Reinhart's *Theta System* was found to match these demands in an ideal way, and it was therefore adopted. Reinhart's notation supplies a trivial answer to the *interface problem*. Binary features are legible by the computational system, and they can easily be interpreted as neo-Davidsonian predicates in the semantic component.

The stage has now been set to investigate the most interesting question of lexical semantics, the *mapping problem*. In chapter 2, the (lexical and syntactic) argument structure of a set of German verbs will be described in some detail. Chapter 3 then develops a theory of syntactic projection that accommodates both the facts of chapter 2, and the conceptual demands argued for in this chapter: a listed lexicon, and an autonomous syntax.

Notes

[1] Notice that this is not the case for formulations in terms of thematic positions and visibility, rather than discrete roles, as in Chomsky (1986:97): "*Each argument A appears in a chain containing a unique visible theta position P, and each theta position P is visible in a chain containing a unique argument A.*"

[2] "*Movement* is used here in the full sense used by Michotte (1963), which includes 'changes in shape', which he classifies as the special movement of the 'kinaesthetic amoeba' (pp.204-206). Thus, a plant growing toward the sun, or an amoeba engulfing a paramecium would equally count as movements" (Opfer 2002:100).

[3] Notice that this formulation of the merging instructions predicts that a verb selecting two mixed-value clusters should have variable argument realization. A case at hand would be the German verb *faszinieren* (to impress). It will be argued in chapter 2 that this is not true. [+c-m] cannot be assigned to an internal argument.

Chapter 2
German verbs: lexical representation and argument realization

In this chapter, Reinhart's notation in terms of two binary features, [+/-m] and [+/-c] is applied to a set of German verbs. After a detailed examination of a significant set of verbs, the syntactic realization of these verbs will be examined with respect to the predictions of the *Theta System*. The facts presented in this chapter will supply the empirical basis for the theoretical discussion in chapters 3 and 4.

The chapter is organized as follows: Section 1 gives an overview of thematic features, and on how they (do not) compare with traditional role labels. Section 2 applies the feature notation to a set of German verbs, and exemplifies the reasoning that allows us to postulate specific lexical representations. It then describes the realization of thematic feature clusters in a pre-theoretical way. The syntactic properties of thematic role realization are examined in more detail in section 3. This section will conclude that the predictions of the *Theta System* are largely correct. The most important deviation from the *Theta System* defended in that section is with respect to underspecified [-] clusters. It is argued that such clusters can be assigned to a VP-external subject. Section 4 discusses the reflexive alternation in German. The conclusion reached in that section is less straightforward. Standard unaccusativity tests do not supply conclusive evidence in favor of, or against an unaccusative analysis of non-causative German reflexives.

1. Introduction: features and roles

The notation adopted from Reinhart (2000) allows the combination and underspecification of features, such that there are eight distinct feature-clusters. Each of these clusters has an interpretation in the semantic component. Marelj (2004) argues that each thematic role cluster can be interpreted as a role predicate in the sense of neo-Davidsonian semantics (Parsons 1990). In what follows, I will be referring to clusters as *Θ-roles* in this sense. Strictly speaking, feature clusters have little in common with traditional, atomistic Θ-roles. First, their number is defined. We cannot 'discover' new roles by inspection of empirical facts. This greatly limits the arbitrariness of role-lists mentioned in chapter 1. Second, the notation defines natural classes of events, and thus tackles the super-role problem. Finer distinctions are described with reference to fully specified clusters. Grosser generalizations are captured by natural classes of clusters. For example, the set of all clusters containing a [/+c] specification corresponds to Levin and Rappaport's *immediate cause*. The following table sketches the interpretation of possible feature combinations.

(1)

cluster	specified for:	not specified for:
[+c+m]	physically and mentally active	
[+c-m]	physically active, object of thought	
[-c+m]	target of *force*, mentally active	
[-c-m]	target of *force*, object of thought	
[+c]	physically active	sentience
[+m]	mentally active	*force*
[-c]	target of *force*	sentience
[-m]	object of thought	*force*

At the top end of this set, we find the fully specified [+]-cluster [+c+m]. An argument to which this cluster is assigned is interpreted as an agent with respect to the verb-event in both domains of event interpretation, the physical and the mental. Since a co-occurrence of mental activity and physical causation is perceived by the human mind as volitional control (Wegner and Wheatley 1999), an argument bearing the [+c+m] cluster is interpreted as an agent in volitional control of the event.

The fully specified [-]-cluster [-c-m] occupies the other end of this scale. [/-c] specifies a patient in the domain of mechanical action. [/-m] does the same for the mental domain. In this sense, [-c-m] corresponds to traditional roles like *theme*, *affected/effected object* and the like.

[-c+m] differs from [-c-m] with respect to the mental domain. An argument bearing this cluster is still a target of *force*, but it must be a mental agent. The object-role of *frighten* is an example. When somebody is frightened, an external force triggers the mental state *fear* in the argument. Usually, [-c+m] corresponds to the role label *experiencer*. However, it likewise applies to goals and addressees, if such roles appear with a condition of sentience.

The other mixed value cluster is [+c-m]. Its [/+c] specification requires that the argument it is assigned to is an agent with respect to physics, while

[/-m] requires that it is an object in the domain of minds. Typically, this is the case with instruments. They bring about a physical event, and they are likewise objects of an intention. It also applies to the argument of internally caused change of state verbs like *bloom, blossom, flower*. Since these events are represented as internally caused, their subject must be specified as an agent with respect to physics. At the same time, these verbs exclude any reference to intentionality. Therefore, their subjects must be specified as objects in the mental domain.

Underspecified clusters allow for a wider range of interpretations. [+c] requires agency in the physical domain, but does not give any instruction with respect to the mental domain. An argument assigned [+c] can be interpreted as an agent, a cause, or an instrument, depending on many factors including world knowledge: *Max/the wind/the key opened the door.*

[+m] requires agency in the mental domain, and leaves physical aspects unconstrained. For example, the subject in *The madman loves his sheep* can, but does not need to be physically active. Rapp (1997) observes that emotions have this property in general. They can be read as either activities, or as states. Rapp describes this variability with two base predicates, *PSYCH-DO* vs. *PSYCH-BE*. In the feature-notation, it follows from underspecification.

The underspecified [-] clusters give rise to the biggest freedom of interpretation. [-c] requires that an argument receives a passive interpretation in the physical domain. It does not specify mental requirements or constraints. Therefore, *experiencer*, *theme*, *goal*, and similar interpretations are compatible with [-c]. [-m] states the same requirement for the mental domain, and thus allows interpretations like *theme*, *goal*, *source* and *instrument.*

The underspecified [-] clusters share a number of properties with each other, and with other clusters. Therefore, it is important to be aware of the differences. [-m] must be postulated as opposed to [-c], if an argument can be read as *theme/goal*, and allows an additional *instrument*, *source*, or other force-bearing interpretation. An example of this latter reading is the subject of stative *contain* in *the jar contains water.*

[-m] differs from [+c-m] at the other end of the force-scale. [+c-m] excludes an affectedness-reading, while [-m] would allow it. An example is the contrast between *fill* and *spray.* The substance used to *fill* something cannot be read as an affected object, but the substance used for *spraying* can. So it is ungrammatical to say that **John filled water into the bottle*, while it is grammatical that *he sprayed paint on the wall. Fill* selects [+c-m], *spray* selects [-m].

[-c] differs from [-c+m] in that it does not refer to the mental domain at all. For example, when we observe an alternation between goal and experiencer, the verb selects [-c]. However, if the goal is always required to intentionally cooperate, then we must postulate [-c+m].

Both [-c] and [-m] differ from [-c-m] in that they allow for alternations that are unavailable, had [-c-m] been selected. [-c] allows intentionality, [-m] causation.

2. Role sets and realization patterns

This section introduces a set of verbs that will constitute the empirical basis of the discussion to follow. The section is based to a considerable degree on Rapp (1997), which is helpful for the present discussion because of the importance it attributes to the role of causality in the mapping from the lexicon into syntax. For an overview of more aspect-oriented theories the reader is referred to Engelberg (2000). For an extensive collection of data, cf. Schumacher (1986).

2.1. Agent verbs: [+c+m]

I call a verb an *agent verb*, if it selects a [+c+m] cluster. The class of agent verbs can be distinguished on the basis of further clusters selected.

2.1.1. Agent-patient verbs

There are many two-place verbs that select both a [+c+m] cluster, and a [/-c] cluster. A first class in the set of agent verbs comprises those that select a theme along with the agent:

(2) [+c+m], [-c-m]
bauen 'build', *besteigen* 'climb', *betreten* 'enter/walk on', *erklimmen* 'climb-terminative', *kämmen* 'comb', *malen* 'paint', *rasieren* 'shave', *überdachen* 'cover/ build a roof over'

An agent-theme verb is the nearest we can get to the proto-entailments of Dowty (1991). One of its arguments is required to contribute both mental and physical activity. Since this is equivalent to full volitional control, imperatives are very natural (the (b) examples below), and the volitional attitude of the agent can be modified (the (c) examples).

(3) a. *Hans betritt den Raum.*
Hans enters the room
b. *Betritt jetzt das Zimmer!*
enter now the room
'Enter the room now!'
c. *Hans betrat den Raum absichtlich/gern.*
Hans entered the room on-purpose/with-pleasure

(4) a. *Bau/Mal/Überdache ein Zimmer!*
build/paint/cover a room
b. *Besteig/Erklimm den Berg!*
climb/climb the mountain
c. *Kämme/Rasiere mich!*
comb/shave me

The other argument is required to be a target of force, and the object of an intention. These requirements can be fulfilled in different ways. The argument can be effected (5a), affected (5b) or the target of a terminative motion, as in (5c). Recall that contact is a requirement of folk physics. Since a terminative motion requires contact, the respective verb selects [/-c].

(5) a. *Hans baut ein Haus.*
Hans builds a house
b. *Hans kämmt seinen Bart.*
Hans combs his beard
c. *Hans erklomm den Gipfel.*
Hans climbed the summit
'Hans reached the summit.'

A second set of agentive verbs selects an experiencer along with the agent:

(6) [+c+m] [-c+m]
beraten 'advise'

Agent-experiencer verbs differ minimally from agent-theme verbs. As above, one argument is understood as a volitional agent, and the other one as a patient. In contrast to the verbs above, both arguments must generate truth-conditionally relevant mental activity. The subject does so in the form of volitional action. This action triggers the mental activity in the object. Since German *beraten* 'advise' requires mental activity by its object, inanimate objects are impossible (7b).

(7) a. *Hans beriet Helmut.*
Hans advised Helmut
b. **Hans beriet das Projekt.*
Hans advised the project

A third set comprises ditransitive agentive verb. The following verb exemplifies this class:

(8) a. [+c+m] [-c+m] [-c-m]
mitteilen 'pass on'

The direct object of *mitteilen* 'inform' refers to something that is both being said ([/-c]), and the object of an intention ([/-m]). The dative likewise denotes the target of an activity: it is being addressed, and realizes [/-c]. At the same time, it must intentionally cooperate, and inanimates are ungrammatical (9c). Therefore, the dative realizes [-c+m]. Notice that the dative can be omitted (9b), but this sentence is read as referring to a discourse-salient addressee, indicating that the dative is selected, not free.

(9) a. *Hans hat mir die Nachricht mitgeteilt.*
Hans has to-me the news on-passed
'Hans passed the news on to me.'
b. *Hans hat die Nachricht mitgeteilt.* (salient addressee)
Hans has the news on-passed
'Hans passed the news on.'
c. **Hans hat dem Projekt einige Änderungen mitgeteilt.*
Hans has to-the project some amendments on-passed

The verb *mitteilen* 'pass on/inform' differs from similar verbs with respect to the role assigned to the dative. Consider *beibringen* 'teach/inflict/supply', to be discussed below in the section on underspecified [+c]. *beibrin-*

gen 'teach/produce' differs minimally from *mitteilen* 'pass on information' with respect to the role it assigns to the dative. On one reading, the dative must clearly be sentient (10a). There is another reading, though, where the dative refers to an inanimate goal (10b, c). Notice the contrast in acceptability between (9c) above, and (10c) below:

(10) a. *Hans hat uns das Singen beigebracht.*
Hans has to-us the singing taught
'Hans taught us how to sing.'
b. *Hans hat uns eine Niederlage beigebracht.*
Hans has to-us a defeat produced
'Hans defeated us.'
c. *Hans hat dem Projekt einen Rückschlag beigebracht.*
Hans has to-the project a setback produced
'Hans caused a setback for the project.'

The fact that the inanimate goal in (10c) is realized in a dative indicates that the dative case does not introduce an animacy restriction. The restriction we observe in (9) must therefore be a property of the lexical entry of *mitteilen* 'pass on'.

2.1.2. Agent-instrument verbs

Reinhart (2001) discusses a class of verbs she calls *manner verbs*, which alternate between an agentive and an instrumental use. An example is *to peel.*

(11) a. *Max peeled the apple (with the knife).*
b. *The knife peeled the apple.*

A similar pattern of behavior is described by Rapp (1997) under the heading of *indirect causation* ("Wirkungsverben"). The agent in the following example is understood to trigger the event described by the verb by doing something else. The immediate cause of the event can be referred to by an *argument-adjunct*, in Rapp's terminology.

(12) *Hans schont die Wäsche, indem er sie kalt wäscht.*
Hans protects the clothes in-that he them cold washes
'Hans protects the clothes by washing them cold.'

Like Reinhart's manner verbs, Rapp's verbs of indirect causation alternate between an agentive (12) and an instrumental use (13).

(13) *Kaltes Waschen schont die Wäsche.*
cold washing protects the clothes

The common property of both *indirect causation* and *manner verbs* is the perception that certain events cannot be caused by a single event participant alone. This perception is encoded in the lexicon by the presence of two [/+c] clusters.

The set of agent-instrument verbs can be divided into sub-classes depending on the further arguments they select. Consider as a first sub-class verbs that select a theme direct object:

(14) [+c+m] [+c-m] [-c-m]
abweisen 'reflect/reject', *schmücken* 'decorate', *schonen* 'protect/spare', *umgeben* 'surround', *umhüllen* 'cover', *umrahmen* 'frame', *verraten* 'betray/give away'

The accusative is both affected by an action, and the object of an intention. The presence of two [/+c] clusters is shown in two steps. First, these verbs alternate between an agentive and an instrumental use, as illustrated in the (a) vs. (b) examples below.

(15) a. *Hans weist einen Antrag ab.*
Hans rejects an application prt
'Hans is rejecting an application.'
b. *Der Stoff weist Flüssigkeiten ab.*
the fabric reflects liquids prt
'The fabric reflects liquids.'

(16) a. *Hans schmückt den Balkon mit Blumen.*
Hans decorates the balcony with flowers
b. *Blumen schmücken den Balkon.*
flowers adorn the balcony

(17) a. *Hans schont die Natur.*
Hans protects the nature
b. *Das Medikament schont den Magen.*
the drug protects the stomach

(18) a. *Hans umgibt das Dorf mit einer Mauer.*
Hans surrounds the village with a wall
b. *Eine Mauer umgibt das Dorf.*
a wall surrounds the village

(19) a. *Hans umhüllt sein Gesicht mit einem Tuch.*
Hans covers his face with a cloth
b. *Ein Tuch umhüllt sein Gesicht.*
a cloth covers his face

(20) a. *Hans umrahmt den Empfang mit einer Gesangsdarbietung.*
Hans frames the reception with a singing-performance
b. *Eine Gesangsdarbietung umrahmt den Empfang.*
a singing-performance frames the reception

(21) a. *Hans verrät ein Geheimnis.*
H. gives-away a secret
b. *Sein Vorgehen verrät geringen Sachverstand.*
his action betrays poor expert-knowledge

Second, it is impossible to account for this alternation in terms of under-specification. If these verbs selected underspecified [+c], we would expect non-intentional, inanimate causes in eventive environments. However, this is not the case (22). The eventive use of these verbs implies the realization of the agent cluster. Therefore, agent and instrument must be distinct roles.

(22) a. **Der Krieg weist mehr Anträge ab als gewöhnlich.*
the war rejects more applications than usual
b. **Der Frühling schmückt den Garten mit Blüten.*
the spring decorates the garden with flowers
c. ??*Der milde Winter schont das Wildleben.*
the mild winter protects the wildlife

d. ??*Der Krieg umgibt das Dorf mit feindlichen Garnisonen.*
the war surrounds the village with enemy garrisons
e. ??*Der Krieg umhüllt das Dorf mit Rauch.*
the war covers the village with smoke
f. **Der Zeitdruck umrahmt den Empfang mit einem gekürzten Streichquartett.*
the time-constraint frames the reception with a shortened string-quartet
g. ??*Das Licht verrät die Schwächen des Aggressors.*
the light betrays the weaknesses of-the aggressor

A second sub-class comprises verbs that select an experiencer internal argument:

(23) [+c+m] [+c-m] [-c+m]
beleidigen 'insult', *demütigen* 'humiliate', *enttäuschen* 'disappoint'

The direct object of these verbs is still a target of force, but it is also required to generate truth-conditionally relevant mental activity. Notice that, in some cases, the direct object may name the elicited mental state in place of its bearer (24b). Reference to non-sentient objects is clearly impossible.

(24) a. *Hans beleidigte Helene.*
Hans insulted Helene
b. *Diese Bemerkung beleidigt den guten Geschmack.*
that comment insults the good taste
c. **Hans beleidigte das schlechte Kunstwerk.*
Hans insulted the bad work-of-art

(25) a. *Helene demütigte Hans.*
Helene humiliated Hans
b. **Helene demütigte die Armbanduhr ihres Freundes.*
Helene humiliated the wrist-watch of-her friend

(26) a. *Hans enttäuschte Helene.*
Hans disappointed Helene
b. **Hans enttäuschte das Projekt.*
Hans disappointed the project

The subject alternation remains the same as above. Eventive sentences have agent subjects, subject matter subjects correlate with a cognitive-state/attitude interpretation. Although judgments about eventivity in the (b) examples vary, consider the contrast between (a), (b) and (c) below. The subject of these verbs can be a volitional agent in (a), or a subject matter, as in (b), but it cannot be a non-intentional cause distinct from the subject matter (c). Underspecified [+c] would allow the (c) examples. Therefore, we must postulate {[+c+m], [+c-m], ...}, as opposed to {[+c], [+c-m], ...}.

(27) a. *Hans beleidigte Helene mit einer sexistischen Bemerkung.*
Hans insulted Helene with a sexist remark
b. *Die sexistische Bemerkung beleidigte Helene.*
the sexist remark insulted Helene
c. **Der Krieg beleidigte Helene (mit/durch gesteigerten Sexismus).*
the war insulted Helene with/through increased sexism

(28) a. *Helene demütigte Hans mit einer öffentlichen Abweisung.*
Helene humiliated Hans with a public rebuffal
b. *Die öffentliche Abfuhr demütigte Hans.*
the public rebuffal humiliated Hans
c. **Der Krieg demütigte Hans (mit/durch den Wegfall aller Privilegien).*
the war humiliated Hans with/through the loss of-all privileges

(29) a. *Hans enttäuschte Helene mit seiner Illoyalität.*
Hans disappointed Helene with his illoyalty
b. *Seine Illoyalität enttäuschte Helene.*
his illoyalty disappointed Helene
c. **Der Krieg enttäuschte Helene (mit/durch die verlogene Berichterstattung).*
the war disappointed Helene through the false reporting

2.2. Underspecified causation: [+c]

Underspecified [+c] does not introduce the constraints observed above for double causation. As long as an argument can be understood as a bearer of *force*, it can realize this cluster, no matter whether the predicate is interpreted eventively or not, or whether the argument is animate or not.

2.2.1. Cause-theme verbs

(30) [+c] [-c-m]
begrenzen 'limit', *behindern* 'obstruct', *gefährden* 'endanger', *halten* 'hold', *holen* 'get/fetch', *rollen* 'roll', *schieben* 'push', *schleppen* 'tow/drag', *verbrennen* 'burn'

All of these verbs allow agents, causes, instruments, and similar roles as subjects. This freedom of interpretation is characteristic of underspecification.

(31) a. *Hans/seine Politik/der Investitionsstop begrenzte die Einnahmen.*
Hans/his policies/the investment-stop limited the revenue
b. *Der Zaun begrenzt den Garten.*
the fence limits the garden

(32) *Hans/ das schlechte Wetter/ die Blockade behindert den Verkehr.*
Hans/the bad weather/the barrier obstructs the traffic

(33) *Hans/ die Parteikrise/ der Ministerwechsel gefährdet das Projekt.*
Hans/the party-crisis/the government-reshuffle endangers the project

(34) a. *Hans/ ein dünner Faden hielt die Tasche.*
Hans/a thin thread held the bag
b. *Der Krieg hielt den Kurs hoch.*
the war held the rate high

(35) a. *Hans holt einen Wein.*
Hans fetches a wine
b. *Der Herbst holte die Blätter von den Bäumen.*
the autumn fetched the leaves from the trees

(36) a. *Hans/ der Sturm rollt die Dornen zu Bündeln.*
Hans/the gales rolled the thorns to bundles

b. *Die Maschine rollt den Zwirn auf die Spule.*
the machine rolls the thread on-to the spool

(37) a. *Hans/ die Zugmaschine schob den Wagen in die Scheune.*
Hans/the tractor pushed the carriage in-to the barn
b. *Der Gletscher schob die Moräne bis in die Kaiserau.*
the glacier pushed the debris up to the Kaiserau

(38) a. *Hans schleppt eine Tasche.*
Hans carries a bag
b. *Die Zugmaschine schleppt einen Anhänger.*
the tractor pulls a trailer

(39) a. *Hans und Helmut/ die Flammen verbrennen unsere Bücher.*
Hans and Helmut/the flames burn our books
b. *Die Sonne verbrennt seine Haut.*
the sun burns his skin

The objects are always passive both on the physical and on the mental scale. They realize fully specified [-c-m].

A small subset of transitive causatives has a non-causative variant, which refers to an externally caused event affecting the subject. This is the case for *rollen* 'roll', *verbrennen* 'burn':

(40) a. *Der Ball ist ins Tor gerollt.*
the ball is in-the goal rolled
'The ball rolled into the goal.'
b. *Das Haus ist verbrannt.*
the house is burned
'The house has burned down.'

Notice that the alternation between [+c] and [-c-m] differs from the one we observed above between [+c+m] and [+c-m]. With [+c+m]/[+c-m], the alternation is fully productive. It does not have an exception. With [+c]/[-c-m], it affects just a tiny, lexically defined subset of verbs. This asymmetry will be relevant in the formalization of diathesis alternations in sections 3 and 4 below.

2.2.2. Verbs of indirect and double causation

Underspecified [+c] is compatible with double causation. Since [+c] alone allows any physically active role interpretation, the co-occurrence of [+c] with [+c-m] cannot be argued for on the basis of excluded configurations. However, the double or indirect causation denoted by these verbs can be observed in various other ways.

In some cases, a verb selects a subject that triggers the event by causing a mediating event. Rapp (1997) observes that these verbs allow their imperative to be paraphrased as a bi-clausal imperative that separates [+c] (interpreted as an agent) and [+c-m] (interpreted as a mediating event). Such paraphrases are unavailable for verbs that lack the additional [/+c] cluster. Notice that some speakers find the paraphrases slightly less acceptable than the simple imperatives, but there is still a contrast between (41b) and (42b).

(41) a. *Senke die Ausgaben!*
lower the expenses
b. *Mache etwas, wodurch du die Ausgaben senkst!*
do something by-which you the expenses lower
'Do something by which you lower the expenses!'

(42) a. *Schieb den Wagen zur Seite!*
push the cart to-the side
b. ??*Mach etwas, wodurch du den Wagen zur Seite schiebst!*
do something by-which you the cart to-the side push

Rapp's test is applicable wherever [+c-m] is interpreted as a mediating event. However, not every [+c-m] cluster is interpreted in this way. Indeed its most natural interpretation is instrumental. This poses a problem, because instrumental adjuncts are often not selected, but free adjuncts licensed by an agent in subject position.

(43) *Hans baut ein Haus mit seinen eigenen Händen.*
Hans builds a house with his own hands

However, only volitional agents license unselected instruments. With an inanimate cause subject, a free instrumental adjunct is marginal at best:

(44) a. *Hans rollt mit bloßen Händen den Faden auf die Spule.*
Hans rolls with bare hands the thread on the spool
b. ??*Die Maschine rollt mit einem Haken den Faden auf die Spule.*
the machine rolls with a hook the thread on the spool

This constraint gives us the test we are looking for. When an instrument/source co-occurs with an inanimate subject, it must be selected. I claim it realizes [+c-m].

(45) *Die Chemische Industrie verschmutzt den Fluss mit Abwässern.*
the chemical industry contaminates the river with sewage

Consider as a first set psychological double causatives, exemplified by the following verb:

(46) [+c] [+c-m] [-c+m]
erschrecken 'frighten/scare'

Underspecified [+c] is called for by variable subject interpretation. We can find a volitional agent, an inanimate cause, or a subject matter of emotion.

(47) a. *Hans erschreckt Helmut.*
Hans scares Helmut
b. *Der Brief des Arztes erschreckt Helmut.*
the letter by-the doctor frightens Helmut
c. *Der Inhalt des Briefs des Arztes erschreckt Helmut.*
the content of-the letter by-the doctor frightened Helmut

The presence of the second [/+c] cluster can be observed in examples with a cause subject and a subject-matter adjunct.[1]

(48) a. *Hans erschreckte Helmut mit einem lauten Schrei.*
Hans frightened Helmut with a loud scream
b. *Die Presseerklärung erschreckte mich mit ihrer Aggressivität.*
the press-statement scared me with its aggressiveness

The verb *erschrecken* 'scare/frighten' has a non-causative variant, on which the experiencer role is assigned to the subject. In the following example, the event is interpreted as externally caused, and the subject is affected by it. Notice that non-causative *erschrecken* 'get scared' belongs to a different inflectional class than its causative counterpart. The causative verb is *weak* (it marks tense by affixation, (48)), the non-causative form is *strong* (it marks tense by a stem vowel change, (49)). This fact will be relevant in the discussion of the locus of reduction in section 3.1 below.

(49) *Hans erschrak.*
Hans scared
'Hans got scared.'

Another set of double-causatives selects a theme internal argument:

(50) [+c] [+c-m] [-c-m]
anregen 'propose/stimulate', *bedecken* 'cover', *dämpfen* 'dim/diminish', *erschweren* 'make difficult', *hemmen* 'impede', *schädigen* 'harm', *senken* 'lower', *transportieren* 'transport', *verschmutzen* 'contaminate'

As above, [+c] is supported by the variable interpretation of subjects with the verbs of this class:

(51) a. *Hans/der Krieg/die Kapitalspritze regte die Produktion an.*
Hans/the war/the capital investment stimulated the production prt
b. *Hans/der Sturm bedeckte das Dorf mit einer Staubschicht.*
Hans/the storm covered the village with a dust-layer
c. *Hans/ der Krieg/ die Vereinbarung dämpfte unsere Erwartungen.*
Hans/the war/the agreement lowered our expectations
d. *Hans/ der Fluss/ die Strömung transportiert Geschiebe.*
Hans/the river/the current transports debris
e. *Hans/ die Industrie/ das Abwasser verschmutzt den Rhein.*
Hans/the industry/the sewage contaminates the Rhine
f. *Hans/ der Krieg/ die Blockade erschwert die Durchfahrt.*
Hans/the war/the blockade makes-difficult the passing
g. *Hans/ die Krise/ sein Taktieren hemmt den Fortschritt.*
Hans/the crisis/his caution impedes the progress
h. *Hans/ die Krise/ sein Taktieren schädigt unsere Interessen.*
Hans/the crisis/his causation harms our interests
i. *Hans/ die Krise/ der Investitionsstop senkte den Ertrag.*
Hans/the crisis/the investment-stop lowered the revenue

The additional [+c-m] cluster is supported for the following verbs by the co-occurrence of a cause subject and a subject matter PP:

(52) a. *Der Krieg regte mit einer gesteigerten Nachfrage die Produktion an.*
the war stimulated with an increased demand the production prt
b. *Der Sturm bedeckte das Dorf mit einer Staubschicht.*
the storm covered the village with a dust-layer
c. *Die Vereinbarung dämpfte durch weitgehende Zugeständnisse an den Aggressor die Hoffnung auf baldigen Frieden.*
the agreement lowered through extensive concessions to the aggressor the hope for early peace
d. *Der Inn transportiert mit seiner starken Strömung viel Geschiebe.*
the river-Inn transports with its strong current much debris
e. *Die Industrie verschmutzt den Rhein mit Abwässern.*
the industry contaminates the Rhine with sewage

In the other cases, Rapp's indirect imperatives show the presence of the additional [+c-m] cluster.

(53) a. *Erschwere die Aufgabe!*
make-difficult the task
b. *Mach etwas, wodurch du die Aufgabe erschwerst!*
do something by-which you the task make-difficult
'Do something to make the task more difficult!'

(54) a. *Hemme den Fortschritt!*
impede the progress
b. *Mach etwas, wodurch du den Fortschritt hemmst!*
do something by-which you the progress impede
'Do something to impede the progress!'

(55) a. *Schädige seine Interessen!*
harm his interests
b. *Mach etwas, wodurch du seine Interessen schädigst!*
do something by-which you his interests harm
'Do something to harm his interests!'

(56) a. *Senke die Ausgaben!*
lower the expenses
b. *Mach etwas, wodurch du die Ausgaben senkst!*
do something by-which you the expenses lower
'Do something to lower the expenses!'

In this rather numerous set of verbs, we find one that has a non-causative variant: *senken* 'lower/sink'. The alternation is morphologically marked by a stem-vowel alternation. The non-causative variant of *senken* 'lower' is *sinken* 'fall':

(57) *Mein Kontostand ist weiter gesunken.*
my account-balance is further sunk
'My account balance has fallen further.'

2.2.3. Cause and source

The verbs of double and indirect causation discussed above select a fully specified [+c-m] cluster along with [+c]. This cluster differs from underspecified [-m], exemplified by the non-causative stative use of the following verb:

(58) [+c] [-c-m] [-m]
tragen 'carry/bear'

The verb *tragen* 'carry/bear' is problematic for Rapp (1997:147), because it has two uses that cannot be derived from each other: a stative use (59a), and an activity use (59b) – the examples are adapted from Rapp's (40b), p. 147. The stative use is represented in Rapp's (32) on p. 146 by the base predicate LOC, the activity use by DO.

(59) a. *Ein Pfeiler trägt das Dach.*
a pillar supports the roof
b. *Eine Frau trägt das Dach.*
a woman carries the roof

Rapp does not discuss another use of the verb *tragen* 'carry', which is neither locational, nor an activity:

(60) *Der Wind hat den Gleiter in eine luftige Höhe getragen.*
the wind has the glider in a airy height carried
'The wind lifted the glider to a great altitude.'

The verb *tragen* 'carry' in (60) cannot be represented as *DO(x,y)*, because its subject is an inanimate cause, not a volitional actor. It cannot be represented as *LOC(x,y)*, because it refers to a causative movement, rather than a state. So a third representation is called for, probably a causative extension of the LOC variant. In the features notation, both eventive variants are natural interpretations of underspecified [+c]. As a matter of fact, even the stative example (59a) can be read in this way: *a pillar supports the roof.*

Rapp (1997:147) observes that the DO variant apparently extends the grammatical spectrum of the stative variant. In contrast to non-causative statives, verbs like *tragen* 'carry' passivize even on the stative use (Rapp's 1997:147 example (40b), gloss and translation by MH):

(61) *Das Dach wurde von einer Frau/von einem Pfeiler getragen.*
the roof was by a woman/by a pillar supported
'A woman/a pillar supported the roof.'

However, passivization of a stative depends on the availability of the quasi-causative *support*-reading. The verb *tragen* actually has a non-causative stative variant too, which is not discussed in Rapp (1997). This reading is lost under passivization. If no causative reading is available, then the passive is ungrammatical – (63b) is much worse than (61).

(62) a. *Das Dokument trägt das Siegel der Stadt.*
the document bears the seal of-the city
b. *Das Siegel der Stadt wird (vom Sekretär/*von dem Dokument) getragen.*
the seal of-the city is (by the clerk/by the document) carried
'The seal of the city is being carried by the clerk.'

(63) a. *Hans trägt die Schuld an dem Problem.*
Hans carries the blame at the problem
'Hans is to blame for the problem.'

b. ??*Die Schuld wird von Hans getragen.*
the blame is by Hans carried

Sentences of this kind express an assessment. Their subject realizes underspecified [-m], because it is being assessed ([/-m]), and it may be to blame (no [/-c]). The direct object must be passive with respect to both the mental and the physical domain, on all readings of the verb. It is assigned fully specified [-c-m].

2.2.4. Cause and goal

The other underspecified [-] cluster can co-occur with transitive [+c] verbs too. We find this configuration with the following verbs:

(64) [+c] [-c-m] [-c]
beibringen 'teach/inflict/supply', *bringen* 'bring/take', *geben* 'give', *erhalten* 'keep/receive'

All of these verbs assign underspecified [+c] to the subject:

(65) a. *Hans hat uns das Lesen beigebracht.*
Hans has us the reading taught
'Hans taught us how to read.'
b. *Die letzten Wahlen haben ihm eine empfindliche Niederlage beigebracht.*
the recent elections have him a painful defeat inflicted
'He suffered painful losses in the recent elections.'

(66) a. *Hans brachte uns Flöhe.*
Hans brought us flees
'Hans brought us flees'
b. *Der Winter bringt Schnee.*
the winter brings snow
'There is snow in wintertime.'

(67) *Die Ärzte/die Instrumente haben den Patienten am Leben erhalten.*
the doctors/the instruments have the patient at-the life kept
'The doctors/the instruments kept the patient alive.'

(68) *Hans/die Arbeit hat ihrem Leben einen Sinn gegeben.*
Hans/the job has her life a sense given
'Hans/the job gave sense to her life.'

The direct object realizes fully specified [-c-m] in all cases. The accusative systematically excludes any inherently caused physical activity, and it is an object in the mental domain.

The third argument is always interpreted as a goal, which indicates [/-c]. For some of the verbs, sentience seems required on some readings. However, this is not a general condition imposed by the thematic grid of the verb. Since inanimate goals are always possible, we are dealing with underspecified [-c]. (69) exemplifies the variable realization of the third argument of *beibringen, bringen.*

(69) a. *Er hat uns/dem Projekt eine Niederlage beigebracht.*
he has to-us/to-the project a defeat inflicted
'He inflicted a defeat on him/the project.'
b. *Der Winter bringt ihm/dem Land seine Einnahmequelle, den Schnee.*
the winter brings to-him/to-the country his source-of income the snow
'The winter is responsible for his/the country's main source of income, snow.'

With respect to role reduction, the verbs in this class do not exhibit a systematic behavior. One member of the class allows a non-causative use (70b):

(70) a. *Hans hat sein Haus in einem guten Zustand erhalten.*
Hans has his house in a good state kept
'Hans kept his house in a good state.'
b. *Das Haus hat einen neuen Anstrich erhalten.*
the house has a new coating received
'The house received a new coating.'

The fact that the other verbs in this class do not exhibit a similar alternation is a remarkable fact, because the alternations we have been observing with [+m]/[-m], and with [/+c]/[+c-m] apply systematically, without exception. By contrast, alternations in the configuration [+c]/[-c] are subject to lexical constraints. We will come back to this observation in section 3 below.

2.3. Minder verbs: [+m]

Some verbs select a mentally active subject, but they do not pose conditions with respect to an external cause of that mental activity. Such verbs select an underspecified [+m] cluster. The subject of such verbs is ambiguously specified as either an agent, or an experiencer of an emotion. Its interpretation may vary with context.

A typical example of a [+m] verb is *hören*. This verb denotes a partly mental activity, so it selects [/+m]. But the verb does not specify whether the *hearing* event it denotes is intentional, or coincidental. In the example below, the agent-reading is supported by a directional phrase (71a), the experiencer reading is supported by a source phrase (71b).

(71) a. *Hans hört (absichtlich, gern etc.) auf mich.*
Hans listens (on-purpose, with-pleasure etc.) to me
b. *Hans hörte das Wort (??absichtlich) im Radio.*
Hans heard the word (on-purpose) on-the radio

In order to have a name for the [+m] cluster, let us call it *minder*.

2.3.1. Minder and represented object

Mental events can be constrained to the mind, or extend into the physical world. Consider the following verbs:

(72) [+m] [-m]
bewundern 'admire', *erkennen* 'recognize/realize', *lieben* 'love', *verachten* 'despise'

Some of these verbs tend to take objects which are part of the physical world, and these objects may even be affected by the event, at least in some sense. However, this is not a necessary condition. As a subject matter of emotion, the object need only be represented in the mind of the subject, and such a representation may actually trigger the respective sentiment. This is a good sign that we are dealing with underspecified [-m].

Turning to the subject, the absence of [/+c] is evidenced by the fact that imperatives tend to be slightly marginal:

(73) a. ?*Bewundere Hans!*
admire Hans
b. ?*Erkenne die Lösung deines Problems!*
realize the solution of-your problems
c. ?*Liebe Hans!*
love Hans
c. ?*Verachte diese dummen Leute!*
despise those silly people

All of these imperatives are marginal, because the respective verbs do not *require* a causative interpretation of their minder-subjects. However, they *allow* such an interpretation. In some cases, it is enough to exclude any reference to the physical world, and the imperative becomes acceptable: in the mental domain, mental activity is self-sufficient (74a). In other cases, a first person direct object helps (74b,c). In (74d,e), the extra-linguistic context is intended to hint at volitional control. This shows that the external Θ-role cannot be specified as [/-c]. [/-c] would exclude imperatives in all contexts.

(74) a. *Erkenne die Wahrheit!*
realize the truth
b. *Bewundere mich!*
admire me
c. *Liebe mich!*
love me
d. (?)*Verachte diese Leute doch einfach nach Belieben!*
despise those people prt simply according liking
'Despise those people as you please!'

I conclude that the verbs in (72) select underspecified [+m]. This conclusion is supported by data like the following, from van Riemsdijk (pc):

(75) *Hortensien lieben dieses Klima/ den feuchten Boden.*
hydrangeas love this climate / the wet soil

In (75), the verb *lieben* 'love' is used in a metaphorical way. An utterance of (75) indicates that a speaker talks of flowers, as if they were sentient individuals, and this reading is created by the [+m] feature selected by the verb used. It would not arise, if [/+m] were not selected by the respective verb.

Consider as an example the contrast between *essen* 'eat' and *fressen* 'eat/ feed on'. While *essen* is normally used with human subjects only (76a), *fressen* applies to both humans and animals (76b). This indicates that *essen* differs from *fressen* with respect to the feature *m*. *Essen* selects fully specified [+c+m], while *fressen* selects underspecified [+c]. In fact, *fressen* allows inanimate subjects in some variants of German (76d) vs. (76c).

(76) a. *Hans / ?die Sau isst einen Apfel.*
Hans/ the sow eats an apple
b. *Hans / die Sau frisst einen Apfel.*
Hans / the sow eats an apple
c. **Die Maschine hat den Faden gegessen.*
the machine has the thread eaten
d. *Die Maschine hat den Faden gefressen.*
the machine has the thread eaten
'The machine consumed/pulled in the thread.'

Recently, the verb *essen* is increasingly used with animals, in particular, when people speak about their pets. Again, the [/+m] specification provided by the lexical entry of *essen* allows speakers to express an attitude: the fact that they consider their pets as sentient individuals. A traditionalist farmer would never use *essen* with *cattle* (unless, of course, they appear in direct object position).

2.3.2. Ditransitive minder verbs and the intentional alternation

There is a set of ditransitive minder verbs: the verbs in this class exhibit an alternation between an intentional/psychological, and a dimensional use, which will be referred to as *intentional alternation* from now on. The following verbs exemplify this set:

(77) [+m] [-c-m] [-m]
besitzen *'own', finden* 'find', *kennen* 'know'

The presence of [/+m] is evidenced in the variant that denotes intentional states or attitudes, which include possession in (78a) – cf. Rapp (1997), who uses the base-predicate PSYCH to represent the intentional variant of possession. Apart from the intentional use, all of these verbs have a dimensional variant, illustrated below in (82).

(78) a. *Herbert besitzt ein Haus in Florida, das er noch nie gesehen hat.*
Herbert owns a house in Florida, which he prt never seen has
'Herbert owns a house in Florida that he hasn't ever seen.'
b. *Sie findet das großartig/zum Kotzen.*
she finds this great/to puke
'She finds this great/disgusting.'
c. *Herbert kennt einen Zahnarzt in der Stadt (zumindest kann er dir eine Adresse geben).*
Herbert knows a dentist in the town (at least can he to-you an address give)
'Herbert knows a dentist in town (at least he can give you an address).'

Underspecified [+m] is supported by the observation that the subject does not need to be in a physical relation to the object in any of the above examples. With *besitzen* 'own' and *kennen* 'know', the possession relation can be purely conceptual, as in (78), or embedded in a context of action, as below in (79). *finden* 'find' has a reading in which the subject must become physically aware of the object (79b).

(79) a. *Claudia besitzt das Haus seit gestern.*
Claudia owns the house since yesterday
'Claudia owns the house as of yesterday.'
b. *Er fand den Schlüssel auf dem Boden.*
he found the key on-the floor
'He found the key on the floor.'
c. *Sie kennt diesen Zahnarzt schon lange persönlich.*
she knows this dentist already long personally
'She has personally known this dentist for a long time.'

With respect to the latter examples, there is a clear intuition that the subject is active, rather than affected. For *besitzen* 'own' and *kennen* 'know', we observe combination of psychological involvement and activity. For *finden* 'find', Rapp (1997) assumes the representation of an optional preparatory activity in the lexical entry. We must conclude from this that the subject cannot be assigned a [/-c] role.

At the same time, imperatives are generally very marginal, if not excluded at all (80). Only *finden* 'find' allows a fully acceptable imperative, if reference to a preparatory activity is possible (81). Taken together with the impression of activity, the marginality of imperatives is evidence for underspecified [+m].

(80) a. **Finde um 9 Uhr deine Schlüssel wieder!*
find at 9 o'clock your keys again
b. ??*Besitz doch endlich eine Wohnung!*
own prt finally a flat
c. ??*Kenne doch endlich die Leute!*
know prt finally the people

(81) *Finde doch endlich eine eigene Wohnung!*
find prt finally a own flat
'Get moving and find yourself a flat!'

Now consider the other clusters. The object of a cognitive predicate is always mentally represented, and therefore [/-m]. In contrast to verbs like *lieben* 'love', the object cannot be interpreted as a trigger of the respective mental state. Therefore, we are dealing with fully specified [-c-m], rather than underspecified [-m].

In addition to [+m], [-c-m], the verbs in the *finden* 'find'-class select an underspecified cluster [-m]. This cluster can be observed, when the verbs are used as dimensional predicates:

(82) a. *Das Grundstück besitzt eine Ausdehnung von 32 km^2.*
the estate owns an extension of 32 sqkm
'The estate is 32 sqkm large.'
b. *Die Beziehung fand ein Ende.*
the relationship found an end
'The relationship came to an end.'

c. *Sein Reichtum kennt Grenzen.*
his wealth known limits
'His wealth is limited.'

On the dimensional use, the subject is interpreted as being evaluated. This is an indication that [/-m] has been assigned. As for the physical domain, the verbs do not introduce a constraint on interpretation. On the one hand, we could interpret the sentences in (82) as denoting a property *extends up to a limit*. Such a property can be viewed as an instance of movement in the broad sense, as introduced in chapter 1. This interpretation is incompatible with [/-c]. On the other hand, sentences like those in (82) can be paraphrased as *X is limited by Y boundary*. Such a paraphrase interprets the subject as affected by, rather than extending to the respective boundaries. Its availability excludes [/+c]. In sum, the subject of the sentences in (82) is assigned underspecified [-m].

The direct object, like the subject, must be interpreted as affected by an evaluating act. This supports the feature [/-m]. At the same time, the sentences in (82) mean that the subject extends up to, and indeed touches its limits. If a contact is not established, the verbs are falsely used: the estate would be smaller than stated, the relationship would still be existing, his wealth be unlimited. This contact requirement is a feature of the commonsense theory of physics, and it supports the assumption of [/-c]. The direct object realizes a fully specified [-c-m] cluster.

To conclude, verbs like *finden* 'find' select three clusters: [+m], [-c-m], [-m], and the two underspecified clusters compete for realization as a subject.

2.3.3. Indirect causation in the mental domain: sensations

Indirect causation extends into the domain of mental events. Sensations are a good example of indirectly caused mental events. They require both a sentient mind, and a sensory organ to occur. Consider two example verbs:

(83) sensations
sehen 'see/look', *hören* 'hear/listen'

Indeed, these verbs select either a sentient individual, or a medium as a subject.

(84) a. *Hans sah das Ende.*
Hans saw the end
b. *Alle Augen sahen das Licht.*
all eyes saw the light

(85) a. *Hans hörte einen Laut.*
Hans heard a sound
b. *Alle Ohren hörten einen Laut.*
all ears heard a sound

Notice that the medium, realizing a [+c-m] cluster, does not need to denote a sensory organ. In an appropriate context, it can also be an artifact capable of mediating the respective sensation:

(86) *Der Computer sieht die Festplatte.*
the computer sees the hard-disk

When the subject of a sensation verb refers to a sentient individual, this individual may, but does not need to be interpreted as a physical agent. Correspondingly, imperatives require specific contexts (in this case directional PPs) to be acceptable. As above, I take this behavior to indicate that such subjects realize an underspecified [+m] cluster.

(87) a. ?*Sieh die Gans!*
see the goose
b. *Sieh mal dort hin!*
see once there to
'Look over there!'

(88) a. ?*Hör den Sinuston!*
hear the sinus-tone
b. *Hör auf mich!*
hear to me
'Listen to me!'

The examples in (87)-(88) already indicate that sensation verbs can be used with either a direct object NP, or with a directional PP. The two types of complement are in complementary distribution (89).[2] This indicates that directionals and direct object NPs compete for a single thematic role cluster.

(89) a. *Hans sah die Mickeymaus.*
Hans saw the Mickey
b. *Hans sah auf die Uhr.*
Hans saw at the watch
'Hans looked at the watch'
c. **Hans sah die Mickeymaus auf die Uhr.*
Hans saw the Mickey at the watch

This single thematic role cannot be specified as [/-c], because *Mickey's* appearance in (89) can be interpreted as (at least partly) triggering the sensation. This is particularly clear in the case of *hören* 'hear'. The presence of a sound is a sufficient condition for a normal individual to hear it. All this indicates that the object is assigned underspecified [-m].

(90) [+m] [+c-m] [-m]
sehen 'see/look', *hören* 'hear/listen'

2.4. Special event verbs

Up to now, we have seen verbs that denote complete events. The events were complete in the sense that the respective verbs select arguments specified for both values of a given feature. Verbs that select both [/+c] and [/-c] refer to physical events from the perspective of both causer and target. Verbs that select [/+m] and [/-m] refer to mental events from the perspective of both the minder, and the represented object. In this sense, and in this sense only, such events are complete.

The verbs we will now turn to are incomplete in this sense. A first set comprises verbs that select mixed value and [-] clusters. These verbs are classified under special events, because their subject is always both an agent in one domain of event interpretation, and a patient in the other domain. A second set of verbs selects only [-] clusters. Put metaphorically, the denotation of these verbs grays out the active portion of an event, and focuses on the passive event participants. Later on, we will turn to the formalization of this graying out phenomenon. For the time being, let us take stock of the facts.

2.4.1. Mixed value clusters

There are two mixed-value clusters: [-c+m] and [+c-m]. Consider first verbs that assign an experiencer role to the subject, exemplified by *erblicken* 'catch sight of':

(91) [-c+m] [-c-m]
erblicken 'catch sight of'

Verbs that select a [-c+m] subject differ minimally from those that select underspecified [+m]. While [+m] verbs have a reading in which the subject causes the event, a [-c+m] subject must be affected by an external trigger of the respective sensation. Rapp (1997:63) represents this observation by embedding a psychological state under the change of state predicate *BECOME*.

The object to *erblicken* is mentally represented, therefore [/-m]. In contrast to sensation verbs like *hören* 'hear', the presence of the object is not sufficient to trigger the sensation. It is equally affected by a change of state as the subject. In Rapp's representation, this observation is captured by embedding under BECOME. In the present notation, both the subject and the object must be assigned [/-c].

Now consider the other mixed value cluster, [+c-m]. This cluster is usually selected in conjunction with a [+] cluster. However, some rare verbs exhibit it in isolation. One of them is *faszinieren*:

(92) [+c-m] [-c+m]
faszinieren 'impress'

The interesting fact about *faszinieren* is that its subject is clearly understood as causing the described state. So the subject supposedly realizes a [/+c] cluster. We therefore expect fully grammatical imperatives. However, imperatives are anomalous (93c), as are modifiers of intentionality (93d).

(93) a. *Hans fasziniert Helmut.*
Hans impresses Helmut

b. *Seine Dummheit fasziniert Helmut.*
his silliness impresses Helmut
c. ??*Fasziniere uns doch!*
impress us prt
d. ??*Hans fasziniert absichtlich Helmut, und nicht Johanna.*
Hans impresses on-purpose Helmut and not Johanna

This is the behavior of a [+c-m] cluster. It is interpreted as a cause, which lacks any intentional control over the event. When a sentient individual realizes a [+c-m] cluster, it cannot control the denoted event/state itself. However, it may have control over another, mediating event, which in turn causes the verb-event/state. This is the standard behavior of indirect or double causation as discussed above. As with double causatives, an indirect imperative is fully acceptable. The verb *faszinieren* is special, because it does not select a second [/+c] role. In the indirect imperative (94), the agent-role is assigned by the matrix verb *machen* 'do'.

(94) *Mache etwas, wodurch du uns fasziniersti!*
do something whereby you us impress
'Do something to impress us!'

As for the object, it is clearly assigned [-c+m]. It is both affected, and emotionally involved.

2.4.2. Transitive [-] verbs

I call a verb a [-] verb, if none of the features in the clusters it selects has a positive value. Genuine [-] verbs are in fact quite rare. In many cases that we have already seen above, apparent [-] verbs have a causative or intentional counterpart. In this section, we will be considering those [-] verbs that do not have a lexically related causative/intentional counterpart.

Verbs that exclusively select [-] clusters can nevertheless be transitive, at least in the traditional sense of the term. They take a subject in nominative case, and an object in accusative case. What such verbs lack is reference to the active part of an event, be it in the mental, or in the mechanical domain. This is what appears to foster the intuition that such verbs should, in some way, be related to unaccusatives or passives. Section 3.6 will take up this intuition and partly reject it. Before that, the data need to be laid out without bias.

Consider first verbs that select two [/-c] clusters. In what follows, I will call this set *theme-goal verbs*. The following two verbs do not have a lexically related causative/intentional counterpart. They roughly correspond to the (non-alternating) causative verb *geben* 'give'. Notice that some speakers consider the verb *kriegen* 'get' non-standard.

(95) [-c-m] [-c]
bekommen 'receive', *kriegen* 'get'

Both the subject and the object of these verbs is interpreted as a target of *force*. The object undergoes an externally-caused movement, and this movement ends at, and touches the subject. In contrast to the object (which must not), the subject may contribute mental activity. We can observe this mental activity in the possessional use of the verbs in (96a,b). With Rapp (1997), I assume that possession implies psychological activity. An even stronger indication for the availability of an intentional interpretation is the performative use of these verbs, as in (96c). On the other hand, intentionality is by no means obligatory (97). Therefore, the verbs assign underspecified [-c] to the subject.

(96) a. *Hans bekommt ein Auto.*
Hans receives a car
b. *Helene kriegt den Preis.*
Helene gets the prize
c. *Ich bekomme/kriege das Wiener Schnitzel und ein Bier.*
I receive/get the escalope and a beer
'I would like to have the escalope and a beer.'

(97) a. *Das Haus bekommt einen neuen Anstrich.*
the house receives a new painting
b. *Die Wand kriegt einen neuen Anstrich.*
the wall gets a new painting

Consider next the set of verbs that select two [/-m] clusters. Genuine examples for this class seem to be particularly rare, but notice that there is a productive alternation between [+m] and [-m], and some verbs exhibit an alternation between [+c] and [-m]. Most instances of the grid {[-m] [-c-m]}

are therefore reduced forms of more complex lexical entries. An example of a theme-source verb without an intentional or causative variant is *enthalten* 'contain'. This verb roughly corresponds to the causative verb *füllen* 'fill'. As an aside, notice that German *füllen* differs sharply from English *fill* in that it takes part in a spray-lead alternation (98a, b), but it cannot be used as a non-reflexive unaccusative (98c).

(98) a. *Hans füllte das Becken mit Wasser.*
Hans/water filled the pool with water
'Hans filled the pool with water.'
b. *Hans füllte Wasser in das Becken.*
Hans filled water into the pool
'Hans poured water into the pool.'
c. *Das Becken füllte *(sich) langsam mit Wasser.*
the pool filled refl slowly with water
'The pool slowly filled with water.'

(99) [-m] [-c-m]
enthalten 'contain'

The subject of *enthalten* 'contain' is best described as a container. This container can (but does not need to) be perceived as emitting *force* in the sense that it constrains the extension of the object. Therefore [/-c] is excluded. However, the subject can equally well be interpreted as just being filled. This excludes a specification as [/+c]. Since intentionality is systematically excluded (100), the subject must realize underspecified [-m]. The object is both mentally inert and physically constrained by the container, therefore [-c-m].

(100) a. *Die Kanne enthält Wasser.*
the jar contains water
b. *Der menschliche Körper enthält etliche Liter Blut.*
the human body contains several liters blood
c. **Hans enthält absichtlich etliche Liter Blut.*
Hans contains on-purpose some liters blood

Rapp (1997:146) assumes a lexical representation *LOC(x,y)* for *enthalten* 'contain'. This representation accounts well for the fact that *enthalten* 'contain' is a stative, locational predicate. However, Rapp (1997:60) holds that the first argument of LOC must be realized higher than its second argument, and that the first argument of LOC denotes the located object, the second one a location. All other things being equal, we thus erroneously expect (100a) to mean that there is a jar in the water.

Verbs like *enthalten* 'contain' and *kriegen* 'get' are likewise problematic for the Theta System, if they turn out to take a VP-external subject. This is so, because all [-] clusters should be assigned inside VP by the marking conventions. Section 3 will take up this issue and suggest an alternative to Reinhart's original marking conventions that allows external assignment of underspecified [-] clusters.

2.4.3. Intransitive [-] verbs

Consider first dying verbs like the following examples:

(101) [-c]
sterben 'die', *verhungern* 'starve to death', *verdursten* 'die of thirst'

Since the subject is necessarily affected by the event, it must be assigned [/-c]. The typical participant in a dying event is alive. This suggests at first sight that such verbs select a fully specified cluster [-c+m]. However, animacy is not a requirement. Depending on largely pragmatic factors, abstract objects, especially actions, are grammatical with *sterben, verhungern*. With *verdursten*, an absence of mental activity does not diminish grammaticality, as long as the subject fulfills a condition of *biological* life. We must conclude that the subject of dying verbs is assigned underspecified [-c].

(102) a. *Hans ist gestorben.*
Hans is died
'Hans died.'
b. *Der Plan ist gestorben.*
the plan is died
'The plan is dead.'

(103) a. *Hans ist verhungert.*
Hans is starved-to-death
'Hans starved to death.'

b. *Der Schuss ist noch vor dem Tor verhungert.* (Austrian)
the shot is still before the goal starved-to-death
'The shot did not reach the goal.'

(104) *Die Leute/die Pflanzen sind verdurstet.*
the people/the plants are died-of-thirst
'The people/the plants died of thirst.'

Underspecification is supported by the fact that even imperatives are possible in contexts where an intentional contribution to the event is plausible. This is a clear sign that the verbs cannot select [/-m]:

(105) *Stirb/Verhungere/verdurste doch, wenn du nicht essen/trinken willst!*
die/starve-to-death/die-of-thirst prt if you not eat/drink want
'You are most welcome to die, if you refuse to eat/drink!'

Consider next some emission verbs. This class falls in two sub-classes. In one class, we observe an alternation between an intentional and a non-intentional reading. This sub-class includes *leuchten* 'shine', *klappern* 'rattle' in the following sentences. An agent cluster is supported for these verbs by the fact that modifiers of intention and imperatives are fully grammatical.

In the absence of an agent, an instrument cluster is assigned. The subjects in (109) are all interpreted as non-intentional emitters of force. This is true even if world knowledge tell us that the cause of the event is, ultimately, something else. For example, we know that the moon only reflects the light of the sun, but this knowledge does not change the perception that the moon itself (and not the sun) shines brightly in a clear night. This is exactly the interpretation we expect of an instrument cluster [+c-m]. In sum, the verbs *leuchten* 'shine', *klappern* 'rattle' must be analyzed as double causatives.

(106) [+c+m] [+c-m]
leuchten 'shine/light', *klappern* 'rattle'

(107) a. *Hans leuchtet (absichtlich/gern) mit seiner Taschenlampe.*
Hans lights on-purpose/happily with his torch
'Hans lights the way with his torch (on purpose/happily).'

b. *Leuchte hier hin!*
light here to
'Shine your torch this way!'

(108) a. *Hans klappert (absichtlich/gern) mit seinen Zähnen.*
Hans rattles on-purpose/happily with his teeth
'Hans rattles his teeth (on purpose/happily).'
b. *Klappere doch noch etwas weiter bitte!*
rattle prt still some further please
'Keep on rattling a bit more please!'

(109) a. *Die Lampe leuchtet.*
the torch lights
'The torch is on.
b. *Seine Zähne klapperten.*
his teeth rattled rather loudly
'His teeth were rattling.'

A second kind of emission verbs is truly monadic. This class includes *aufblühen* 'flower', *verwelken* 'wilt', *wachsen* 'grow'.

(110) [-c-m]
aufblühen 'come into bloom', *verwelken* 'wilt', *wachsen* 'grow'

Aufblühen 'come into bloom' denotes a change of state by which the subject is affected. The cause of this change must be distinct from the subject: *the spring* in (111a), *the separation* in (111b). Intentional contribution is likewise excluded. The verb *aufblühen* 'come into bloom' selects fully specified [-c-m].

(111) a. *Im Frühling blüht der Garten wieder richtig auf.*
in-the spring bloom the garden again really prt
'In the spring, the flowers in the garden come into bloom again'
b. *Nach der Trennung ist sie richtig aufgeblüht.*
after the separation is she really prt-bloom
'After the separation she really brightened up.'

With *verwelken* 'wilt', the subject undergoes an externally caused physical change, to which it cannot contribute any intentional activity. Sentient individuals cannot be the subject of *verwelken*. Again, we are dealing with fully specified [-c-m].

(112) *Die Blumen/*die Leute sind in der Sonne verwelkt.*
the flowers/the people are in the sun wilted
'The flowers wilted in the sun.'

The verb *wachsen* 'grow' denotes a change of state that is completely unaffected by the mental state of its undergoer. Even though one can imagine to use growth-enhancing drugs in order to voluntarily cause some growing, this is not a meaning of the verb *wachsen* 'grow' – (113b) is still unacceptable.

(113) a. *Der Baum/das Defizit wächst*
the tree/the deficit grows
'The tree/the deficit is growing.'
b. **Hans wuchs absichtlich noch ein Stück, indem er Hormone einnahm.*
Hans grew on-purpose still a bit in-that he hormones ingested

The verb *blühen* 'flower/bloom' differs from the above verbs. It refers to a non-intentional state. The subject may, but does not need to contribute causal force towards the existence of this state. For example, the economic boom in (115b) may be the result of massive state-intervention. *Blühen* 'flower' assigns underspecified [-m].

(114) [-m]
blühen 'flower/bloom'

(115) a. *Die Blume blüht.*
the flower flowers
'The flower is blooming.'
b. *Die Wirtschaft blüht.*
the economy flowers
'The economy is booming.'

2.5. Realization patterns

We can start to address the *mapping problem*. In this subsection, we will be revisiting the verb classes introduced above, and state initial generalizations about the relation between thematic role clusters and grammatical functions. These generalizations will be the topic of a more thorough syntactic discussion in sections 3 and 4.

2.5.1. Agent verbs

(116) [+c+m], [-c-m]
bauen 'build', *besteigen* 'climb', *betreten* 'enter/walk on', *erklimmen* 'climb-terminative', *kämmen* 'comb', *malen* 'paint', *rasieren* 'shave', *überdachen* 'cover/ build a roof over'

Agent-theme verbs realize their clusters in a homogeneous way. [+c+m] is always assigned to the subject, [-c-m] to the object.

(117)

SU		DO
[+c+m]		[-c-m]
Hans	*baut*	*ein Haus*
Hans	builds	a house

(118) [+c+m] [-c+m]
beraten 'advise'

Agent-experiencer verbs are very similar in this respect. [+c+m] is assigned to the subject [-c+m] to the direct object.

(119)

SU		DO
[+c+m]		[-c+m]
Hans	*berät*	*einen Freund*
Hans	advises	a friend

(120) [+c+m] [-c+m] [-c-m]
mitteilen 'inform'

When an agentive verb selects both [-c-m] and [-c+m], the theme cluster is assigned to the direct object, the experiencer cluster to the indirect object.

(121)

SU		IO	DO	
[+c+m]		[-c+m]	[-c-m]	
Hans	*teilte*	*mir*	*die Nachricht*	*mit*
Hans	passed	to-me	the news	prt

(122) [+c+m] [+c-m] [-c-m]
abweisen 'reflect/reject', *schmücken* 'decorate', *schonen* 'protect/spare', *umgeben* 'surround', *umhüllen* 'cover', *umrahmen* 'frame', *verraten* 'betray/give away'

Agentive double causatives appear in two argument realization frames. If [+c+m] is realized at all, it is assigned to the subject. In this case, [+c-m] can be assigned to a PP-adjunct. If [+c+m] is not realized, [+c-m] is assigned to the subject. [-c-m] is always assigned to the direct object.

(123)

SU		DO	PP
[+c+m]		[-c-m]	[+c-m]
Hans	*schmückt*	*den Balkon*	*mit Blumen*
Hans	decorates	the balcony	with flowers
[+c-m]		[-c-m]	
Blumen	*schmücken*	*den Balkon*	
flowers	decorate	the balcony	

(124) [+c+m] [+c-m] [-c+m]
beleidigen 'insult', *demütigen* 'humiliate', *enttäuschen* 'disappoint'

Psychological double causatives behave alike. The two [/+c] clusters compete for realization in subject position, and [-c+m] is consistently assigned to the direct object.

(125)

SU		DO	PP
[+c+m]		[-c+m]	[+c-m]
Helene	*demütigte*	*ihn*	*mit einer Abweisung*
Helene	humiliated	him	with a rebuffal

[+c-m]		[-c+m]
Die Abweisung	*demütigte*	*ihn*
the rebuffal	humiliated	him

For agent verbs, this leaves us with the following patterns. (126a) gives the distribution of roles in a fully realized context, (126b) gives the reduced distribution, with [+c+m] missing. A first generalization that emerges from this picture is that a [/+c] cluster cannot be realized in direct object position, and that the fully specified [-] cluster is always assigned to the direct object. Both mixed value clusters are subject to variation. [+c-m] can be a PP-adjunct or a subject, [-c+m] an accusative or a dative. Further options will turn out to be available below.

(126)

	SU	IO	DO	PP
a.	[+c+m]		[-c-m]	
	[+c+m]		[-c+m]	
	[+c+m]	[-c+m]	[-c-m]	
	[+c+m]		[-c-m]	[+c-m]
	[+c+m]		[-c+m]	[+c-m]
b.	[+c-m]		[-c-m]	
	[+c-m]		[-c+m]	

2.5.2. Cause verbs

(127) [+c] [-c-m]
begrenzen 'limit', *behindern* 'obstruct', *gefährden* 'endanger', *halten* 'hold', *holen* 'get/fetch', *rollen* 'roll', *schieben* 'push', *schleppen* 'tow/drag', *verbrennen* 'burn'

Like agent-theme verbs, cause-theme verbs always realize [-c-m] in direct object position. [+c] is consistently assigned to the subject.

(128)

SU		DO
[+c]		[-c-m]
Hans	*begrenzt*	*einen Garten*
Hans	limits	a garden

Double causatives alternate. As above, the [/+c] roles compete for realization in subject position, and [-c-m] must be assigned to the direct object.

(129) [+c] [+c-m] [-c-m]
anregen 'propose/stimulate', *bedecken* 'cover', *dämpfen* 'dim/diminish', *erschweren* 'make difficult', *hemmen* 'impede', *schädigen* 'harm', *senken* 'lower', *transportieren* 'transport', *verschmutzen* 'contaminate'

(130)

SU		DO	PP
[+c]		[-c-m]	[+c-m]
Er	*bedeckte*	*das Dorf*	*mit Staub*
he/it	covered	the village	with dust
[+c-m]		[-c-m]	
Staub	*bedeckt*	*das Dorf*	
dust	covers	the village	

The same holds for psychological double causatives. [/+c] roles compete for the subject position, [/-c] is realized as an object.

(131) [+c] [+c-m] [-c+m]
erschrecken 'scare/frighten'

(132)

SU		DO	PP
[+c]		[-c+m]	[+c-m]
Sie	*erschreckte*	*mich*	*mit ihrer Härte*
she/it	scared	me	with her/its roughness
[+c-m]		[-c+m]	
Ihre Härte	*erschreckte*	*mich*	
her/its roughness	scared	me	

Transitive causatives with an additional source role alternate between a causative and a non-causative use. On the causative use, [+c] is assigned to the subject, and [-c-m] to the direct object. On the non-causative use, [-m] is assigned to the subject, and [+c] remains unassigned.

(133) [+c] [-c-m] [-m]
tragen 'carry/bear'

(134)

SU		DO
[+c]		[-c-m]
Der Wind	*trug*	*den Gleiter*
the wind	carried	the glider
[-m]		[-c-m]
Er	*trägt*	*die Schuld*
he	carries	the blame

Transitive causatives with an additional goal cluster exhibit some variation. They assign their underspecified [-] cluster either to a dative, or to a PP. If a verb in this class allows a non-causative use, then [-c] is assigned to the subject on this use. The theme is always assigned to the direct object.

(135) [+c] [-c-m] [-c]
beibringen 'teach/apport/inflict', *bringen* 'bring/take', *geben* 'give', *erhalten* 'keep/receive'

(136)

SU		IO	DO	PP
[+c]		[-c]	[-c-m]	[-c]
Instrumente	*erhielten*		*den Patienten*	*am Leben*
instruments	kept		the patient	alive
Der Winter	*brachte*	*uns*	*Schnee*	
the winter	brought	us	snow	
[-c]			[-c-m]	
Er	*erhielt*		*das Stipendium*	
he	received		the grant	

In sum, we find the following distribution of thematic roles with cause verbs. (137a) gives the distribution under full role-realization. (137b) gives the reduced pattern, with [+c] unrealized.

(137)

	SU	IO	DO	PP
a.	[+c]		[-c-m]	
	[+c]		[-c-m]	[+c-m]
	[+c]		[-c+m]	[+c-m]
	[+c]		[-c-m]	[-c]
	[+c]	[-c]	[-c-m]	
b.	[+c-m]		[-c-m]	
	[+c-m]		[-c+m]	
	[-m]		[-c-m]	
	[-c]		[-c-m]	

2.5.3. Minder verbs: [+m]

Verbs that denote psychological events/states assign [+m] to the subject and [/-m] to the direct object.

(138) [+m] [-m]
bewundern 'admire', *erkennen* 'recognize/realize', *lieben* 'love', *verachten* 'despise'

(139)

SU		DO
[+m]		[-m]
Hans	*bewundert*	*Helmut*
Hans	admires	Helmut

If a verb selects more than one [/-m] cluster, fully specified [-c-m] is assigned to the direct object. [-m] competes with [+m] for realization as a subject.

(140) [+m] [-c-m] [-m]
besitzen 'own', *finden* 'find', *kennen* 'know'

(141)

SU		DO
[+m]		[-c-m]
Hans	*fand*	*den Schlüssel*
Hans	found	the key
[-m]		[-c-m]
Sein Reichtum	*kennt*	*Grenzen*
his wealth	knows	boundaries

Mental double causatives exhibit a fully regular alternation: the [+] cluster competes with the instrument cluster [+c-m] for realization as a subject.

(142) [+m] [+c-m] [-m]
sehen 'see/look', *hören* 'hear/listen'

(143)

SO		DO	PP
[+m]		[-m]	[+c-m]
Hans	*sah*	*das Unglück*	*mit eigenen Augen*
Hans	saw	the accident	with his-own eyes
[+c-m]		[-m]	
Alle Augen	*sahen*	*das Licht*	
all eyes	saw	the light	

The [-m] cluster gives rise to additional variability. It can be assigned either to the direct object, or to a directional PP.[3]

(144)

SO		DO	PP
[+m]		[-m]	
Hans	*sah*	*das Licht*	
Hans	saw	the light	
[+m]			[-m]
Hans	*sah*		*auf die Uhr*
Hans	looked		at the watch
[+c-m]		[-m]	
Alle Augen	*sahen*	*das Licht*	
all eyes	saw	the light	

Summing up the results with mental verbs, the following patterns have been observed. (145a) gives the patters of full realization, (145b) the reduced patterns, where [+m] remains unassigned.

(145)

	SO	DO	PP
a.	[+m]	[-m]	
	[+m]	[-c-m]	
	[+m]	[-m]	[+c-m]
	[+m]		[-m]
b.	[-m]	[-c-m]	
	[+c-m]	[-m]	

A few further observations are in order here. A [+] cluster is always assigned to a subject, a fully specified [-] cluster is always assigned to a direct object. This distribution confirms the generalizations about thematic role realization in Reinhart (2000). In addition, we observe that a [/+c] cluster is never assigned to a direct object, and that the assignment of both underspecified [-] clusters is free.

2.5.4. *Special event verbs*

(146) [-c+m] [-c-m]
erblicken 'spot/glimpse'

When two fully specified [/-c] clusters are selected, [-c-m] still behaves as above. It must be assigned to the direct object. [-c+m] is realized as a subject here:

(147)

SU		DO
[-c+m]		[-c-m]
Hans	*erblickt*	*einen Fisch*
Hans	spots	a fish

(148) [+c-m] [-c+m]
faszinieren 'impress'

When a verb selects two mixed value clusters, the [/+c] cluster is assigned to the subject, the [/-c] cluster to the object.

(149)

SU		DO
[+c-m]		[-c+m]
Seine Dummheit	*fasziniert*	*sogar Hans*
his sillyness	impresses	even Hans

When a verb selects only [-] clusters, the fully specified [-] cluster must be assigned to the direct object, and the underspecified cluster is realized as a subject.

(150) [-c-m] [-c]
bekommen 'receive/get', *kriegen* 'receive/get'

(151) [-c-m] [-m]
enthalten 'contain'

(152)

SU		DO
[-c]		[-c-m]
Hans	*bekommt*	*ein Auto*
H	receives	a car
[-m]		[-c-m]
Die Kanne	*enthält*	*Wasser*
the jar	contains	water

Intransitive double causatives behave exactly like their transitive counterparts. A [+] cluster competes with [+c-m] for realization as a subject.

(153) [+c+m] [+c-m]
leuchten 'shine/light', *klappern* 'rattle'

(154)

	SU		PP
a.	[+c+m]		[+c-m]
	Hans	*leuchtet*	*mit der Lampe*
	Hans	lights	with the torch
b.	[+c-m]		
	Die Lampe	*leuchtet*	
	the torch	lights	

This leaves us with the following patterns of argument realization for special event verbs that assign more than one cluster:

(155)

SU	DO
[-c+m]	[-c-m]
[+c-m]	[-c+m]
[-c]	[-c-m]
[-m]	[-c-m]
[+c+m]	
[+c-m]	

On the one hand, this pattern confirms Reinhart's generalization that both mixed value clusters can be assigned to the subject. On the other hand, it strengthens the observation made here with respect to underspecified [-] clusters. These clusters pattern with mixed value clusters, rather than with [-c-m] in that their assignment is, in principle, free.

This observation is important, when we turn to intransitive verbs that do not assign any [+] cluster. Some, indeed most of these verbs are usually analyzed as unaccusatives. However, the fact that underspecified [-] clusters can be assigned to the subject of a transitive predicate excludes surface thematic role configurations as primary evidence for an unaccusative analysis. Unaccusativity can of course follow from thematic role configurations, if we assume with Reinhart (2000) that unaccusative verbs are derived by reduction of a [+c] cluster. In sum, the fact that all of these verbs assign a [-] cluster to the subject must be considered with caution.

(156) [-c]
sterben 'die', *verhungern* 'starve to death', *verdursten* 'die of thirst'

(157) [-c-m]
aufblühen 'come into bloom', *verwelken* 'wilt', *wachsen* 'grow'

(158) [-m]
blühen 'flower'

2.5.5. Summary

In terms of generalizations, we get the following final result. (159) excludes the intransitive [-] verbs just discussed, and abstracts away from the options of role reduction, and of leaving a cluster unrealized, respectively.

(159)

cluster	generalization
[+]	always assigned to a subject
[-c-m]	always assigned to a direct object
[/+c]	never assigned to a direct object

By and large, this distribution corresponds to the observation about the prominence of causing over affected arguments in syntactic argument structure (Croft 1990, 1991, 1998; Jackendoff 1990; Rapp 1997; Wunderlich 1997). It extends this observation in one fundamental respect: psychological agency, encoded as [+m], is grouped together with causation as a property that determines thematic prominence. This approach promises an account of the notoriously problematic set of psychological predicates along the lines of Reinhart (2002).

Another fact must be pointed out here. The distribution of underspecified [-] clusters is similar to the distribution of mixed-value clusters, not to that of fully specified [-c-m]. The assignment of underspecified [-] clusters is, in principle, free.

Finally, the assignment of [-] clusters to the subject of intransitive verbs has been excluded from this generalization in the hope that the facts can be made to follow from the correct formalization of thematic role reduction.

3. The syntax of thematic alternations

Consider the following pair of sentences:

(160) a. *The ice melted.*
b. *The sun melted the ice.*

(160) exemplifies the causative alternation. A given verb can be used both as a transitive causative verb, and an intransitive, non-causative one.

In principle, we would expect to find the causative alternation with all verbs that select a [/+c] role. In fact, straightforward examples can only be found with verbs that select underspecified [+c]. No agent verb in the German set discussed so far has an intransitive non-causative counterpart, and even within the set that selects underspecified [+c], only a few alternating examples can be found. Only the following three verbs exhibit what looks like a robust alternation:

(161) [+c] [-c-m]
halten 'hold', *rollen* 'roll', *verbrennen* 'burn'

(162) a. *Der Haken hält jetzt endlich mal.*
the hook holds now finally prt.
'The hook is finally fixed.'
b. *Die Kugel rollt.*
the ball rolls
'The ball is rolling.'
c. *Das Dokument verbrannte.*
the document burned

Let us consider the thematic interpretation of the subject in these examples. With *verbrennen* 'burn', the subject is clearly undergoing a change of state, so it probably realizes [/-c]. It cannot intentionally contribute to this change of state, so the role assigned to the subject of *verbrennen* 'burn' in (162c) is [-c-m].

The situation is slightly less clear with *rollen* 'roll' in (162b). The subject is undergoing a change of location, and it seems possible to imagine that this change of location is internally caused. However, this impression is misleading. If we construct a scenario in which external causation is unlikely as in (163), acceptability decreases. Both *rollen* 'roll' and *verbrennen* 'burn' are non-causative on their intransitive use.

(163) ?*Die Kugel rollte plötzlich den Berg hinauf.*
the ball rolled suddenly the mountain up

The situation is different with *halten* 'hold'. In (162a), the subject can easily be read as an emitter of *force*, which is not itself affected by the event/state it causes. This indicates that intransitive *halten* 'hold' remains a causative verb. Its subject is assigned [+c]. The difference between *halten* 'hold' and *rollen* 'roll', *verbrennen* 'burn' is corroborated by auxiliary selection (cf. chapter 4 below). Intransitive *rollen* 'roll', *verbrennen* 'burn' select the unaccusative auxiliary *sein* 'be'. *Halten* 'hold' selects the transitive auxiliary *haben* 'have':

(164) a. *Der Haken hat/*ist dann doch gehalten.*
the hook has/is then prt. held
'In the end the hook this not give way.'
b. *Die Kugel ist/*hat gerollt.*
the ball is/has rolled
c. *Das Dokument ist/*hat verbrannt.*
the document is/has burned

I conclude that only *rollen, verbrennen* exhibit a causative alternation.

(165) causative alternation: [+c] [-c-m] -> [-c-m]
rollen 'roll', *verbrennen* 'burn'

The small size of this class, and the failure of the large majority of causative verbs to alternate, is strong evidence to the effect that that the causative alternation cannot be the product of a syntactic operation. If it were, we would expect it to apply in a much more generalized fashion. Alternating causatives must be listed in the lexicon. While this confirms an independent argument in Reinhart and Siloni (2005), it might be challenged by some observations about morphological complexity, which are the topic of the next section. At closer inspection, it will turn out that these data are further evidence for the lexical designation of alternating causatives.

3.1. Causation and morphological complexity

Some transitive causative verbs have morphologically (or lexically) related intransitive counterparts. While there are many ways of morpho-lexical marking available, most notably verbal prefixes and particles (Stiebels 1996), let us concentrate here on a small set of verbs that mark the causative alternation by means of a stem vowel alternation. This alternation stands out, because it is directional.

Take the pair in (166). The causative verb has stem vowel /e/, the anticausative/inchoative one has /i/.

(166) *sinken* 'sink/fall', *senken* 'lower'

a. *Der Wasserspiegel s**i**nkt.*
the water-level falls
'The water level is falling.'

b. *Die Dürre/der Schleusenwärter s**e**nkt den Wasserspiegel.*
the drought/the lock operator lowered the water-level

The stem-vowel alternation is accompanied by a shift in inflectional class membership. Inchoatives can be *strong*:[4] the past tense of inchoative *sinken* 'fall' is formed by means of a stem-vowel alternation (167b). Derived causatives are exclusively *weak*: the past tense of causative *senken* 'lower' is formed by means of affixation (167a). This change of class membership can be used as evidence for the morphological complexity of the respective verbs.

(167) a. *Die Dürre senk-**te** den Wasserspiegel.* (causative, weak)
the drought lower-past the water-level

b. *Der Wasserspiegel s**a**nk.* (inchoative, strong)
the water-level sank

Consider first the strong, inchoative verb. In Bendjaballah and Haiden (2003) it is argued that the stem of a strong verb projects the bare prosodic structure depicted in (168a) (cf. chapter 3 below for details and justification). (168a) represents the fact that stress falls on the first of three CV units that make up the majority of *strong* stems.

A prosodic configuration like (168a) has an interpretation in syntax. In (168b), the interpretation of a strong verb is depicted. The fact that CV_1 is mapped on the syntactic head T establishes a link between the melodic alternation that takes place at this site, and its interpretation as a tense marker.

(168) a. prosodic structure

C V_1
C V_1 C V_2
C V_1 C V_2 C V_3
z i n k
[ziŋk]

b. mapping into syntax

C	V_1					~>	T
C	V_1	C	V_2				
C	V_1	C	V_2	C	V_3	~>	V
|	|	|		|			
z	a	n		k			

[zaŋk]

Now consider *senken* 'lower', the causative counterpart of *sinken* 'fall'. Several observations indicate that the causative form is derived from the inchoative one. First, the phonological complexity of the vowel /e/ is higher than the complexity of /i/. /e/ is composed of the elements A and I. /i/ is basic (Kaye, Lowenstamm and Vergnaud 1985). The same complexity differential holds for most other pairs of this type, like /a/-/e/ (A vs. A.I), and /i/-/ø/ (I vs. A.I.U). In all cases, the vowel of the causative verb is more complex than the vowel of the non-causative one.

(169)

non-causative		causative	
fallen	'fall'	*fällen*	'fell'
A		**A.I**	
fließen	'flow'	*ein-flößen*	'fill'
I		**I.A.U**	

Second, causatives and inchoatives behave differently at the phonology-syntax interface. While inchoatives can map their stem vowel on tense (170), derived causatives do not have this option. They inflect by means of affixation (171):

(170)

present	past	
sinken	***sank***	'sink'
fallen	***fiel***	'fall'
fließen	***floss***	'flow'

(171)

present	past	
senken	*senk-**te***	'lower'
fällen	*fäll-**te***	'fell'
ein-flößen	*flöß-**te** ein*	'fill'

This observation follows, once we assume that the causative alternants are overtly marked by means of a stem-vowel alternation. If they are, their stem vowel maps on V, rather than T. Consequently, the melodic alternation hosted by this site cannot be interpreted as a marker of tense.[5]

(172) mapping of causativized stems

```
C V                 ~> V
C V C V
C V C V C V ~> V    C V ~> T
| | |     |         |
z e n     k         t
[zɛŋktə]
```

Consider *erschrecken* 'frighten/scare':

(173) [+c] [+c-m] [-c+m]
erschrecken 'frighten/scare'

Like *senken* 'lower', this verb has an inchoative, *strong* counterpart. Unlike the *senken/sinken* pair, there is only one infinitive form for both causative and inchoative *erschrecken*.

(174) a. *Hans erschreck-te die Leute.* (causative, weak)
Hans scared the people
b. **Hans erschrak die Leute.*
Hans scared the people

(175) a. *Hans erschrak.* (inchoative, strong)
Hans scared
'Hans got scared'
b. **Hans erschreck-te.*
Hans scared

Although there is no indication of a causative marker in the melodic shape of the infinitive, Bendjaballah and Haiden (2003) argue that the stem vowel of the causative alternant maps on a causativizing head. As above, this explains its inflectional class membership. If the stem vowel maps on V, it cannot map on T, and tense must be expressed by an affix.

To conclude, we have observed in this section that some causative verbs are asymmetrically related to their non-causative counterparts: the causative form is derived from the non-causative one.

3.2. On the independence of morpho-syntactic and lexical complexity

If causatives are morpho-syntactically derived from inchoatives, we might want to take this as evidence for the claim that the inchoative forms are *lexically* basic, and extend this claim to the set of Θ-roles selected by the respective verb. The claim would then be that causative interpretation is contingent on the presence of a causativizing syntactic head. Correspondingly, we would assume that there are no causative verbs in the lexicon.

This is in fact a popular hypothesis (Kratzer 1996; Pesetsky 1995), and it is justified as such. However, this hypothesis does not follow from the morphological data above, or from similar observations about *morphological* complexity, because morphological data are contradictory with respect to lexical-semantic complexity.

First a considerable number of strong verbs is causative, like for example *springen* 'jump' in (176a). Since this verb inflects by means of a stem vowel alternation, it cannot be zero-derived. It is basic. Hence, causative meaning thus does not imply morphological complexity.

Second, the causative base *springen* 'jump' can be subject to a stem-vowel derivation. The output of this operation is *sprengen* 'detonate', which is equally causative. In this case, we can observe a systematic correlation, but this correlation is strictly confined to morphology. The fact that *sprengen* 'detonate' is stem-derived implies that it must change inflectional class. While the base *springen* 'jump' marks tense by a stem-vowel change (176a), derived *sprengen* 'detonate' marks it by an affix (176b).

(176) a. *Hans spr**a**ng über den Tisch.*
Hans jumped over the table
b. *Die Polizei spreng**te** das verdächtige Auto.*
the police detonated the suspicious car

Finally, does morphological complexity imply causative meaning? Not at all. There are numerous examples of non-causative verbs that are morphologically derived from causative ones. Consider the pair in (177). The base verb *treten* 'kick' is clearly causative. The non-causative verb *eintreten* 'occur' is derived from it as an idiomatic verb-particle combination.[6]

(177) a. *Hans trat den Hund.*
Hans kicked the dog
'Hans kicked the dog.'
b. *Das Ereignis ist um 15.00 eingetreten.*
the event is at 15.00 occurred
'The event occurred at 15.00.'

To be precise, none of the above shows that causatives could not be derived from unaccusatives in syntax. The only safe conclusion that we can draw from these facts is that morphological complexity cannot be used as an argument in support of such a hypothesis.

So can we conclude anything useful at all from the morphological facts discussed in this section? – Indeed we can. It was observed in the previous section that the causative alternation can only apply to a small sub-set of causative verbs. We have now found that the causative alternation tends to be accompanied by an unproductive morphological alternation. Both observations suggest that the causative alternation cannot apply freely in syntax. It can only affect verbs that are lexically designated to alternate. This is empirical support for the claim in Reinhart and Siloni (2005) that causative reduction must apply in the lexicon.

3.3. Tests for the position of NP

Several tests have been suggested in the literature to determine the position of a NP with respect to the VP (Grewendorf 1989). One set of tests is related to the status of NP with respect to government. In the Government and Binding framework, extraction out of an NP is licit only if the NP is properly governed by V. This is true for the direct object, but not for the subject. If extraction out of NP is grammatical, then we must conclude that NP is properly governed, and therefore, VP-internal.

A second set of tests is related to constituency. If an NP can be fronted together with a participle, it must form a constituent with it. This is so, because only a single constituent can precede the finite verb in a German main clause. Admittedly, this test does not show that the constituent in question is VP, as opposed to one of its functional extended projections.

However, this is irrelevant as long as we can find a sufficiently clear contrast between movable and unmovable NP-V sequences. Even Haider (1993), who denies the existence of a VP-external subject position in German, assumes that the direct object forms a constituent with V that excludes the subject. With this in mind, I will call a nominative *VP-internal*, if it can be fronted with a participle. I call it *VP-external*, if it cannot.

A third kind of tests involves Binding asymmetries. Such tests try to establish an asymmetric prominence relation between co-arguments. The assumption is that a pronoun can only be bound by a quantifier, if the quantifier c-commands it. Binding asymmetries appear to be good evidence to establish an unaccusative analysis of non-monadic verbs, for example Pesetsky's *appeal*-class, or our German verbs that assign underspecified [-] clusters to the subject of a transitive sentence, e.g., *bekommen* 'reveive/get', *enthalten* 'contain', etc. If we find that a pronoun embedded under the object systematically resists binding by a quantifier in subject position, this is strong evidence for an unaccusative analysis of such verbs.

Additional tests that have been proposed in the literature are the availability of an attributive past participle, the impersonal passive, and auxiliary selection. The attributive past participle is a reliable test for the unaccusativity of a monadic verb. If such a verb can be used as an attributive participle, then it is unaccusative. The availability of an impersonal passive is supposed to show that an intransitive verb is unergative. Finally, selection of the perfect auxiliary *sein* 'be' is supposed to show that a verb is unaccusative.

3.3.1. Government-related tests

German allows the topicalization of partial noun phrases (den Besten and Webelhuth 1987; den Besten 1989, van Hoof 2004; van Riemsdijk 1989). The result of this operation is a fronted 'small' NP, and a stranded determiner and/or adjective:

(178) ***Austern*** *hat er schon* ***viele*** *gegessen.*
oysters has he already many eaten
'As for oysters, he has already eaten many of them.'

It has been argued by den Besten (1981, 1989), den Besten and Webelhuth (1987), van Riemsdijk (1989) and subsequent work that split topicalization affects VP-internal NPs, but not subjects:

(179) a. ***Austern*** *hat er schon* ***viele*** *gegessen.*
oysters has he already many eaten
b. ****Engländer*** *haben schon* ***viele*** *Austern gegessen.*
Englishmen have already many oysters eaten

Provided this generalization is accurate, the availability of split topicalization is a test for VP-internal position.

Unfortunately, split topicalization gives no more than a rough guide for the position of an NP. Embedded in an appropriate quantificational and focus structure, subjects are quite acceptable as split topics (Haiden 1995):

(180) *Engländer haben hier schon viele getrunken, aber noch nie ein einziger Franzose.*
Englishmen have here already many drunk but not ever one single Frenchman

Another movement operation has been used to test the position of a DP. This type of movement has become known as *subextraction*, or *was für split* (den Besten 1981, 1989; Broekhuis 1992; de Hoop and Kosmeijer 1995; van Riemsdijk 1989). *Was für split* produces questions that ask for the quality of some N.

(181) ***Was*** *habt ihr* ***für Sachen*** *gemacht?*
what have you for things done
'What kind of things were you up to?'

As above with split topicalization, the source of extraction usually cannot be a subject.

(182) a. *Was habt ihr für Sachen gemacht?*
what have you for things done
b. **Was haben für Engländer Bier getrunken?*
what have for Englishmen beer drunk

As above, however, this generalization is prone to exceptions. Not all objects allow subextraction with equal ease, and some transitive subjects give rise to pretty acceptable examples.

(183) a. ??*Was haben sie für Hunde geliebt?*
what have they for dogs loved
b. *Was haben euch dort für Leute gesehen? - Hoffentlich keine zivilen Polizisten!*
what have you there for people seen - hopefully no plain-clothes police
'What kind of people saw you there? - I hope no plain-clothes police!'

Like remnant movement, subextraction is not an adequate test to identify the position of NP with respect to VP.

3.3.2. Constituency-related tests

A German VP can be fronted, and such a fronted VP may (but does not need to) contain an accusative NP (184b). By contrast, a transitive subject cannot be fronted with the participle (184c).

(184) a. *Er hat ein Bier getrunken.*
he has a beer drunk
b. *Ein Bier getrunken hat er nicht.*
a beer drunk has he not
'He hasn't had a beer.'
c. **Ein Engländer getrunken hat kein Bier.*
an Englishman drunk has no beer

It might be argued that the offending property of (184c) is the stranded object. However, this cannot be the only reason. In (185a) the object is included in the fronted constituent, and the sentence is equally ungrammatical. Dropping the object alltogether (185b) does not significantly improve the sentence either. The same holds for a bare plural subject in the fronted constituent (185c). All of these facts follow, if a transitive subject does not form a movable constituent with the participial verb.

(185) a. **Ein Engländer ein Bier getrunken hat heute wohl schon oft.*
an Englishman a beer drunk has today prt already often
b. **Ein Engländer getrunken hat hier schon oft.*
an Englishman drunk has here already often
c. **Engländer getrunken haben hier schon immer*
Englishmen drunk have here already always

Although these data seem solid enough, they are repeatedly challenged in the literature. For example, Haider (1993:156) claims that subjects can be topicalized with VPs. This claim forms part of an argument that seeks to deny the existence of a VP-external subject position in German. However, nearly all of Haider's examples involve unaccusative verbs. The subjects of unergative verbs are marginal at best. The following examples, including judgments, are from Haider (1993) – gloss and translation by MH:

(186) a. ?*Ein Außenseiter gewonnen hat hier noch nie.*
an outsider won has here prt never
'An outsider has never ever won here.'
b. ?*Kinder gespielt haben hier noch nie.*
children played have here still never
'Children have never ever played here.'

Comparable data are reported by Meurers (1999). In Meurers' judgment, Haider's sentence (186a) is grammatical. In addition, he reports examples like the following:

(187) *Die Hände gezittert haben ihm diesmal nicht.*
the hands trembled have him this-time not
'This time his hands did not tremble' (Meurers 1999:179)

Constructions of this kind do exist, but they are rare, and they always involve intransitive verbs. The verbs *gewinnen* 'win' and *spielen* 'play' above are interesting in this respect, because they are optional intransitives with a transitive variant. Now observe the sharp contrast between the intransitive examples in (186a) above, and their transitive counterparts in (188):

(188) a. **Aussenseiter Rennen gewonnen haben hier noch nie.*
outsiders races won have here still never

b. ??*Kinder Klavier gespielt haben hier noch nie.*
children piano played have here still never

The only configuration in which such examples are (marginally) possible is with an accusative clitic to the right of the finite verb (examples and judgments from Haider 1993:153; translation and gloss by MH):

(189) a. **Ein Aussenseiter gewonnen hat damals wohl keines der wichtigsten Derbies.*
an outsider won has then prt none of-the most-important derbies
b. ?*Ein Aussenseiter gewonnen hat es damals zwar nicht, aber...*
an outsider won has it then prt not, but
'An outsider hasn't won it back then, but...'

Haider (1993:153f.) claims that the ungrammaticality of (189a) is caused by an unlicensed object-gap inside the fronted VP. For (189b) he argues that the clitic, which is right-adjoined to C, can govern into the fronted VP and thus licenses the object gap. Whatever the correct analysis turns out to be, the contrast between (188) and (189a) shows that a constituent composed of the nominative and the participle must include the accusative. This is exactly the point that we are interested in here. The nominative asymmetrically c-commands the accusative.

There is a special kind of VP-topicalization that den Besten and Webelhuth (1987) call *remnant VP topicalization.* In this construction, an NP is fronted together with a participle, while the NP's determiner is stranded.

(190) a. *Hans hat schon viele Biere geleert.*
Hans has already many beers emptied
'Hans has already downed many pints.'
b. *[**Biere** geleert] hat Hans schon **viele**.*
beers emptied has Hans already many
'As for downing pints, Hans has done a lot of it.'

Again, we find a subject-object asymmetry ((190b) vs. (191)).

(191) ??[*Engländer getrunken] haben hier schon viele, aber noch nie ein einziger Franzose (gegessen).*
Englishmen drunk have here already many but not yet a single Frenchman eaten

Remnant VP-topicalization implies the existence of a salient contrast set. In (191), the contrast set is explicitly introduced in the continuation, but it does not safe the fronted subject. In the following, data from VP topicalization will only be considered relevant, if ungrammaticality persists in spite of the availability of a stable contrast set.

3.3.3. Binding asymmetries

A stable binding asymmetry between co-arguments does not show that the binder is a VP-external argument, but it does supply good evidence for the c-command relation between NPs. Following Brandt (2003), Reinhart (1983), binding asymmetries will be tested in configurations with a universally quantified NP and a coindexed possessive embedded in another NP. The availability of a bound variable reading of the possessive indicates c-command. (192) – from Brandt (2003:76) is supposed to show that *erscheinen* 'appear' is construed as an unaccusative verb. Its nominative argument is c-commanded by the dative.

(192) a. *Es erschien [jedem Autoren]$_i$ sein$_i$ Lektor.*
it appeared [every writer]$_i$-DAT his$_i$ reader-NOM
b. *?*Es erschien [jeder Autor]$_i$ seinem$_i$ Lektor.*
It appeared [every author]$_i$-NOM his$_i$ reader-DAT

Asymmetries of this kind initially appear to be good evidence with respect to reduced transitive forms and transitive [-] verbs. Notice, however, that judgments are often contaminated by independent factors. The clear contrast in the above example depends, at least to a considerable degree, on the presentational construction with initial expletive *es* 'it'. If the nominative occupies its unmarked sentence-initial position (193a), or if it precedes the dative in an embedded clause (193b), nothing much seems wrong with a bound variable reading of the possessive.

(193) a. *[Jeder Autor]$_i$ erschien seinem$_i$ Lektor.*
each author appeared his reader
b. *dass [jeder Autor]$_i$ seinem$_i$ Lektor erschien.*
that each author his reader appeared

One might want to argue that the availability of both the Dat>Nom and the Nom>Dat configuration derives from the fact that *erscheinen* 'appear' is a two-place unaccusative verb. If both the theme and the goal are assigned inside VP, then the actual merging order of nominative and dative could be free, and both c-command configurations can be derived. For a comprehensive criticism of binding data as an indication for the original position of NP cf. Frey (1993).

Binding facts will be considered good evidence, if binding from A into B is consistently possible, binding from B into A consistently excluded, and if these results are corroborated by independent evidence, for example constituency tests.

3.3.4. Attributive past participle

When a past participle is used as a modifier of a noun, then the modified noun identifies the internal, but not the external argument of the participle. This is obvious with transitive verbs:

(194) a. *Hans hat ein Buch geschrieben.*
Hans has a book written
'Hans wrote a book'
b. *das geschriebene Buch*
the written book
c. **der geschriebene Hans*
the written Hans

With intransitive verbs, we find a clear contrast between two classes. Verbs like *verwelken* 'wilt' can be used as attributive participles, verbs like *arbeiten* 'work' cannot. We can conclude from this that verbs like *verwelken* 'wilt' assign their only thematic role to an internal argument. Verbs like *arbeiten* 'work' assign it to an external argument.

(195) a. *die verwelkte Blume*
the wilted flower
b. **die gearbeitete Kollegin*
the worked colleague

3.3.5. Impersonal passive

It is generally assumed that an impersonal passive is possible in German, if the respective verb is unergative. Unaccusatives do not normally appear in an impersonal passive. Unfortunately, this generalization is not exactly accurate. Rapp (1997) observes that a number of verbs that pass other unaccusativity tests still form an impersonal passive, if certain semantic conditions are met. The verb *sterben* 'die' behaves like this ((196b) is due to Rapp 1997:129). The impersonal passive therefore cannot be used as a reliable unaccusativity test.

(196) a. *der um 13 Uhr gestorbene Patient*
the at 13 hours deceased patient
'the patient who passed abay at 3 o'clock'
b. *In Bosnien wird weiter gestorben.*
in Bosnia is more died
'People are still dying in Bosnia.'

3.3.6. Auxiliary selection

Auxiliary selection is likewise unreliable. It is normally the case that an unaccusative verb selects the perfect auxiliary *sein* 'be' as opposed to *haben* 'have', which appears with transitives and unergatives. However, agentive motion verbs select *sein* 'be' (197a), and some non-causative reflexives select *haben* 'have' (197b).

(197) a. *Hans ist immer gern auf Urlaub gefahren.*
Hans is always with-pleasure in-holidays gone
'Hans always liked going on holiday trips'
b. *Ein neues Problem hat sich ergeben.*
a new problem has refl. result
'There appeared a new problem.'

This pattern contradicts other unaccusativity tests. For example, the subject of *fahren* 'drive/go' cannot be fronted inside VP, but the subject of *sich ergeben* 'result' marginally can. Auxiliary selection therefore cannot be used as a reliable test for unaccusativity.

(198) a. **Touristen gefahren sind in die Alpen.*
tourists gone are to the alps
b. (?)*Probleme ergeben haben sich hier schon öfter.*
problems resulted have refl here already more-often
'On many occasions we have come across problems here.'

In summary, it appears that none of the unaccusativity tests that have been proposed in the literature is solid enough to supply firm evidence. In the following sections, a verb will be analyzed as unaccusative, if a number of tests point in the same direction. Otherwise, the evidence will be discarded as inconclusive.

3.4. The causative alternation

The following verbs have been identified as alternating between a causative and a non-causative use:

(199) alternating causatives
erschrecken 'scare/frighten', *rollen* 'roll', *senken/sinken* 'lower/sink', *verbrennen* 'burn'

All of these verbs select the unaccusative auxiliary *sein* 'be' on their intransitive use:

(200) a. *Hans hat ein Kind erschreckt.*
Hans has a child scared
b. *Viele Kinder sind erschrocken.*
many children are scared
'Many children got scared.'

(201) a. *Hans hat den Ball gerollt.*
Hans has the ball rolled
b. *Viele Köpfe sind gerollt.*
many heads are rolled
'There were many casualties.'

(202) a. *Hans hat seine Erwartungen gesenkt.*
Hans has his expectations lowered
b. *Das Ruderboot ist gesunken.*
the rowing boat is sunk

(203) a. *Hans hat sein Haus verbrannt.*
Hans has his house burned
b. *Viele Häuser sind verbrannt.*
many houses are burned

Let us consider the movement tests first. *Erschrecken* 'get scared' immediately raises the issue of contrast sets. The problem here is that the denoted event is instantaneous, and it does not lead to a lasting resultant state. Therefore, it is hard to compare individuals in it. With this effect balanced, the nominative can be fronted with VP. Inchoative *erschrecken* is an unaccusative verb.

(204) a. *Schulkinder erschrocken sind hier natürlich schon oft.*
school-children scared are here naturally prt often
'Of course, school children would often get scared here.'
b. *Schulkinder erschrocken sind hier natürlich schon viele.*
school-children scared are here naturally prt many
'As for school children, they would often get scared here.'

Anti-causative *rollen* 'roll' yields fully acceptable sentences with the nominative inside a fronted VP. It is unaccusative too.

(205) a. *Köpfe gerollt sind bis jetzt noch nicht.*
heads rolled are until now still not
'There still aren't any casualties.'
b. *Köpfe gerollt sind bei dieser Affaire schon viele.*
heads rolled are in this affair already many
'There have already been many casualties in this affair.'

With *sinken* 'fall/sink', the use of a compounded nominative does the trick, especially when the first part of the compound is stressed. The examples in (206) are then read as introducing a contrast between the sinking of rowing boats and other vessels. *Sinken* 'fall/sink' passes the unaccusativity test.

(206) a. *Ruderboote gesunken sind hier schon oft.*
rowing-boats sunk are here prt often
b. *Ruderboote gesunken sind hier schon viele.*
rowing-boats sunk are here already many
'It regularly occurs that a rowing boat would sink here.'

With *verbrennen* 'burn', the presence of a dative clitic (read as an *out-of-control* agent) helps. In the presence of the dative clitic, the subject easily fronts with VP.

(207) a. *Dokumente verbrannt sind ihm in letzter Zeit schon öfter.*
documents burned are to-him in recent time already more-often
'Recently, he has accidentally burned more than one document.'
b. *Dokumente verbrannt sind ihm bis jetzt zum Glück noch keine.*
documents burned are to-him until now to-the luck still none
'Fortunately, he hasn't accidentally burned documents so far.'

So far, the data are very clear. The [/-c] cluster of an anti-causative verb must be assigned to an internal argument. The verbs above project unaccusative syntax. This conclusion is confirmed by the availability of an attributive past participle:

(208) a. *ein erschrockener Gast*
a scared guest
b. *eine gerollte Kugel*
a rolled ball
c. *ein gesunkenes Boot*
a sunk boat
d. *ein verbranntes Dokument*
a burned document

For the fully specified cluster [-c-m], assignment to an internal argument is expected without further assumption. However, it is not so obvious why the mixed value cluster [-c+m] of psychological unaccusatives like *erschrecken* 'get scared' should be assigned to an internal argument.

Recall that the mixed value cluster [-c+m] is not affected by the marking convention in the Theta System:

(209) Lexicon marking ((27) in Reinhart 2002)
Given an n-place verb-entry, n>1,
a. Mark a [-] cluster with index 2.
b. Mark a [+] cluster with index 1.
c. If the entry includes both a [+] cluster and a fully specified cluster [/α,/-c], mark the verb with the ACC feature.

Since the experiencer unaccusative *erschrecken* 'get scared' is lexically related to the object-experiencer verb *erschrecken* 'scare/frighten', there are two options to proceed now, in the framework of Reinhart (2002). The unaccusative can be derived either by role reduction, or by non-realization.

Consider first reduction. Since the causative form is assumed to be lexically basic, clause (c) of the marking convention applies, and the verb is assigned an ACC feature. Since this feature must be checked in syntax, an internal argument must be projected. However, the accusative feature is deleted by the reduction operation:

(210) Decausativization: Reduction of an external [+c] role ((67a) in Reinhart and Siloni 2005)
$V_{acc}\ (\Theta_{1[+c]}, \Theta_2) \rightarrow V\ (\Theta_2)$

Once reduction has applied to causative *erschrecken*, the accusative feature is of no help any more, and syntactic argument structure must be projected on the basis of the merging instructions:

(211) CS merging instructions ((29) in Reinhart 2002)
a. When nothing rules this out, merge externally.
b. An argument realizing a cluster marked 2 merges internally. An argument with a cluster marked 1 merges externally.

The result is clear: in the absence of a marked cluster, the unmarked mixed value cluster [-c+m] must be assigned externally, as it does with subject experiencer verbs like *fürchten* 'fear'. However, *erschrecken* 'get scared' assigns the experiencer to an internal argument. Reduction therefore cannot be the correct derivation.

The second option was non-realization. This option would be based here on the condition that [+c] can remain unrealized, if a verb selects two [/+c] clusters (causative *erschrecken* 'scare/frighten' assigns both [+c] and [+c-m]). In contrast to reduction, non-realization does not touch the ACC feature of the verb. Therefore, there must be an internal argument to check the ACC feature. The experiencer is thus forced into VP.

The account in terms of non-realization would find independent support in the fact that non-causative *erschrecken* 'get scared' selects a prepositional object (212), which refers to a stimulus, i.e., it realizes [+c-m]. Since this cluster is linked to the selected preposition, it is not available as a structural argument, and the experiencer must be realized as an internal argument.

(212) *Er erschrak vor ihr.*
he scared before her
'He got scared by her'

The unaccusativity of *erschrecken* 'get scared' is now consistent with the general approach of the Theta System to object-experiencer verbs, but recall an apparently marginal detail. The causative-unaccusative pair *erschrecken* is morphologically marked by a change in inflectional class membership (cf. section 3.1). In the Theta System, it is assumed that non-realization is typically not marked morphologically. Rather, the presence of a morphological marker can be taken as an indication that reduction has applied; cf. section 3.8 below for an account in terms of reduction that relies on a slight modification of the marking procedure.

3.5. The intentional alternation

In the *Theta System*, there are two scenarios in which a [+] cluster may remain unrealized: (i) if two [/+c] clusters are present, then one of them may remain unrealized; (ii) if two clusters in the lexical verb entry are indistinguishable, then one of them may remain unrealized. Neither of these options is available in the intentional alternation. The verbs in this set are not double causatives, and [+m] is obviously distinct from [-m]. Nevertheless, [+m] competes with [-m] for realization as a subject.

(213) [+m] [-c-m] [-m]
besitzen 'own', *finden* 'find', *kennen* 'know'

Notice furthermore that an analysis of the intentional alternation in terms of reduction is impossible, because [/+m] cannot be reduced by hypothesis in the *Theta System*. Let us therefore add an empirical statement to the scenarios that allow non-realization:

(214) intentional generalization
[+m] may remain unrealized in the context {[+m], [-c-m], [-m]}

The intentional alternation pairs two transitive uses of a verb, an intentional and a dimensional use. In the (a) examples below, the subject must intentionally contribute to the event. In the (b) examples, the subject is being evaluated.

(215) a. *Hans besitzt eine Ratte.*
Hans owns a rat
b. *Das Grundstück besitzt eine Ausdehnung von 25m^2.*
the estate owns an extension of 25 sqm

(216) a. *Hans fand den Schlüssel im Bad.*
Hans found the key in-the bath
b. *Der Krieg fand ein Ende.*
the war found an end

(217) a. *Kans kennt das Prozedere.*
Hans knows the procedure
b. *Sein Reichtum kennt Grenzen.*
his wealth knows boundaries
'His wealth is limited.'

The question that we want to ask now is whether the [-m] role of the subject in the (b) examples is assigned inside VP or not. In other words, we want to know if the dimensional use of verbs in the intentional alternation implies unaccusative syntax.

According to the implementation of the lexicon-syntax mapping in the *Theta System*, all [-] clusters are marked with an index 2 (cf. (209) above), and this index instructs the computational system to merge an NP inside VP (cf. (211) above). Therefore, the verbs must be unaccusatives on their dimensional use.

The prediction of unaccusativity is disconfirmed by the data. On the dimensional use, the subject cannot be fronted with the participial verb. Notice that this cannot be blamed on the unavailability of contrast sets. The compounds used in the examples make them clearly available. We are therefore dealing with ungrammaticality, not information-structural malfeasance.

(218) a. **Baugrundstücke besessen haben eine große Ausdehnung wohl nicht.*
building-estates owned have a great extension prt not
b. **Baugrundstücke besessen haben eine große Ausdehnung viele.*
building-estates owned have a great extension many

(219) a. **Nahostkriege gefunden haben ein schnelles Ende wohl schon oft.*
middle-east-wars found have a swift end prt already often
b. **Nahostkriege gefunden haben ein schnelles Ende schon viele.*
middle-east-wars found have a swift end already many

(220) **(Sein) Reichtum gekannt hat nicht oft Grenzen.*
his wealth known has not often boundaries

Not even Haider's (1993) strategy with clitic object pronouns saves these examples. Notice that (221a) has a grammatical reading, in which *sie* refers to a possessor subject 'they', rather than a dimension.

(221) a. **Baugrundstücke besessen haben sie/so eine große Ausdehnung wohl kaum.*
building-estates owned have her/such a large extension prt not
b. **Nahostkriege gefunden haben es wohl nicht - ihr rasches Ende.*
middle-east-wars found have it prt not - a swift end
c. **(Sein) Reichtum gekannt hat sie nicht.*
his wealth known has them not

It seems tempting to speculate that the clitic strategy does not work, because the dimensional use does not allow referential objects, and the clitics are incompatible with a non-referential use. This is not immediately relevant, though. If the nominative were a VP-internal argument, it should not depend on the clitic strategy in the first place. We must conclude that the subjects of *besitzen 'possess'*, *finden* 'find', *kennen* 'know' are VP-external arguments, even where they have been assigned a [-m] role.

The other unaccusativity tests confirm this conclusion. A nominative quantifier can bind a pronoun embedded under the accusative, but an accusative quantifier cannot bind a pronoun embedded under the nominative. This is true even if the quantifier precedes the pronoun. The nominative asymmetrically c-commands the accusative.

(222) a. *weil jedes Grundstück$_i$ seine$_i$ Abmessungen besitzt.*
because each estate its measurement owns
'because each estate has its specific dimensions.'
b. **weil jede Abmessung$_i$ sein$_i$ Grundstück besitzt.*
because each measurement its estate owns
(223) a. *weil jeder Krieg$_i$ sein$_i$ Ende gefunden hat.*
because each war its end found has
'because each war has found its end.'
b. **weil jedes Ende$_i$ sein$_i$ Krieg gefunden hat.*
because each end its war found has
(224) a. *weil jeder Aufwand$_i$ seine$_i$ Grenzen kennt.*
because each effort its limits knows
'because there is a limit to each effort.'
b. **weil jede Grenze$_i$ seinen$_i$ Aufwand kennt.*
because each limit its effort knows

Auxiliary selection points in the same direction. In all uses of the verbs in this class, the auxiliary *haben* 'have' must be used. It is thus safe to conclude that [-m] can be assigned to an external argument. This suggests the following modification to the marking conventions, where the modified section is highlighted with italics:

(225) Lexicon marking (modified)
Given an n-place verb-entry, n>1,
a. Mark a *fully specified* [-] cluster with index 2.
b. Mark a [+] cluster with index 1.
c. If the entry includes both a [+] cluster and a fully specified cluster [/α,/-c], mark the verb with the ACC feature.

It remains to be checked whether this modification can account for all underspecified [-] clusters, in particular for the behavior of [-c].

3.6. Transitive non-causatives

Transitive non-causatives can be derived from three-place verbs, or they can be lexically basic, lacking a lexically related causative counterpart. Let us first consider derived transitive non-causatives. Depending on the remaining clusters, we can distinguish two classes, exemplified by *tragen* 'carry/bear' and *erhalten* 'keep/receive'. On the non-causative use, the former assigns [-m] to the subject, the latter assigns [-c].

(226) a. *Das Dokument trägt ein Siegel.*
the document bears a seal
b. *Die Wand erhält einen neuen Anstrich*
the wall gets a new coating

If it is true that underspecified [-] clusters must be assigned to an internal argument, as assumed in the *Theta System*, then these verbs must be two-place unaccusatives. If the modified version of lexicon marking in (225) is correct, then it should be possible to assign both [-m] and [-c] to an external argument.

VP-fronting suggests that the underspecified clusters are assigned externally. The nominative cannot be fronted within VP.[7]

(227) a. **Qualitätsprodukte getragen haben diese Auszeichnung schon viele.*
quality-products carried have her/the distinction prt many
b. **Wände bekommen haben den Anstrich schon viele.*
walls got have the coating already many

Judgments for such examples tend to be unstable, because cooperative speakers apply repair strategies. They often repeat the respective sentences with a different word order, and then judge them as grammatical. It is therefore important to compare (227) with their grammatical counterparts below. Indeed there is a significant contrast in grammaticality between (227) and (228).

(228) a. *Qualitätsprodukte haben die Auszeichnung schon viele getragen.*
quality-products have the distinction prt many carried
'As for quality products, many of them were awarded the distinction.'

b. *Wände haben schon viele einen neuen Anstrich bekommen.*
walls have already many a new coating got
'Many a wall has got a new coating.'

Consider next binding data. While one could argue that the ungrammaticality of (227) is weak, binding into the subject is completely impossible. The asymmetry firmly establishes the conclusion that the nominative is VP-external.

(229) a. *dass jedes Dokument$_i$ sein$_i$ Siegel trägt.*
that each document its seal carries
'that each document bears its seal.'
b. *dass jede Wand$_i$ ihre$_i$ Farbe erhält.*
that each wall its color gets
'that each wall gets its respective color.'

(230) a. **dass jedes Siegel$_i$ sein$_i$ Dokument trägt.*
that seal each seal its document carries
b. **dass jede Farbe$_i$ ihre$_i$ Wand erhält.*
that each color its wall gets

Auxiliary selection corroborates this conclusion. Non-causative *tragen* 'bear', *erhalten* 'receive/get' select *haben* 'have', not *sein* 'be'. Both underspecified [-] clusters can be assigned to an external argument. The modified version of the marking conventions in (225) is thus confirmed.

Let us consider next underived non-causatives. In the description above, we have come across the following examples: *bekommen* 'receive/get', *kriegen* 'receive/get' assign [-c] to their subject, *enthalten* 'contain' assigns [-m]. Judgments are once more unstable for VP-fronting, but as above there is a clear acceptability contrast between the (a) and (b) examples below, which suggests that the nominative is not inside VP.

(231) a. **Häuserwände bekommen haben diesen Anstrich nicht viele.*
facades got have this coating not many
b. *Häuserwände haben viele diesen Anstrich bekommen.*
facades have many this coating got
'As for facades, many of them were treated with this coating.'

(232) a. **Kinder gekriegt haben diese Krankheit nicht viele.*
children got have this disease not many
b. *Kinder haben schon viele diese Krankheit gekriegt.*
children have already many this disease got
'As for children, many of them have been infected by this disease.'

(233) a. **Krüge enthalten haben soviel Wasser nicht viele.*
jars contained have so-much water not many
b. *Krüge haben schon viele soviel Wasser enthalten.*
jars have already many so-much water contained
'As for jars, many of them contained this quantity of water.'

Binding data supply a sharper contrast. A nominative quantifier can bind into the accusative, but an accusative quantifier cannot bind into the nominative, even if it precedes it. The nominative asymmetrically c-commands the accusative.

(234) a. *dass jede Wand$_i$ ihre$_i$ Farbe bekommt.*
that each wall its color gets
'that each wall gets its respective color.'
b. **dass jede Farbe$_i$ ihre$_i$ Wand bekommt.*
that each color its wall gets

(235) a. *dass jedes Kind$_i$ sein$_i$ Geschenk bekommt.*
that each child its present gets
'that each child gets his/her respective present.'
b. **dass jedes Geschenk$_i$ sein$_i$ Kind bekommt.*
that each present its child gets

(236) a. *dass jeder Krug$_i$ seine$_i$ Menge Wasser enthält.*
that each jar its amount water contains
'that each jar contains its respective quantity of water.'
b. **dass jede Menge Wasser$_i$ sein$_i$ Krug enthält.*
that each amount water its jar contains

Auxiliary selection confirms this conclusion: in all cases, *haben* 'have' must be used, and *sein* 'be' is ungrammatical. The modified version of the marking conventions in (225) is thus once more confirmed: underspecified [-] clusters can be assigned to a VP-external argument.

3.7. The instrumental alternation

In the instrumental alternation, a [+] cluster competes with a [+c-m] cluster for realization as a subject. In the *Theta System* the alternation is considered an instance of non-realization. The transitivity of both alternants is not an issue. However, a specifically interesting configuration obtains with psychological double causatives.

(237) [+c+m] [+c-m] [-c+m]
beleidigen 'insult', *demütigen* 'humiliate', *enttäuschen* 'disappoint'

These verbs select two mixed value clusters: [+c-m] and [-c+m]. The original version of lexicon marking and merging instructions do not order these two clusters with respect to each other. Either one of them should be equally available in internal and external position. In fact, only [-c+m] can be assigned to the direct object. [+c-m] must be assigned to the subject.

(238) a. **Der Mann demütigt den dummen Witz.*
the$_{\text{Nom}}$ man humiliates the$_{\text{Acc}}$ silly joke
b. *Der dumme Witz demütigt den Mann.*
the$_{\text{Nom}}$ silly joke humiliates the$_{\text{Acc}}$ man

The offending cluster in (238a) must be the instrument cluster [+c-m], because it is a well established fact that the experiencer cluster can be assigned to an external argument (cf. subject-experiencer verbs of the *fear* class). By contrast, it would be surprising to find a cause in direct object position. Let us just state this observation as follows:

(239) Instrument-Observation
Do not assign [/+c] to a direct object.

Observation (239) is reminiscent of the *cause principle* in Rapp (1997:59). This principle states that an argument, which is or can be the first argument of a base predicate CAUSE is always higher in the thematic hierarchy than an argument, which is or can be the second argument of CAUSE. The present approach acknowledges this observation, and rephrases it as an absolute condition on the realization of thematic role clusters.

3.8. Intransitive [-] Verbs

The following verbs have been introduced above. Not all of them are [-] verbs. A comparison is nevertheless instructive.

(240) a. [-c]
sterben 'die', *verhungern* 'starve to death', *verdursten* 'die of thirst'
b. [+c+m] [+c-m]
leuchten 'shine/light', *klappern* 'rattle'
c. [-c-m]
aufblühen 'come into bloom', *verwelken* 'wilt', *wachsen* 'grow'
d. [-m]
blühen 'flower'

As a first indication, observe that auxiliary selection groups double causatives and [-m] together. Both select the transitive auxiliary *haben* 'have'. By contrast, the [/-c] verbs select the unaccusative auxiliary *sein* 'be'.

(241) a. *Hans ist gestorben/verhungert/verdurstet.*
Hans is died/starved-to-death/died-of-thirst
'Hans died/of starvation/of thirst.'
b. *Die Blume ist aufgeblüht/verwelkt/gewachsen.*
the flower is flowered-up/wilted/grown
'The flower started flowering/wilted/grew.'

(242) a. *Das Objekt hat geleuchtet/geklappert.*
the object has lighted/rattled
'The object rattled/glowed.'
b. *Die Blume hat geblüht.*
the flower flowered
'The flower was blooming.'

Since these verbs are typically intransitive, VP-fronting and binding do not contribute conclusive evidence. The subject of unergatives can (marginally) be fronted with VP, and there is no second argument with respect to which a binding asymmetry could be tested. However, intransitives lend themselves to another test, the attributive use of the past participle. Indeed, the classes established by auxiliary selection are confirmed. The [/-c] verbs can be used as attributive past participles, if independent conditions are met. For example, the availability of a result state must be supported by an adverb for *wachsen* 'grow'. The other class does not allow an attributive past participle at all.

(243) a. *ein gestorbener/verhungerter/verdursteter Freund*
a died/died-of-starvation/died-of-thurst friend
'a friend who died/of starvation/of thirst'
b. *eine aufgeblühte/verwelkte Blume*
a flowered-up/wilted flower
'a flower in full bloom/a wilted flower'
c. *ein hier gewachsener Baum*
a here grown tree
'a tree that has grown here'

(244) a. **eine geleuchtete Lampe*
a lighted lamp
b. **ein geklappertes Rad*
a rattled wheel
c. **eine geblühte Blume*
a flowered flower

Their behavior of most of these verbs is not surprising at all, given the previous discussion. Double causatives should realize either one of their two [/+c] clusters in external position. Likewise, a fully specified [-] cluster should be assigned to an internal argument. For underspecified [-m], we have seen evidence to the effect that it, too, should be assigned externally, if no [+] cluster is assigned. A question arises with respect to underspecified [-c] in the class of dying verbs. If these verbs are lexically basic, then their [-c] cluster should be assigned to an external argument, given the modified version of lexicon marking.

Notice now that *sterben* 'die' selects the preposition *an* 'at'. The argument introduced by *an* refers to the immediate cause of dying. It realizes a [+c-m] cluster.

(245) *Hans starb an Krebs*
Hans died at cancer
'Hans died of a cancer.'

This fact is interesting, because it recalls the behavior of *erschrecken* 'get scared', which selects *vor* 'before'. The fact that these prepositions are semantically vacuous shows that they are selected, and the fact that they are selected is in turn evidence for the presence of an additional thematic role cluster in the lexical entry of these verbs.

[+c-m] cannot be realized in a PP, if the verb itself already encodes the cause of dying. This is true for *verhungern* 'die of starvation' and *verdursten* 'die of thirst'. In these cases, [+c-m] is lexically frozen, which means, it cannot be assigned in syntax (Reinhart and Siloni 2005). In the lexical entry, it is present. The correct representation of dying verbs is as follows:

(246) [-c] [+c-m]
sterben 'die', *verdursten* 'die of thirst', *verhungern* 'die of starvation'

An explanation for the unaccusativity of such verbs is now within reach. The only adjustment we need to make is an additional statement in clause (c) of the marking conventions. As above, parts that differ from Reinhart's original formulation are highlighted by italics:

(247) Lexicon marking (modified 2)
Given an n-place verb-entry, n>1,
a. Mark a *fully specified* [-] cluster with index 2.
b. Mark a [+] cluster with index 1.
c. Mark the verb with an ACC feature, if its entry includes
(i) both a [+] cluster and a fully specified cluster [/α,/-c], or
(ii) both a [/+c] cluster and a [/-c] cluster.

Admittedly, this new formulation is somewhat redundant, and clause (c.ii) should obviously be related to the instrument-observation (239). These issues will be addressed in chapter 3. For the time being, just notice that dying verbs are marked with the ACC feature by clause (c.ii). Therefore, [-c] must be assigned VP-internally.

3.9. Intermediate conclusion

The patterns of syntactic argument realization that we have so far observed confirm the *Theta System*. In particular, a small set of universal conditions is sufficient to determine the realization of thematic role clusters in syntactic positions. The modifications that have been introduced affect empirical details of the theory. In particular, it was argued that

(i) non-realization is an option for underspecified clusters in the configuration {[+m], [-c-m], [-m]},

(ii) only fully specified [-] clusters are marked with index *2*,

(iii) a [/+c] cluster cannot be assigned to a direct object, and

(iv) the presence of both [/+c] and [/-c] in a lexical entry triggers the assignment of an ACC feature.

4. The reflexive alternation

A dominant question in the literature on reflexivization is whether the argument of a reflexive predicate is an internal, or an external argument (Grimshaw 1982, 1990; Marantz 1984; Pesetsky 1995; Reinhart and Siloni 1999; Sportiche 1998). This question is particularly interesting in the case of anti-causative reflexives. The thematic role assigned by such predicates is [-c-m], and the argument that realizes this role is a subject. Since [-c-m] must be assigned to an internal argument, the *Theta System* predicts that anti-causative reflexives project unaccusative syntax. If anti-causative reflexives are syntactically transitive, then we have identified a serious problem.

To set up the problem, notice that there exists an overt case paradigm for reflexive pronouns in German. Notice, however, that a case distinction is visible only for first and second person singular pronouns. In the plural, we find a syncretism between accusative and dative, and the third person has just a single form, *sich*. A nominative form does not exist, and the genitive is ignored here.

(248)

	1sg	2sg	1pl	2pl	3
dat	*mir*	*dir*	*uns*	*euch*	*sich*
acc	*mich*	*dich*	*uns*	*euch*	*sich*

In a reflexive sentence, the full noun or pronoun is realized in the nominative case, the reflexive in the accusative.

(249) *Du hast dich als Langeweiler erwiesen.*
you$_{nom}$ have refl$_{acc}$ as bore shown
'You turned out to be a bore.'

Taken together with the selection of the auxiliary *haben* 'have' in the perfect tense, the distribution of cases hints at a syntactically transitive analysis of German reflexive. Worse still, it looks as if a [-c-m] role could be assigned to the VP-external subject in such constructions.

However, before jumping to a premature conclusion, we need to control a number of variables involved in reflexive constructions. First, it is not always obvious which role is actually assigned in a reflexive sentence. While the example in (249) above has been chosen for its exceptionally clear anti-causative meaning, most reflexives allow both a causative and a non-causative interpretation:

(250) *Hans hat sich verbrannt.*
Hans has refl burned
'Hans burned himself.' or
'Hans suffered a burn.'

Second, auxiliary selection and the distribution of case alone are not sufficient support for the claim that a construction is syntactically transitive. Additional evidence, in particular constituency related tests are called for.

Finally, even a syntactically transitive analysis of German anti-causative reflexives would not entail that [-c-m] must merge VP-externally. Building on von Stechow (1995), Sæbø (2001) argues that the internal Θ-role of an anti-causative reflexive is inherited by a VP-external subject from the reflexive pronoun in direct object position.

4.1. Thematic roles in reflexive constructions

Consider the following set of agent verbs:

(251) [+c+m], [-c-m] - reflexive
kämmen 'comb', *rasieren* 'shave'

(252) [+c+m] [-c+m] [-c-m] - reflexive
mitteilen 'inform'

(253) a. *Hans rasiert sich.*
Hans shaves refl
b. *Hans kämmt sich.*
Hans combs refl

(254) *Hans teilt sich (uns) mit.*
Hans informs refl (to-us) prt
'Hans expresses himself (to us)'

There is clear indication that the agent cluster [+c+m] is left intact under reflexivization. Modifiers of intentionality and imperatives are fully acceptable.

(255) a. *Hans rasierte sich absichtlich, um nicht erkannt zu werden.*
Hans shaved refl on-purpose for not to recognized be
'Hans shaved on purpose, in order not to be recognized.'
b. *Kämme dich!*
comb refl.
c. *Teile dich mit!*
inform refl. prt
'Express yourself!'

What about the other clusters? (254) already shows that [-c+m], assigned to the dative, is still present. As for the theme-role [-c-m], it seems to be assigned by *rasieren* and *kämmen*, because the subject is undergoing a change of state. This intuition fails to emerge with *mitteilen*, unless maybe in a metaphorical way. The following section is dedicated to a test that is intended to clarify our intuitions about the theta-roles assigned in reflexive sentences.

4.1.1. The selbst *test*

In order to determine the referential status of a reflexive pronoun, we can use stressed post-nominal, or "intensifying" *selbst* 'self' (Eckardt 2001; Hole 2002; König 1992; König and Siemund 1996, 2000; Siemund 2000).

This particle emphasizes the identity of the individual referred to by the preceding noun, as opposed to others in his or her vicinity. Stressed post-nominal *selbst* must be distinguished from the unstressed focus particle *selbst*, which appears to the left of a focus. (256)-(257) exemplify intensifying *selbst* in its stressed, post-nominal position. (258) gives an example of the unstressed focus particle *selbst*.

(256) a. *[Hans selbst] schreibt die Todesurteile, nicht sein Sekretär.*
Hans self writes the death-sentences, not his secretary
'It is Hans himself, not his secretary, who writes the death sentences.'
b. *Der Sturm überraschte [den Diktator selbst] (und nicht seinen Doppelgänger).*
the storm surprised the dictator self (and not his look-alike)
(257) a. *[Er selbst] schreibt die Todesurteile.*
He self writes the death-sentences
b. *Er malte am liebsten [sich selbst].*
he painted at-the dearest refl self
'Above all, he liked painting himself'

(258) *Er hat [selbst die geringste Mühe] immer gescheut.*
he has self the slightest effort always shied
'He always shied away from making even the slightest effort.'

Intensifying *selbst* is interesting as a test, because it can attach to a reflexive, as in (257b). At the same time, *selbst* introduces sortal restrictions. Usually, "it can only combine with proper names and definite NPs denoting single individuals or groups [...]" (Eckardt 2001:380). If both the subject and the object can be selectively identified by *selbst*, then chances are that both an internal and an external Θ-role is present. At the very least, a reflexive marker of role-reduction should not allow intensification by *selbst*.

Notice in passing that an intensified reflexive in German cannot be compared with the Dutch complex anaphor *zichzelf* without further qualification. First, the simplex German anaphor *sich* is used in all reflexive contexts. This is not the case for Dutch *zich* (Reinhart and Reuland 1993). Second, the German reflexive *sich* and the intensifier *selbst* are not a morphological unit. The two elements do not even have to be string adjacent. (259a) exemplifies floating *selbst* in a non-reflexive context. Stressed *selbst* can emphasize either the identity of *Johanna*, or that of the president. (259b) gives a reflexive context.

(259) a. *Johanna hat den Präsidenten selbst begrüßt.*
Johanna has the president self welcomed
'It was Johanna herself who welcomed the president.' or
'It was the president himself, who Johanna welcomed.'
b. *Johanna hat sich nur selbst gemalt.*
Johanna has refl only self painted
'Johanna only ever painted images of herself.' or
'Johanna painted all self portraits herself.'

The ambiguity disappears in topicalization. In the following sentences, stressed *selbst* can only intensify the immediately preceding constituent.

(260) a. *[Johanna selbst] hat den Präsidenten begrüßt, (nicht ihr Sekretär).*
Johanna self has the president welcomed, not her secretary
'It was Johanna herself who welcomed the president, (not her secretary).'
b. *[Den Präsidenten selbst] hat Johanna begrüßt, (nicht seinen Sekretär).*
the president self has Johanna welcomed, not his secretary
'It was the president himself who Johanna welcomed, (not his secretary).'

Finally, intensifying *selbst* can be used in a *by-phrase*. The use of *von selbst* 'by self' indicates that an event takes place by itself, as opposed to being instigated by an external agent. The expectation of such an agent can be based on the meaning of the respective verb, as in (261a), but this is not always the case: (261b) is most appropriate in a situation in which the child normally needs the help of his parents to eat. In contrast to intensifying *selbst*, the use of by-phrase *selbst* is very natural in contexts of reduced argument structure.

(261) a. *Die Kugel rollte von selbst nach links.*
the ball rolled by self to left
'The ball rolled to the left by itself.'

b. *Das Kind aß von selbst.*
the child ate by self
'The child ate by himself.'

4.1.2. Agent verbs

Armed with *selbst* as a test for the argument status of a reflexive, we can now reconsider the reflexive sentences above. Both *sich rasieren* 'shave' and *sich kämmen* 'comb' freely allow *selbst* with both the subject and the reflexive object. The verbs assign both an internal and an external Θ-role.

(262) a. *Der Friseur hat sich selbst rasiert.*
the barber has refl self shaved
b. *Der Friseur selbst hat sich rasiert.*
the barber self has refl shaved
'The barber himself shaved.'
c. *Sich selbst hat der Friseur rasiert.*
refl self has the barber shaved
'The barber shaved himself.'

(263) a. *Der Friseur hat sich selbst gekämmt.*
the barber has refl self combed
b. *Hans selbst hat sich gekämmt.*
Hans self has refl combed
'Hans combed himself.'
c. *Sich selbst hat der Friseur gekämmt.*
refl self has the barber combed
'The barber combed himself.'

With *sich mitteilen* 'express oneself', intensifying *selbst* is appropriate with the full noun (264b), but not with the reflexive (264c).

(264) a. ?Hans hat sich selbst mitgeteilt.
Hans has refl self informed
b. Hans selbst hat sich mitgeteilt.
Hans self has refl informed
'It was Hans who expressed himself.'

c. *Sich selbst hat Hans mitgeteilt.
refl self has H informed

The fact that the nominative can, and the reflexive cannot be intensified appears to suggest that the internal Θ-role of *sich mitteilen* 'express oneself' is not assigned in the reflexive construction. While such a conclusion will turn out to be premature, let us take note of the observation and list *sich mitteilen* 'express oneself' in a group of *agent reflexives*.

(265) agent reflexive
sich mitteilen 'express oneself'

Now consider agentive double causatives in the reflexive construction. Notice that *sich schmücken* 'make oneself pretty' is not accepted in all varieties of German.

(266) [+c+m] [+c-m] [-c-m]
schmücken 'decorate', *schonen* 'protect', *verraten* 'give a-way/betray'

(267) a. *Hans schmückt sich.*
Hans decorates refl
'Hans makes himself pretty.'
b. *Hans schmückt sich wohl selbst.*
Hans decorates refl prt self
'Hans makes himself pretty (he does it himself).'
(268) a. *Hans schont sich.*
Hans protects refl
'Hans takes good care of himself.'
b. *Hans schont sich wohl selbst.*
Hans protects refl prt self
'Hans independently takes good care of himself.'
(269) a. *Hans verriet sich.*
Hans betrayed refl
'Hans betrayed himself.'
b. *Hans verriet sich wohl selbst.*
Hans betrayed refl prt self
'Hans betrayed himself (he did it himself).'

In all of these examples, it looks as if the subject is, or at least can be in volitional control of the event. Furthermore, in all of the examples, both the full NP nominative and the reflexive accusative can be intensified by *selbst*:

(270) a. *Hans selbst hat sich geschmückt.*
Hans self has refl decorated
'Hans makes himself pretty (he does it himself).'
b. *Hans selbst hat sich geschont.*
Hans self has refl protected
'Hans independently took good care of himself.'
c. *Hans selbst hat sich verraten.*
Hans self has refl betrayed
'Hans betrayed himself (he did it himself).'

(271) a. *Sich selbst hat Hans geschmückt.*
refl self has Hans decorated
'Hans made himself pretty (not somebody else).'
b. *Sich selbst hat Hans geschont.*
refl self has Hans protected
'Hans took good care of himself (not of somebody else).'
c. *Sich selbst hat Hans verraten.*
refl self has Hans betrayed
'Hans betrayed himself (not somebody else).'

In addition, *sich verraten* 'betray' has a somewhat different reading with a non-sentient subject:

(272) *Der Truppenaufmarsch verriet sich durch die große Staubentwicklung.*
the military-build-up betrayed refl through the great dust-production
'The military build-up showed by the amount of dust produced.'

In this context, the *by-phrase* use of *selbst* is most natural. The intuition here is that the subject is both a target of *force* and the content of a propositional attitude. We can see that the subject does not realize the instrument cluster [+c-m], because the immediate cause of the event can be made explicit in a PP headed by *durch* 'through'. In this context, neither the full noun, nor the reflexive can easily be intensified by *selbst*. The only way we can make intensifying *selbst* grammatical is by biasing a theme-reading of the nominative. This is done in (273c) by contrasting the subject of the reflexive sentence (*der Truppenaufmarsch* 'the military buildup') with the internal argument of the antecedent clause (*das Angriffsdatum* 'the date of the attack').

(273) a. *Der Truppenaufmarsch verriet sich (durch die große Staubentwicklung) von selbst.*
the military-build-up betrayed refl (through the great dust-production) by self
'The military build-up inevitably showed by the amount of dust produced'
b. ??*Der Truppenaufmarsch selbst hat sich verraten.*
the military-buildup self has refl. betrayed
c. *Das Angriffsdatum kannte man schon aus der Zeitung,*
the attack-date knew one already from the paper
und der Truppenaufmarsch selbst hat sich durch die große Staubentwicklung verraten.
the military-buildup self has refl through the great dust-production betrayed
'The date of the attack had already been in the papers, and the military buildup itself betrayed itself by the amount of dust produced.'

Once the non-causative reading of *sich verraten* 'betray oneself' is established, we expect it to be available even with a sentient subject. This is indeed the case. In the following example the non-causative reading is biased by the *durch*-PP and by-phrase *selbst*:

(274) *Hans hat sich durch seine Dummheit von selbst verraten.*
H has refl through his silliness by self betrayed
'Because of his silliness, Hans gave himself away without doing anything.'

In sum, we have found a first example of a non-causative reflexive.[8]

(275) a. agent reflexives: [+c+m] [-c-m] -> [+c+m] (?[-c-m])
sich mitteilen 'express oneself'

b. theme reflexives: [+c+m] [-c-m] -> [-c-m]
sich verraten 'give oneself away'

4.1.3. Cause verbs

Now consider cause verbs. Out of the set of simple cause-theme verbs, the following examples combine with a reflexive without major contextual effort.

(276) [+c] [-c-m]
gefährden 'endanger', *rollen* 'roll', *schieben* 'push', *schleppen* 'drag/tow', *verbrennen* 'burn'

At first glance, all of these verbs allow both sentient and non-sentient subjects.

(277) a. *Hans gefährdet sich.*
Hans endangers refl
'Hans puts himself at risk.'
b. *Das Projekt gefährdete sich jüngst durch eine allzu kreative Finanzgebahrung.*
the project endangered refl recently through a too creative financial-dealings
'The project recently put itself in danger by dodgy financial dealings.'

(278) a. *Hans rollt sich noch etwas weiter.*
Hans rolls refl still some further
'Hans rolls on a little.'
b. ?*Die Kugel rollte sich langsam durch das Labyrinth.*
the ball rolls refl slowly through the labyrinth

(279) a. *Hans schiebt sich an mir vorbei.*
Hans pushes refl at me past
'Hans squeezes past me.'
b. (?)*Der Gletscher schiebt sich langsam ins Tal.*
the glacier pushes refl slowly to-the valley

(280) a. *Hans schleppt sich heim.*
Hans drags refl home
'Hans is dragging himself home.'
b. *Die Vorbereitungen schleppen sich (hin).*
the preparations dragged refl prt.
'The preparations are progressing slowly.'

(281) a. *Hans verbrennt sich*
Hans burns refl
'Hans suffers a burn'
b. *Die Nachricht verbrennt sich 5 Minuten nach dem Öffnen von selbst.*
the message burns refl 5 minutes after the opening by self
'The message will burn itself 5 minutes after having been opened.'

The thematic interpretation of these example varies. Consider first *sich gefährden* 'put oneself at risk'. With a sentient subject, both Θ-roles are assigned. *Selbst* can attach to both the full NP and the reflexive.

(282) a. *Hans hat sich selbst gefährdet.*
Hans has refl self endangered
'Hans put himself at risk.'
a. *Hans selbst hat sich gefährdet.*
Hans self has refl endangered
'Hans put himself at risk (he did it himself).'
b. *Sich selbst hat Hans gefährdet.*
refl self has Hans endangered
'Hans put himself at risk (not somebody elese).'

Trying to push a theme-reflexive reading with a *durch*-instrumental phrase does not succeed in this case. (283a) is properly paraphrased by (283b) and (283c): both arguments can be intensified by *selbst*. By contrast, (283d) (with an agent-canceling by-phrase *selbst*) does not paraphrase (283a). Reflexive *sich gefährden* 'put oneself at risk' still assigns two Θ-roles.

(283) a. *Hans hat sich durch seine Dummheit selbst gefährdet.*
Hans has refl through his silliness refl endangered
'Hans put himself at risk by stupid behavior.'

b. *Hans selbst hat sich durch seine Dummheit gefährdet.*
Hans self has refl throuh his silliness endangered
'It was Hans himself who put himself at risk...' (paraphrases)

c. *Sich selbst hat Hans durch seine Dummheit gefährdet.*
refl self has Hans through his silliness endangered
'It was he himself who Hans put at risk...' (paraphrases)

d. ?*Hans hat sich durch seine Dummheit von selbst gefährdet.*
Hans has refl through his silliness by self endangered
'Hans put himself at risk all by himself ...' (does not paraphrase)

The situation is entirely different with *rollen* 'roll' and *schieben* 'push'. The (a) examples with floating *selbst* are properly paraphrased by the subject-intensifier in the (b) sentences. Intensification of the reflexive in the (c) examples is at best marginal. This suggests that reflexive *rollen* and *schieben* should be put aside together with the agent-reflexive *sich mitteilen* 'express oneself'. They assign an external Θ-role, and the status of the internal role remains to be determined.

(284) a. *Hans rollt sich selbst an mir vorbei.*
Hans rolls refl self at me past
'Hans himself rolls past me.'
b. (?)*Hans selbst rollt sich an mir vorbei.*
Hans self rolls refl at me past (paraphrases)
c. ??*Sich selbst rollt Hans an mir vorbei.*
refl self rolls Hans at me past

(285) a. *Hans schob sich selbst an mir vorbei.*
Hans pushed refl self at me past
'Hans himself shoved past me'
b. (?)*Hans selbst schob sich an mir vorbei.*
Hans self shoved refl at me past (paraphrases)
c. ??*Sich selbst schob Hans an mir vorbei.*
refl self shoved Hans at me past

Schleppen 'drag/tow' behaves like *verraten* 'betray' above. Although floating *selbst* is grammatical (286a), intensification of both the full noun and the reflexive is at best marginal (286b, c). The closest we can get to a paraphrase of (286a) is with the agent canceling by-phrase *selbst* in (286d). As above, intensification of the nominative becomes possible, if a theme interpretation is biased by comparison with the direct object of an antecedent clause, as in (287). This indicates that only [-c-m], but no [+] cluster is assigned. *Sich schleppen* is an anti-causative reflexive.

(286) a. *Hans hat sich wohl selbst heim geschleppt.*
Hans has refl prt self home dragged
'Hans managed to get home by himself.'
b. ??*Hans selbst hat sich wohl heim geschleppt.*
Hans self has refl prt home dragged
c. ??*Sich selbst hat Hans wohl heim geschleppt.*
refl self has Hans prt home dragged
d. *Hans hat sich von selbst heim geschleppt.*
Hans has refl by self home dragged
'Hans managed to get home by himself.'

(287) *Die Vorbereitungen hatten wir schnell abgeschlossen, aber*
the preparations had be swiftly finished but
die Arbeiten selbst schleppten sich dann doch noch sehr (hin).
the works self dragged refl then prt still very prt
'While we had swiftly finished the preparations, the job itself dragged on for much longer.'

The reflexive version of *verbrennen* 'burn' has comparable properties. Its most salient reading is certainly one in which two Θ-roles are assigned: an object causes a burning event, by which it is itself affected. On this reading, the verb refers to a terminative event: the object must be completely destroyed. Apart from this reading, there is one on which *sich verbrennen* means *suffer a (light) burn* (288a). On this reading, an imperative is completely ungrammatical: (288b) contrasts sharply with (288c). This indicates that the *suffer a burn* reading corresponds to an anti-causative reflexive.

(288) a. *Hans hat sich leicht verbrannt.*
Hans has refl. lightly burned
'Hans suffered a light burn.'

b. **Verbrenne dich leicht!*
burn yourself lightly
c. (?)*Sei ein Martyrer und verbrenne dich!*
be a martyr and burn refl
'Be a martyr and burn yourself to death!'

The thematic distinction between the two readings is corroborated by the behavior of intensifying *selbst*. While the reduced *suffer a burn*-reading can be forced with floating *selbst* (289a), unambiguous intensification of both full noun and reflexive exclude it. (289b, c) can only have the martyr reading, which is pragmatically marked. By contrast, by-phrase *selbst* allows both readings again (289d).

(289) a. *Hans hat sich wohl selbst verbrannt.*
Hans has refl prt self burned
'Hans probably burned himself.' or
'It is probably Hans who suffered a burn.'
b. (?)*Hans selbst hat sich wohl verbrannt.*
Hans self has refl prt burned
'It was probably Hans who burned himself.'
c. (?)*Sich selbst hat Hans wohl verbrannt.*
refl self has Hans prt burned
'Hans burned probably himself.'
d. *Hans hat sich wohl von selbst verbrannt.*
Hans has refl prt by self burned
'Hans probably burned himself on his own initiative.' or
'It is nobody's fault that Hans suffered a burn.'

To summarize, we have identified two examples of reduced anti-causative reflexives, and two examples of causative reflexives, for which the status of the internal Θ-role remains to be determined.

(290) a. cause reflexives: [+c] [-c-m] -> [+c] (?[-c-m])
sich rollen 'roll oneself', *sich schieben* 'push/shove oneself'
b. theme reflexives: [+c] [-c-m] -> [-c-m]
sich (hin) schleppen 'drag on', *sich verbrennen* 'suffer a burn'

Now consider double causatives. The following examples seem to have reflexive counterparts:

(291) [+c] [+c-m] [-c-m]
bedecken 'cover', *erschweren* 'obstruct', *senken* 'lower'

Interestingly, the majority of these verbs does not well tolerate sentient subjects under reflexivization. Only *bedecken* 'cover' stands out in this respect. We can take this as a first indication (but not a proof) that these reflexives do not assign [+c].

(292) a. *Hans bedeckte sich mit Schande.*
Hans covered refl with disgrace
'Hans disgraced himself.'
b. *Sein Gesicht bedeckte sich mit einem Ausdruck des Grauens.*
his face covered refl with an expression of-the terror
'His face took on an expression of terror.'
c. *Die Statue bedeckte sich langsam mit Staub.*
the statue covered refl slowly with dust
'The statue slowly got covered with dust.'

(293) a. ??*Hans erschwert sich.*
Hans obstructs refl
b. *Die Arbeiten erschwerten sich.*
the works obstructs refl
'The job was getting difficult.'

(294) a. ?*Hans senkt sich.*
Hans lowers refl
b. *Der Wasserstand senkt sich.*
the water-level lowers refl
'The water level is falling.'

With *sich bedecken* 'get covered/cover oneself', sentient subjects favor an intentional action reading (295a). This reading is paraphrased in (296a,b). However, there is a (remote, pragmatically odd) second reading of (295a), which becomes more obvious in the presence of by-phrase *selbst* in (296c). On this reading, the nominative is read as an affected, non-intentional argument. This latter reading is in fact the only one, if world knowledge rules the nominative out as an agent, as in (295b).

(295) a. *Hans hat sich mit Staub bedeckt.*
Hans has refl with dust covered
'Hans covered himself with dust.' or
'Hans got covered with dust.'
b. *Die Statue hat sich langsam mit Staub bedeckt.*
the statue has refl slowly with dust covered
'The statue slowly got covered with dust.'

(296) a. *Hans selbst hat sich langsam mit Staub bedeckt.*
Hans self has refl slowly with dust covered
'Hans slowly covered himself with dust.'
b. *Sich selbst hat Hans langsam mit Staub bedeckt.*
refl self has Hans slowly with dust covered
'It was he himself, who Hans slowly covered with dust.'
c. (?)*Hans hat sich mit der Zeit von selbst mit Staub bedeckt.*
Hans has refl with the time by self with dust covered
'Hans slowly got covered with dust all by itself.'
(implicature: *Hans* is probably a dead corpse.)

With *sich erschweren* 'get complicated', *sich senken* 'fall', sentient individuals are strictly excluded as subjects, when the verbs are used as reflexives. These verbs will be classified as anti-causative reflexives on the grounds that their subject is clearly affected by, and cannot cause the event. Correspondingly, by-phrase *selbst* in the (b) examples is very natural. Once more, intensifying *selbst* can be used with an inanimate subject, if an antecedent clause biases a theme-interpretation (the (c) examples).

(297) a. *Der Winter erschwerte die Arbeit (duch den einsetzenden Schneefall).*
the winter obstructed the work (through the beginning snow-fall)
'The winter naturally obstructed the work by the beginning snow fall.'
b. *Die Arbeit wird sich noch von selbst erschweren.*
the work will refl still by self obstruct
'The job will get more difficult as we go.'

c. *Wir haben schon die Vorbereitungen gehasst, und*
we had already the preparations hated, and
die Arbeit selbst erschwerte sich dann auch noch durch den fehlenden Einsatz unserer Mitarbeiter.
the work self obstructed refl then also still by the lacking cooperation of-our staff
'We already hated the preparation, but the job itself was complicated even more by the lacking cooperation on the part of our staff.'

(298) a. *Der Schleusenwärter senkte den Wasserstand.*
the lock-operator lowered the water-level
b. *Der Wasserstand senkte sich langsam von selbst.*
the water-level lowered self slowly by self
'The water level slowly fell by itself.'
c. *Man hatte schon gestern alle Schleusen geöffnet, aber*
one had already yesterday all locks opened but
der Wasserstand selbst senkte sich nur langsam.
the water-level self lowered refl only slowly
'They had already opened all locks yesterday, but the actual water level fell very slowly.'

In sum, these double causatives have an anti-causative reflexive alternant.

(299) theme reflexives: [+c] [+c-m] [-c-m] -> [+c-m] [-c-m]
sich bedecken 'get covered', *sich erschweren* 'get complicated', *sich senken* 'fall'

The psychological causative *erschrecken* 'frighten/scare' behaves alike. It has an anti-causative reflexive alternant. Intensifying *selbst* is generally very deviant (301a-c), and by-phrase *selbst* is fine (301d).

(300) *Hans erschreckte sich.*
Hans scared self
'Hans got scared.'

(301) a. ??*Hans erschreckt sich selbst.*
Hans scared refl self

b. ??*Hans selbst erschreckt sich.*
Hans self scared refl

c. ??*Sich selbst erschreckt Hans.*
refl self scared Hans

d. *Hans erschreckt sich oft ganz von selbst, da muß noch nicht mal ein Laut zu hören sein.*
Hans scared refl often all by self there must still not once a sound to hear be
'Hans often gets scared all by itself; not even a whisper is needed for that.'

(302) experiencer reflexive: [+c] [+c-m] [-c+m] -> [+c-m] [-c+m]
sich erschrecken 'get scared'

In the remaining classes of cause-source and cause-goal verbs, the following examples are easily available as reflexives:

(303) a. [+c] [-c-m] [-m]
tragen 'carry/bear'

b. [+c] [-c-m] [-c]
erhalten 'keep ', *geben* 'give'

(304) a. *Das Projekt trägt sich aus Spendengeldern.*
the project carries refl from donations
'The project is supported by donations.'

b. *Hans hat sich ganz passabel erhalten.*
Hans has refl fairly well kept
'Hans is still in pretty good shape'

c. *Hans gibt sich jugendlich.*
Hans gives refl youthful
'Hans presents himself as a young person.'

The first example, *sich tragen aus* 'be supported by' behaves like an anticausative reflexive. Intensification by *selbst* is deviant for both the full noun and the reflexive, unless a theme-reading of the subject is biased, as in (305c).

(305) a. ?*Das Projekt selbst trägt sich aus Spendengeldern.*
the project self carries refl from donations

b. ?*Sich selbst trägt das Projekt aus Spendengeldern.*
refl self carries the project from donations

c. *Die Mitarbeiter werden vom Staat bezahlt, aber*
the employees are by-the state paid, but
das Projekt selbst trägt sich aus Spendengeldern.
the project self carries refl from donations
'Its employees are state-employed, but the project itself is supported by donations.'

The verb *erhalten* 'keep', has two reflexive uses. One of them is intentional, and it roughly means *to support oneself.* In some varieties of German, this reading is expressed by *sich unterhalten* 'support oneself'. The other reading is an anti-causative one, and it roughly means *stay in X condition*. Intensifying *selbst* excludes the anti-causative reading (306a), unless a theme-reading is biased by an antecedent clause (306b). The agent-canceling by-phrase *selbst* is compatible with the anti-causative reading (306c).

(306) a. *Hans hat sich ganz passabel selbst erhalten.*
Hans has refl pretty well self kept
'Hans took care of himself pretty well.'
not: 'Hans is still in good shape.'

b. *Seine Familie sieht schon übel aus, aber*
his family looks already miserable, but
Hans selbst hat sich ganz passabel erhalten.
Hans self has refl pretty well kept
'His family looks pretty miserable already, but Hans himself is still in rather good shape.'

c. *Hans hat sich ganz von selbst so gut erhalten (er lebt eigentlich recht ungesund).*
Hans has refl all by self so well kept (he lives actually pretty unhealthy)
'Hans stayed in good shape all by itself (his lifestyle is in fact pretty unhealthy).'

In contrast to *sich tragen aus* 'be supported by' and *sich erhalten* 'stay in X condition', reflexive *sich geben* 'present oneself' is clearly intentional. This reading is supported by the continuation in (307a). The agent-canceling by-phrase *selbst* in (307b) is not appropriate, and its intended anti-causative meaning would, in any event, not paraphrase *sich geben* in the grammatical example (304c). In sum, the external Θ-role is clearly assigned by *sich geben.* As for the internal role, the situation is less clear. Intensification of the reflexive is deviant (307c). Therefore, *sich geben* will be put aside, together with the other agent/cause reflexives. The status of its theme-role remains to be determined.

(307) a. *Hans selbst gibt sich recht aufgeschlossen (aber seine Frau lässt er das Geschirr abwaschen).*
Hans self gives refl very open-minded (but his wife makes he the dishes wash
'Hans presents himself as very open minded (while he expects his wife to do the dishes).'
b. ??*Hans gibt sich von selbst jugendlich.*
Hans gives refl by self youthful
attempted: 'Hans automatically appears youthful.'
c. ??*Sich selbst gibt Hans jugendlich...*
refl self gives Hans youthful

(308) a. theme reflexive: [+c] [-c-m] [-m] -> [-c-m] [-m]
sich tragen aus 'be supported by', *sich erhalten* 'stay in X condition'
b. cause reflexive: [+c] [-c-m] [-c] -> [+c] (?[-c-m]) [-c]
sich geben 'present oneself as'

4.1.4. Minder verbs

The emotional verbs *lieben* 'love', *verachten* 'despise' have reflexive alternants, but both Θ-roles are assigned in these examples. *Selbst* can be freely associated with both the full noun and the reflexive.

(309) [+m] [-m]
lieben 'love', *verachten* 'despise'

(310) a. *Hans liebt sich.*
Hans loves refl
'Hans loves himself.'

b. *Hans verachtet sich.*
Hans despises refl
'Hans despises himself.'

(311) a. *Hans hat nur sich selbst geliebt.*
Hans has only refl self loved
b. *Hans selbst hat sich geliebt.*
Hans self has refl loved
c. *Sich selbst hat Hans geliebt.*
refl self has Hans loved
'Hans loved only himself.'

(312) a. *Hans hat sich selbst verachtet.*
Hans has refl self despised
b. *Hans selbst hat sich verachtet.*
Hans self has refl despised
c. *Sich selbst hat Hans verachtet.*
refl self has Hans despised
'Hans despised himself.'

The same holds for the perception verbs in our set. Intensification by *selbst* is always fully grammatical; all Θ-roles are assigned.

(313) [+m] [+c-m] [-m]
sehen 'see/look', *hören* 'hear/listen'

(314) a. *Hans sieht sich.*
Hans sees refl
b. *Hans sieht sich selbst.*
Hans sees refl self
'Hans sees himself.'

(315) a. *Hans selbst hat sich (im Spiegel) gesehen.*
Hans self has refl (in-the mirror) seen
b. *Sich selbst hat Hans (im Spiegel) gesehen*
refl self has Hans (in-the mirror) seen
'Hans saw himself in the mirror.'

(316) a. *Hans hört sich (im Radio).*
Hans hears refl (in-the radio)
b. *Hans hört sich selbst (im Radio).*
Hans hears refl self (in-the radio)
'Hans hears himself in the radio.'

(317) a. *Hans selbst hat sich (im Radio) gehört*
Hans self has refl (in-the radio) heard
b. *Sich selbst hat Hans (im Radio) gehört*
refl self has Hans (in-the radio) heard
'Hans heard himself (in-the radio).'

The situation is entirely different with *sich finden* 'find oneself'. Intensifying *selbst* is ungrammatical (319b), unless a theme-reading is biased by an antecedent clause (319c), and by-phrase *selbst* is fine (319d). The reflexive *sich finden* 'find oneself' can only assign its internal Θ-role [-c-m].[9]

(318) [+m] [-c-m] [-m]
finden 'find'

(319) a. *Der Schlüssel fand sich wieder/ im Bad.*
the key found refl again/in-the bath
'The key turned up again/in the bath-room'
b. ??*Der Schlüssel fand sich selbst.*
the key found refl self
c. *Wir hatten seine Spuren zwar im Garten gesehen, aber*
we had his traces though in-the garden seen, but
der Hase selbst fand sich im Stall.
the rabbit self found refl then prt in-the barn
'Though we had seen its traces in the garden, the rabbit itself turned out to be in the barn.'
d. *Der Schlüssel fand sich von selbst wieder.*
the key found refl by self again
'The key turned up again by itself.'

(320) theme reflexive: [+m] [-c-m] [-m] -> [-c-m] [-m]
sich finden 'find oneself'

4.1.5. Special event verbs

There is only one example in this set that appears in a reflexive construction. This verb is *erblicken* 'spot/glimpse', a clear case of full Θ-role realization. Both the full noun and the reflexive can be intensified without contextual effort.

(321) [-c+m] [-c-m]
erblicken 'spot/glimpse'

(322) a. *Hans erblickte sich (im Spiegel).*
Hans spotted refl (in-the mirror)
b. *Hans erblickte sich selbst im Spiegel.*
Hans spotted refl self in-the mirror
'Hans spotted himself in the mirror'

(323) a. *Hans selbst hat sich im Spiegel erblickt.*
Hans self has refl in-the mirror spotted
b. *Sich selbst hat Hans im Spiegel erblickt.*
refl self has Hans in-the mirror spotted
'Hans spotted himself in the mirror.'

4.1.6. Summary of data

Let us take stock of the reflexives we have identified so far. Broadly, they fall in three classes. One class clearly assigns both an internal and an external Θ-role. This class confirms the assumption in Marelj (2004), Reinhart and Siloni (2005) that reflexivization operates in syntax in German. Since the behavior of this class is straightforward, it will be excluded from further discussion.

A second class of reflexives was found to assign a theme or experiencer cluster, but no external role.

(324) theme/experiencer reflexives
a. [+c+m] [-c-m] -> [-c-m]
sich verraten 'give oneself away'

b. [+c] [-c-m] -> [-c-m]
sich schleppen 'drag on', *sich verbrennen* 'suffer a burn'
c. [+c] [+c-m] [-c-m] -> [+c-m] [-c-m]
sich bedecken 'get covered', *sich erschweren* 'get complicated', *sich senken* 'fall'
d. [+c] [+c-m] [-c+m] -> [+c-m] [-c+m]
sich erschrecken 'get scared'
e. [+c] [-c-m] [-m] -> [-c-m] [-m]
sich tragen aus 'be supported by', *sich erhalten* 'stay in X condition'
f. [+m] [-c-m] [-m] -> [-c-m] [-m]
sich finden 'find oneself'

With the exception of the experiencer reflexive *sich erschrecken* 'get scared' (the assignment of [-c+m] is free), this class is interesting for the present discussion, because it allows us to test one of the most stable generalizations of lexical semantics, the assignment of [-c-m] to the direct object position. If [-c-m] is assigned directly to the nominative NP of theme-reflexives, then theme-reflexives must have unaccusative syntax.

There is a third class of reflexives, which have been put aside. In that class, there was evidence for the presence of a [+] cluster, but it was unclear, whether an internal role was assigned. This class will be discussed first. It will turn out that an internal Θ-role is assigned in all cases.

(325) [+] reflexives
a. [+c+m] [-c-m] -> [+c+m] ?[-c-m]
sich mitteilen 'express oneself'
b. [+c] [-c-m] -> [+c] ?[-c-m]
sich rollen 'roll oneself', *sich schieben* 'push oneself'
b. [+c] [-c-m] [-c] -> [+c] ?[-c-m] [-c]
sich geben 'present oneself as'

4.2. [+]-reflexives assign their internal theta-role

In languages where reflexivization operates in syntax, [+] reflexives assign both an internal and an external Θ-role, and these two roles are then bundled. The subject of a reflexive predicate is therefore both the cause and the object of an event.

(326) Reflexivization bundling ((24) in (Reinhart and Siloni 2005)
$[\Theta_i]\ [\Theta_j]$ -> $[\Theta_i - \Theta_j]$, where Θ_i is an external Θ-role.

The difference between a reflexive and an optionally intransitive predicate is very clear, when we compare the following two sentences. In the reflexive sentence (327b), the subject does the shaving, and it must be affected by the event as well. By contrast, the subject of an optionally intransitive sentence like (327a) does not need to be affected by the event.

(327) a. *Hans rasiert normalerweise.*
Hans shaves normally
'Hans usually does some shaving.'
b. *Hans rasiert sich.*
Hans shaves refl
'Hans shaves.'

Now consider again the agent/cause reflexives singled out above. These verbs caused suspicion, because they did not allow intensification of the reflexive. Taking affectedness into account, we can already see that *sich rollen* 'roll oneself' and *sich schieben* 'push oneself' are well behaved. In both cases, the subject is the cause of motion, and it must undergo a change of location too.

(328) a. *Hans hat sich zur Seite gerollt.*
Hans has refl to-the side rolled
'Hans rolled over to one side.'
b. *Hans hat sich durch die Tür geschoben.*
Hans has refl through the door pushed
'Hans shoved himself through the door.'

The situation is still not clear for the remaining two verbs: with *sich mitteilen* 'express oneself' the reference of the subject is not necessarily identical with what is being expressed. The same holds for *sich geben* 'present oneself', where the object of the presentation is not the subject itself, but a certain image of it. Notice, however, that both are cases of metaphorical extension of a literal, truly reflexive meaning. In the case of *sich mitteilen* 'express oneself' the object of the expression necessarily belongs to the subject as one of its propositional attitudes. In the case of *sich geben* 'present oneself', it is always an image of the subject that is being presented, not somebody else's.

(329) a. *Hans hat sich uns mitgeteilt.*
Hans has refl to-us expressed
'Hans expressed himself to us.'
b. *Hans hat sich aufgeschlossen gegeben.*
Hans has refl open-minded given
'Hans presented an open-minded image of himself.'

Other apparently intransitive reflexives behave alike. Take as an example *sich schicken* 'send oneself', which can mean 'hurry up' in some varieties of German. Although the following sentence does not assert that anything is being sent, it does assert that the subject (and not somebody else) is affected by an increase in velocity or activity. Even on the idiomatic reading, the reflexive thus assigns both an internal and an external Θ-role.

(330) *Hans schickt sich.*
Hans send refl
'Hans hurries up.'

I conclude that [+] reflexives are well-behaved in the sense of Reinhart and Siloni (2005). They assign both an internal and an external Θ-role, and the two roles are assigned to the subject in conjunction.

4.3. Are theme-reflexives unaccusatives?

Under standard assumptions regarding unaccusativity (Burzio 1986; Perlmutter and Postal 1984), a verb that does not assign an external Θ-role cannot assign the accusative case. Therefore, the internal argument is raised into the subject position. Applied to German reflexives, this general reasoning introduces a problem. On the one hand, generalizations about thematic role assignment suggest unaccusative syntax: a theme-cluster must be assigned to an internal argument. On the other hand, the distribution of case clearly follows a transitive pattern. In the following example, the anti-causative reading is visible in the idiomatic interpretation *suffer a burn*. Although a causative reading is available too, it is inappropriate in this context, because it would assert that the addressee is dead. As for case, both nominative and accusative are unambiguously marked on the second person singular reflexive.

(331) *Du hattest dich damals verbrannt.*
you$_{nom}$ had refl$_{acc}$ then burned
'You suffered a burn back then.'

Two questions must be asked in relation to this problem. First, are German anti-causative reflexives really transitive? Second, if they are, how can transitive syntax be reconciled with unaccusative argument structure?

As a matter of fact, the evidence is inconclusive with respect to the first question already. Consider first auxiliary selection. While most reflexives select the auxiliary *haben* 'have' (331), some select *sein* 'be', as in the Austrian German example (332). Auxiliary selection in reflexives seems to depend on the auxiliary selected by the base verb, rather than the reduced argument structure of the reflexive.

(332) *Die Prüfung ist sich noch am Vormittag ausgegangen.*
the exam is refl still in-the morning prt-gone
'It was still possible to do the exam in the morning.'

The appositive participle does not attribute entirely conclusive evidence either. The reflexive verbs that have been singled out as theme-reflexives on lexical semantic grounds do not form a class with respect to the appositive participle. In some cases, what looks like a reflexive reading is available (333), but in others it is not (334). These data support an unaccusative analysis for some theme-reflexives, but not for all of them.

(333) a. *deine (mit Staub) bedeckte Statue*
a with dust covered statue
'a dust-covered statue'
b. *die (durch den Regen) erschwerten Arbeiten*
the through the rain complicated works
'the works that have been complicated by the rain'
c. (?)*das aus Spendengeldern getragene Projekt*
the from donations carried project
'the project that is supported by donations'

d. *ein gut erhaltener Senior*
a well kept elderly-man
'an elderly man in good shape'

(334) a. *#der verratene Plan*
the betrayed plan
'the plan that has been betrayed (by somebody)'
b. **die geschleppten Arbeiten*
the dragged works
c. *#der verbrannte Bruder*
the burned brother
'the brother who burned to death'
e. *#der gesenkte Wasserstand*
the lowered water-level
'the water level that has been lowered'
f. *#das erschreckte Kind*
the scared child
'the child that has been scared (by somebody/something)'
g. *#der gefundene Hase*
the found rabbit
'the rabbit that has been found'

Movement data are similarly inconclusive. While split topicalization of the nominative is grammatical in most cases, fronting of the nominative inside VP often is not. Examples are given of those verbs that passed the attributive participle test. It must be stressed that there is considerable variation in judgments among speakers here. The judgments given below summarize the judgments of a set of Austrian speakers. Their insolidity excludes them as evidence for or against any analysis.

(335) a. **Sein Gesicht bedeckt hat sich mit einem Ausdruck des Schreckens.*
his face covered has refl with an expression of-the terror
b. ??*Gesicht bedeckt hat sich noch keines mit einem derartigen Ausdruck des Schreckens.*
face covered has refl still none with a like expression of terror

c. ?*Gesicht hat sich noch keines mit einem derartigen Ausdruck des Schreckens bedeckt.*
face has refl still none with a like expression of terror covered
'No face has yet been overcast by a comparable expression of terror.'

(336) a. ?*Dumme Bräuche erhalten haben sich hier schon immer.*
silly customs survived have refl here already always
b. *Dumme Bräuche erhalten haben sich hier immer welche.*
silly customs survived have refl here always some
c. *Dumme Bräuche haben sich hier immer welche erhalten.*
silly customs have refl here always some survived
'There have always survived some silly customs here.'

(337) a. ??*Die Arbeit erschwert hat sich auf diese Weise schon oft.*
the work obstructed has refl on this way already often
b. ??*Arbeiten erschwert haben sich auf diese Weise schon viele.*
works obstructed have refl on this way already many
c. *Arbeiten haben sich auf diese Weise schon viele erschwert.*
works have refl on this way already many obstructed
'Many jobs have already got complicated in this way.'

(338) a. *Das Projekt getragen hat sich aus so einem kleinen Budget wohl kaum.*
the project carried has refl from such a small budget probably hardly
b. ?*Projekte getragen haben sich aus so einem kleinen Budget wohl kaum.*
projects carried have refl from such a small budget probably hardly
c. ?*Projekt hat sich aus so einem kleinen Budget wohl keins getragen.*
project has refl from such a small budget probably none carried

Once more, we must conclude that the evidence does not support a general analysis of theme-reflexives as unaccusatives. On the other hand, it does not reject such an analysis either. Chapter 3 will develop a theory of argument projection that reconciles the distribution of structural cases with the requirement that fully specified [-c-m] must be assigned to the direct object position.

5. Conclusion

The overall conclusion from this empirically oriented chapter has been that the predictions by the *Theta System* are accurate in most cases. The German facts have made it necessary, though, to introduce a number of minor changes to specific principles and conventions.

First, it was argued that there are three, rather than two contexts that allow non-realization of a thematic role. In the *Theta System*, a [/+c] cluster may remain unrealized, if a verb selects two such clusters. A cluster cannot be realized, if it is indistinguishable from another cluster selected by the same verb. The latter configuration applies primarily to the pair {[+c], [-m]}. A third configuration defended above involves the mental domain. It is repeated as follows:

(339) intentional generalization
[+m] may remain unrealized in the context {[+m], [-c-m], [-m]}

A second adjustment was defended with respect to the marking conventions. While all [-] clusters must be assigned inside VP according to the *Theta System*, underspecified [-] clusters systematically pattern with the mixed value cluster [-c+m] in German. They can be assigned to both internal and external arguments. By contrast, the mixed value cluster [+c-m] can never be assigned to a direct object. These observations suggested the following adaptation of the marking conventions:

(340) Lexicon marking (modified 2)
Given an n-place verb-entry, n>1,
a. Mark a *fully specified* [-] cluster with index 2.
b. Mark a [+] cluster with index 1.
c. Mark the verb with an ACC feature, if its entry includes
(i) both a [+] cluster and a fully specified cluster [/α,/-c], or
(ii) both a [/+c] cluster and a [/-c] cluster.

Finally, it was argued that the reflexive alternation is by and large well behaved. Where a [+] cluster is present, it must be assigned to an external argument. However, standard tests for the syntax of non-causative reflexives did not supply conclusive evidence. The unaccusative analysis of non-causative reflexives can neither be defended, nor rejected on the basis of these data. The syntax of German non-causative reflexives must be determined by an independently motivated syntactic theory.

Notes

[1] The availability of both a cause and a subject matter apparently contradicts Pesetsky's generalization on the unavailability of such combinations. In the present framework, the issue does not immediately arise. If a subject matter realizes underspecified [-m] it cannot co-occur with a cause ([+c]), but if the subject matter realizes fully specified [+c-m], as in the German example in the text, then co-occurrence with [+c] is expected.

[2] (89c) is grammatical if a dative case is used instead of the accusative in the directional PP. However, this change of case turns the selected directional into an unselected local adjunct.

(i) *Hans sah die Mickeymaus auf der Uhr.*
Hans saw the Mickey at the_{DAT} watch

(ii) *Hans sah auf der Uhr eine Mickeymaus.*
Hans saw at the_{DAT} watch a Mickey

[3] A [+c-m] subject does not allow the realization of [-m] in a directional PP. This is a result of the general condition that sensations can only be directed by sentient beings.

(i) **Alle Augen sahen auf die Uhr.*
all eyes looked at the watch

[4] A verb is called *strong* if it marks the tense opposition by means of stem vowel alternation only. Cf. Bendjaballah and Haiden (2003), Grimm (1819), Halle (1953), Ségéral and Scheer (1998) for discussion. A verb is called *weak* if it marks the tense opposition by means of affixation.

[5] A stem-vowel can mark more than one feature, for example tense and mood in the past subjunctive. Bendjaballah and Haiden (2003) argue that such configurations are only possible, if all features in question belong to a single syntactic head; cf. chapter 3 for discussion.

[6] Notice that *eintreten* 'happen/materialize' is strong too. Only stem-vowel and suffixal derivation changes inflectional class membership. Prefixes and particles do not.

[7] With a clitic pronoun instead of a full NP object, the acceptability of the examples improves. However, this just proves the point in question: since the nominative is structurally higher than the accusative, a gap inside the fronted VP must be licensed.

[8] In the *Theta System*, reduction of an agent cluster is impossible, because [/+m] cannot be reduced by hypothesis. An option for the derivation of non-causative

sich verraten 'betray oneself' is non-realization, which would be licensed by the instrument cluster that the verb selects. Non-causative reflexive *verraten* 'betray' could be derived like unaccusative *erschrecken* "get scared". On the other hand, the existence of exceptions does not pose an insurmountable problem, if external role reduction applies in the lexicon, as argued in Reinhart and Siloni (2005).

9 The theme-reflexive *sich finden* 'find oneself' has lost a [+m] cluster, which is not an option in the *Theta System*; cf. note 8.

Chapter 3
A Bare Phrase Structure of Argument Expression

The previous chapter was dedicated to an exploration of lexicon-syntax correspondences for German verbs. A large body of evidence indeed confirms universal generalizations about the realization of thematic roles in syntax, and in particular the implementation of these generalizations in the Theta System.

However, while such generalizations are robust and most probably universal, they are by no means exhaustive. For example, the assignment of a certain type of clusters is, in principle, free. In Reinhart's original version of the Theta System, mixed value clusters can be assigned either internally, or externally. The data presented in chapter two suggest that this freedom of assignment extends to underspecified [-] clusters. There must be conditions outside the domain of lexical semantics, which determine the syntactic projection of such thematic roles.

The behavior of non-causative reflexives is another example. If these verbs are derived by external role reduction, then they should behave as unaccusatives. However, it was observed in chapter 2 that reduced reflexives do not consistently pass unaccusativity tests. Their syntactic structure must be partly determined by conditions outside the domain of lexical semantics, too.

Conceptually, the *semantic bootstrapping* approach to acquisition (Pinker 1984) would favor a reduction of syntactic argument projection to lexical semantics. If basic semantic properties make it possible for a child to acquire syntactic structure, then the child must have access to very robust generalizations on how semantic relations are represented in syntax. Incidentally, semantic bootstrapping is ill supported by evidence from acquisition. Naigles (2002) for instance discusses a number of experimental studies that converge towards the paradoxical generalization that infants score highly in abstract pattern recognition and application tasks, while toddlers seem to have lost this ability. In particular, we find "considerable ability to abstract patterns over specific items and to distinguish natural from unnatural English sentences" (Naigles 2002:157) in infants, while "toddlers appear to be non-abstract, item-specific language users" (Naigles 2002:157). She defends the following solution to this paradox:

> [...] the patterns that infants extract from their linguistic input are not yet tied to meaning; thus, toddlers do not lose these earlier-abstracted forms but their use of them is limited until they have been integrated with meaning. [...] in language acquisition, learning form is easy but learning meaning, and especially linking meanings and forms, is hard. (Naigles 2002:157)

If such studies have any bearing on grammatical theorizing, then the conclusion drawn from them must be that distributional patterns are learnable as such, and that the child does not have access to rules that exhaustively determine the linking of meanings and forms.

This chapter develops a theory of autonomous syntactic projection, which nevertheless allows us to maintain the strongest generalizations about the linking of thematic roles. The chapter is organized as follows. Section 1 outlines the architectural background, a model of parallel, interpreted domains. Starting with observations about the phonology-syntax interface, it formalizes the structure-building algorithm in very simple mathematical terms, and it derives the basic relations of X'-Theory. Section 2 turns back to argument structure. It implements the generalizations of the Theta System in the new model of syntactic projection, and accounts for the distribution of thematic roles in simple, finite sentences.

1. A new architecture: domains and interpretation

It is a fundamental claim of the present approach that thematic roles are properties of lexical verb entries. This approach contrasts with the constructional approach, which holds that thematic role-interpretations are the mere product of specific syntactic configurations. A discussion of the constructional approach as developed in Borer (1991, 1997, 2003) is particularly instructive because of the explanatory weight it places on morphology. While Borer's theory of thematic role interpretation will be rejected, her observations about the morphology-syntax interface form the basis of the model to be developed in this section.

1.1. The role of overt morphology in argument projection: Borer (2003)

According to Borer (1994, 1998, 2003) the thematic interpretation of syntactic arguments is determined exclusively by the position in which they find themselves. Lexical semantic information does not play any significant role in this process. According to Borer, a given lexical item may be more felicitous in some configurations than it is in others, but, in principle, any realization is possible. In Borer (2003), she presents as an example a lexical array composed of the three elements {*dog, boat, sink*}, and the grammatical formatives {*past, the, the*}. In this initial array, any lexical item may be realized either as a noun or as a verb, but only when it is realized as a verb, it takes arguments. As a noun, it refers:

(1) a. *The dog sank the boat.*
b. *The boat dogged the sink.*
c. *The sink boated the dog.*

Certainly, (1a) is more likely to be uttered than (1b), which, in turn, might win over (1c). However, Borer argues, none of these sentences is strictly ungrammatical. A theory of grammar should not be bothered by the fact that (1c) describes a quite unlikely real-world scenario. It should rather offer an explanation for why it is possible to interpret a sentence like (1c) in exactly the way it is interpreted: the first noun refers to an entity that does some action. The action performed is in some way related to the concept boat, and an entity of the type dog is affected by, or undergoes, the action.

Borer's thesis is that a very basic organizational principle of the computational system is responsible for such interpretations: a universal template of clausal projection. Abstracting away form aspectual claims, which have been subject to successive adaptation in the development of the theory (Borer 1994, 1998, 2003), the configuration in (2) is claimed to be common to verbal extended projections. v_1 introduces a specifier position for external arguments (EA). This is not to be interpreted in the conventional way. There is no designated noun phrase that must move to the specifier of v_1 to be licensed there. Things work the other way around. If a constituent comes to occupy the specifier of v_1, it is automatically interpreted as an external argument. The same holds for v_2. It introduces a specifier position for internal arguments (IA). If a constituent occupies this position, an internal argument-interpretation is forced upon it. L-D is an unordered initial array of lexical items. Unlike standard VP, no argument structural relations are defined in L-D.

(2) $[_{v1P}$ [*EA*] $[v_1$ $[_{TP}$ T $[_{v2P}$ [*IA*] [v_2 [L-D]]]]]]

One might want to ask now what the interpretation of an *external* or of an *internal argument* is. For example, why do certain verbs require their external argument to be in volitional control over the event (*bauen* 'build'), while others require it to be a container (*enthalten* 'contain')? What, if any, is the common property to such interpretations? Likewise for *internal argument*. Why do verbs like *bauen* 'build' require the internal argument to be affected, while the internal argument of verbs like *lieben* 'love' need only be represented in the mind of an experiencer, and the experiencer must be the internal argument of still other verbs like *demütigen* 'humiliate'. What, if any, is the interpretation shared by an affected object, a subject of emotion, and an experiencer? It seems rather unlikely that an answer to such questions can be found without invoking lexically specified information of the sort discussed in the previous chapter.

Likewise, we may wonder why there is a stark contrast between Borer's examples in (1) and those in (3):

(3) a. *The sink made the dog look like a boat.*
b. *The sink made the dog feel like a boat.*
c. *Facing the sink, the dog turned into a boat.*

These sentences are still somewhat strange. We would not expect an intelligent person to honestly assert them under normal circumstances. However, they are much less offending than the sentences in (1). It seems plausible to assume that the difference in acceptability is related to the fact that the words in (3) are used in accordance with their lexical specification as verbs, nouns etc, while the words in (1) are not. It seems impossible to construct a theory of syntactic argument structure without reference to lexical information of the kind discussed in chapter two. Borer's (2000)/(2003) article is interesting for the present discussion, because she shows that we cannot discard morpho-phonology either.

Consider the contrast between a complex event nominal as in (4a), and a result nominal as in (4b):

(4) a. *The instructor's (intentional) examination of the student.*
b. *The instructor's examination/exam.*

One of the most important differences between complex event nominals and result nominals is that the former, but not the latter, project argument structure. The question now arises whether the argument structure of a complex event nominal is projected by the noun as such, or by the verbal structure embedded under it.

Borer (2000)/(2003) quotes Grimshaw (1990) for the observation that "[o]nly nouns that are derived from verbs [...] by means of overt affixation can be [complex event] nominals, while nouns which do not have a verbal or adjectival source never are" (Borer 2000:16). She then states that "one is certainly tempted to view argument structure [...] as deriving from the source verb [...], rather than the noun itself" (Borer 2000:16). This would make it possible to assume that event interpretation is always contingent on verbal syntax.

Notice the reference to *overt* affixation in this statement above. Grimshaw's observation does not apply to a lexical-semantic relation between a verb and a complex event nominal, but to a morphological one. Borer (2000:18f.)[1] capitalizes on this observation, to develop an argument for the relevance of phonological shapes for the availability of certain syntactic derivations.

Take a lexical item with the semantic properties of |*transform*|. This lexical item can be inserted in a verbal syntactic frame, to yield the verb /transform/.

(5) |*transform*| + V → [$_{V}$ *transform*]

Then, still without accessing any phonological information, the verb transform can be inserted in a nominal frame, to yield a derived noun:

(6) [$_{V}$ *transform*] + N → [$_{N}$ [$_{V}$ *transform*]]

Finally, [$_{N}$ [$_{V}$ *transform*]] is spelled out phonologically. But here we encounter a problem. The semantic properties of [$_{N}$ *transform*] could be spelled out in various ways, among them the following:

(7) a. [$_{N}$ [$_{V}$ *transform*]] → *transformation*
b. [$_{N}$ [$_{V}$ *transform*]] → *metamorphosis*
c. [$_{N}$ [$_{V}$ *transform*]] → *shift*
d. [$_{N}$ [$_{V}$ *transform*]] → *turn*

As all of these phonological spell-outs have the same core meaning and derivational history, they should have exactly the same syntactic properties. In particular, they should all be argument-taking nouns.

But this is plainly false. Only *transformation*, as a morphologically derived complex event nominal, projects the argument structure of the verb *transform*. Therefore, the spell-out operations (7b-d) must be blocked. *Metamorphosis*, *shift*, *turn* can only be the spell-out of a different derivation, one that inserts the concept in a nominal frame directly, as follows:

(8) a. |*transform*| + N → [$_N$ *transform*]
b. [$_N$ *transform*] → *metamorphosis*/*shift*/*turn*

Thus, the phonological shape associated with a given concept has an influence on the derivational options available for that concept. At least it has to be stipulated that specific derivational operations can bleed specific phonological realizations.

It might be objected at this point that *transformation* differs semantically from *metamorphosis*, *shift*, *turn*, and that this difference in meaning, not the phonological shape of the respective lexical entries, is responsible for their different derivational options. Borer rejects this challenge, quoting an example from Hebrew.

The native Hebrew noun *šinui* 'change/transformation' contrasts with the synonymous borrowed word *transformacia* 'transformation'. Native *šinui* can be used both as an argument-taking event nominal (9a), and as a referential noun (9b) – Borer's example (36):

(9) a. *ha-šinui šel merkaz ha-'ir 'al yedey ha-'iriya*
the-transformation/change of center the-city by city hall
b. *ha-šinuy haya madhim*
the-change/transformation was amazing

By contrast, the borrowed noun *transformacia* can only be used as a referential noun (10b). It does not license arguments (10a) – Borer's example (37):

(10) a. **ha-transformacia šel merkaz ha-'ir 'al yedey ha-'iriya*
the-transformation of center the-city by city hall
b. *ha-transformacia hayta madhima*
the-transformation was amazing

The only difference between the two nouns is that *šinui* is overtly derived from the verb *šina*, while *transformacia* lacks a verbal counterpart. Borer argues that the difference in morpho-phonological shape between the two words is responsible for their different syntactic behavior. She formalizes this conclusion as follows.

Take π to be a "reference to an indexed phonological representation" (Borer 2000:19) that is associated with every lexical item by lexical stipulation. Then, derivations of the following sort can be ruled out on the basis that π refers to the phonological shape *transformation*, not to *metamorphosis*, *shift*, *turn*:

(11) ($[_N$ *transformation*], π) → **metamorphosis/shift/turn*

We must conclude with Borer that morpho-phonological properties of lexical items do have an influence on their syntactic projection potential. More evidence of this sort will be discussed throughout this and the following chapter.

1.2. A parallel architecture of grammatical derivation

Facts of the sort just discussed are problematic for the standard, linear architecture of grammatical derivation, because phonological features must be redundantly represented in syntax, in order to become relevant. Indeed, Borer (1991, 1997) defends a parallel, rather than a linear approach to the syntax-morphology interface. Comparable considerations are endorsed in a much more general way in Jackendoff (2002) and subsequent work by Booij (to appear).

Let us state the essence of the parallel approach in (12). In this diagram, the straight arrows represent derivational operations in each module. Such operations are strictly domain internal. Relations across domains are established by means of interpretation: objects of one domain can be mapped into another domain. Interpretation is represented by squiggly arrows in (12).

(12) parallel derivation and interpretation

phonology		syntax		semantics
c	~>	Z	~>	γ
↑		↑		↑
b	~>	Y	~>	β
↑		↑		↑
a	~>	X	~>	α
↑		↑		↑
Lexical array / numeration				

A few immediate questions arise with respect to (12): First, what is the formal character of the derivation-relation? Is it a single relation, or composed of distinct operations? How are they to be formalized?

Second, what is the formal character of the interpretation-relation? Is it symmetrical or not? If it is asymmetrical, what is the direction of mapping? How should it be formalized?

The questions related to derivation are addressed in section 1.4. The two operations involved are *merge*, which takes two objects and forms a complex object, and *head-of*, which defines the head of a given object by filtering out non-head components. By definition, *merge* and *head-of* have the same properties in all three domains of grammatical derivation. They derive bare structure in phonology, syntax, and semantics.

Interpretation (addressed in section 1.5), is formalized as an asymmetric structure-preserving mapping, a morphism. In agreement with early generative theories like Chomsky (1955), it is assumed that elements in phonology are mapped on elements in syntax, and elements in syntax are mapped on elements in semantics.

The question of convergence now arises in a different way than it does in standard minimalist literature (Chomsky 1995). By hypothesis, the three domains exclusively manipulate features that are interpretable in that domain. Therefore, the condition of Full Interpretation is redundant. It cannot be violated by definition. In the parallel model, a derivation converges, if the objects derived in each domain receive an interpretation in the other domains, which is consistent with their lexical features, i.e., a version of the Projection Principle:

(13) Projection Principle
Lexically stipulated pairings (π, λ) of sounds and meanings remain unaltered throughout a derivation.

Notice that (13) subsumes the *Lexicon Interface Guideline* of Reinhart and Siloni (2005) – their (29):

(14) The Lexicon Interface Guideline
The syntactic component cannot manipulate Θ-grids: Elimination, modification and addition of a Θ-role are illicit in syntax.

Turning back to Borer's argument against late lexical access, the Projection Principle ensures that the phonological object /shift/ is mapped on the syntactic object <N_{shift}>, and not on the syntactic object <$V_{transform}N_{ation}$>, including all relevant properties of the two objects in the respective domains.

Building on Bendjaballah and Haiden (2002, 2003), the following sections first formalize the basic structure building devices, and then exemplify their operation with the morphology of German verbs.

1.3. More overt morphology: templates and features

Chapter 2 discussed causativization by stem-vowel alternation. While it was argued there that the direction of morpho-phonological derivations does not correspond to the direction of lexical-semantic derivations, it is evident that a theory of syntactic argument structure cannot be blind to morpho-phonology. This section uses observations about non-concatenative morphology to develop and exemplify a formalism for the projection of grammatical structure in both morphology and syntax. For extensive discussion of the relation between templatic morphology and argument interpretation, cf. Doron, (2003a, 2003b).

Non-concatenative morphology, in particular the morphological significance of templates, is problematic for standard linguistic theory, because a prosodic configuration, rather than a lexical item, seems to express meaning. In the literature on Semitic (Mc Carthy 1979, 1981), this problem is usually addressed by the assumption that vocalic melody and consonantal frames count as distinct morphemes. Such a solution is unavailable, however, where a single vowel expresses both lexical and inflectional features, as in German strong verbs.

Consider first two verbal forms of the Classical Arabic root *ḍrb* 'hit', the perfective stem *ḍarab* and the imperfective stem *ḍrib*. Assume the two stems can be represented as follows:[2]

```
(15)  a.  perfective stem: ḍarab      b.  imperfective stem: ḍrib
            C V C V C V                    C V C V C V
            | | | | |                      |   | | |
            ḍ a r a b                      ḍ   r i b
```

(15a) and (15b) share a prosodic structure and a consonantal root. They only differ with respect to vowel melody. It is therefore reasonable to assume that the consonantal root and the vowel melody are independent morphemes.

In order to represent this generalization, it is assumed since Mc Carthy (1979, 1981) that root consonants and vowel melody are represented on separate tiers, as in (16) for the perfective stem *ḍarab*. Melodic elements are associated to the C- and V-slots according to the principles of autosegmental theory (Goldsmith 1990; Leben 1978; Mc Carthy 1979).

```
(16)  aspect  ~      a
                    / \
                C V C V C V
                |   |   |
      root    ~ ḍ   r   b
```

(16) derives the independence of root and affix by separating vowels and consonants. If (16) is correct, then templates are simply one form of concatenation.

According to the principles of autosegmental theory, segments/elements are associated to skeletal positions one by one, from left to right. If autosegmental principles apply blindly, then we expect that only the final consonant should geminate. However, Guerssel and Lowenstamm (1990, 1996), Lowenstamm (2003) observe that this is wrong. The intensive stem is formed by gemination of the medial consonant: *ḍarrab* 'hit violently'. The fact that the intensive requires gemination of the medial, not the final consonant must be determined morphologically, not phonologically.

Guerssel and Lowenstamm (1990) therefore suggest to distinguish between root and affixal positions at the level of the template. Their approach is sketched in (17). Root segments blindly attach only to the boxed root positions. Affixal positions (the CV units under *a* and *c*, respectively) are derivationally identified.

(17)

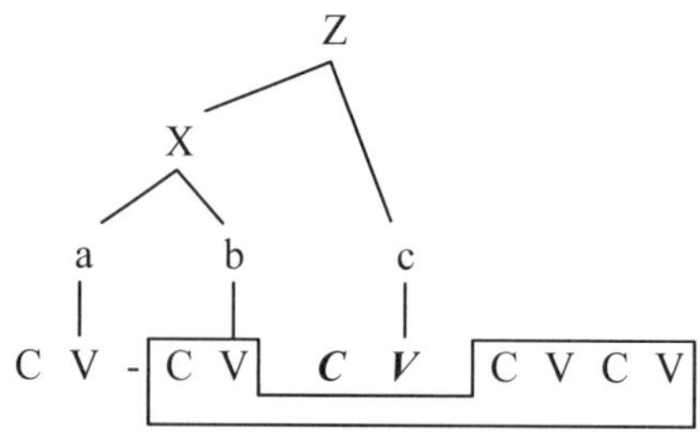

Two questions arise with respect to the implementation of (17). First, how should the association lines between CV units and morpho-syntactic terminals be formalized? (17) suggests that morpho-syntactic structure is prosodic structure. Such a claim is much too strong to be tenable, and it does not seem to be in the spirit of Guerssel and Lowenstamm's theory anyway. But then, what is the relation between CV positions and syntactic heads? Second, (17) shares with (16) the hypothesis that affixal and root positions can be disentangled at the level of the phonological string. This hypothesis is challenged by the behavior of German strong verbs. It will turn out that the parallel architecture (12) provides a natural answer to both questions, and it allows us to maintain the idea behind (17).

Take a German strong verb like *fallen* 'fall'. The phonological representation of the infinitival and past stems, respectively, is as follows (Bendjaballah and Haiden 2002):

(18)

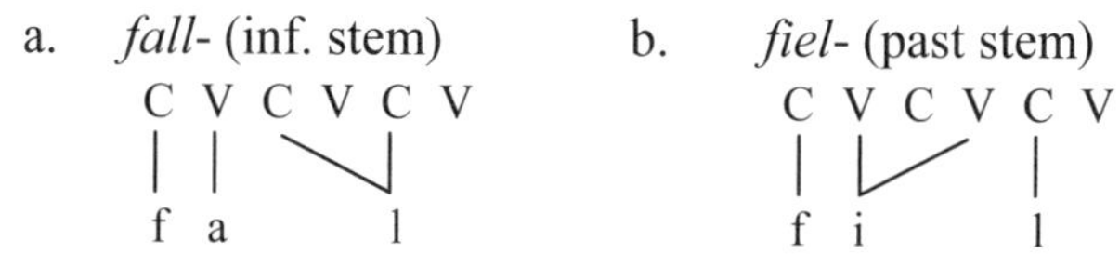

The first V-position is clearly related to tense-marking. However, if we assume with (17) that it is exclusively a tense affix, we cannot account for the fact that this vowel expresses lexical information as well. A significant number of words share the root consonants /*fl*/: *fallen* 'fall' contrasts with *voll* 'full', *füllen* 'fill', *viel* 'much', *fahl* 'pale', and with *fällen* 'fell', the causative counterpart of *fallen* 'fall'. These lexical entries differ only with respect to the length and segmental content of the stem vowel. Clearly, the stem vowel of a German strong verb expresses both lexical and functional information. The existence of such data challenges all theories of templatic morphology proposed so far.

Bendjaballah and Haiden (2002, 2003) take a different approach. They start with the observation that realization of multiple morphological features implies prosodic prominence. For example, the stem vowel of a German strong verb is not only part of the root and a marker of tense. It is also the prosodic head of the verb: it bears stress. On the other hand, the stem-final consonant, which is prosodically weak, bears no independent morphological function. It is morphologically significant exclusively in conjunction with the entire stem.

Thus, there is a parallel structure of prominence in prosody and morphology. In prosody, all segments are visible as part of the terminal string. A subset, the stem vowel, is visible at the level of word-stress too. In morphology, all segments are visible as belonging to the lexical root. A subset, the stem vowel, is visible at the level of tense-marking too. This parallelism can be depicted as follows, for the infinitival stem of *fallen* 'fall'.

```
(19)   C V               ~~  tense
       C V C V
       C V C V C V       ~~  root
       | |  \_|
       f a    l
```

Parallelisms of this kind are most naturally expressed in a framework of parallel, interpreted derivations like the one proposed in (12) above. The following sections formalize the structure-building algorithm, and the interface between grammatical sub-domains.

1.4. Structure-building operations: *merge* and *head-of*

Merge is the basic concatenating operation of human language. It takes two objects and forms a third object. Let us define the operation as a function that takes two variables ranging over the same finite domain E, $x,y \in E^2$, and delivers the product $xy \in E$:

(20) Merge

$$\mu: \begin{array}{l} E^2 \rightarrow E \\ (x, y) \mapsto xy \end{array}$$

By definition, the output of μ is in E, and it can be merged again with another variable of E: $\mu(xy, z)=xyz$.

Defined as a product, merge creates flat structures. The order of subsequent merging operations does not determine any hierarchical relation among variables.

Asymmetrical relations are introduced by a filtering operation that designates the head by eliminating its dependent. This operation can be modeled as a sum. In (21), summation applies with respect to y, so x is the head of xy. y is the complement of x. C is a constant. For the present purposes, its value can be kept to 1, the identity element for μ. Notice that the choice of variable to be eliminated is not a function of *head-of*. We will turn to this issue in the discussion of complement and shell structures in the following section.

(21) head-of

$$\sum_{y \in E} \mu(x, y) = Cx$$

Now take a German strong stem, which is minimally composed of three CV units (Bendjaballah and Haiden 2002): *CVCVCV*. This string is formalized as a product xyz of three variables x, y, z, each representing one CV unit.

The product xyz is a flat structure. It designates a local domain, in the present case the root constituent. Prosodic structure is introduced by subsequent application of *head-of*: $\Sigma\mu(x,y)z$ and $\Sigma\mu(x,y)$, to yield (22), which is a bare prosodic structure. It derives the internal structure of a stressed syllable without reference to derivationally created objects.

(22) bare prosodic structure

x			by *head-of*
x	y		by *head-of*
x	y	z	by *merge*

1.5. Mapping into syntax: the basic relations of X'-theory

A structure like (22) is absolutely opaque. In order to assign a meaning to an object of one domain, we must define a function that maps the elements of the domain into a non-intersecting domain, as follows:[3]

(23) Interpretation

$$f : A \rightarrow B$$

where $A \cap B = \varnothing$

Assume interpretation is structure preserving for *merge*. The task is then to show that *merge* and *head-of* derive meaningful objects in syntax.[4]

Consider again an initial array of three variables *x,y,z*. Assume *x* merges with *y* to form *xy*, and then *head-of* eliminates *y* as a dependent of *x*. Next, *z* merges with the head *x* of *xy*, to form *zx*.

(24)

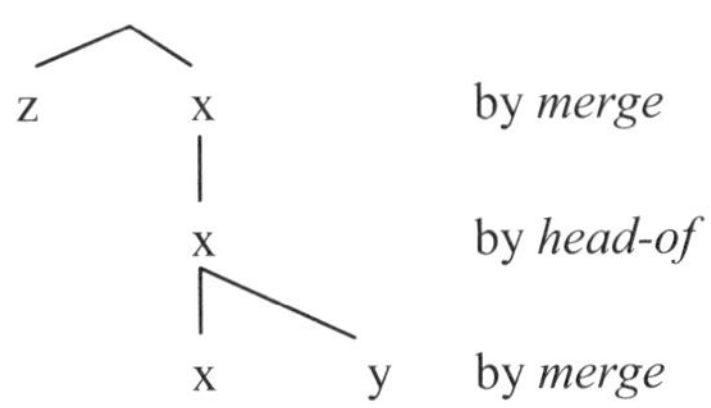

Now there are two options to proceed. Head-of can eliminate *x* as dependent of *z*. This yields a complementation structure (25). By contrast, if *z* is eliminated as a dependent of *x*, the result is a shell- or specifier-structure (26).

(25) complement-structure

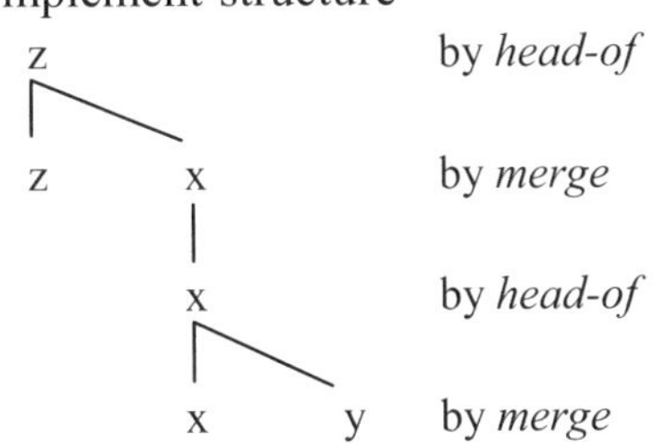

(26) specifier/shell structure

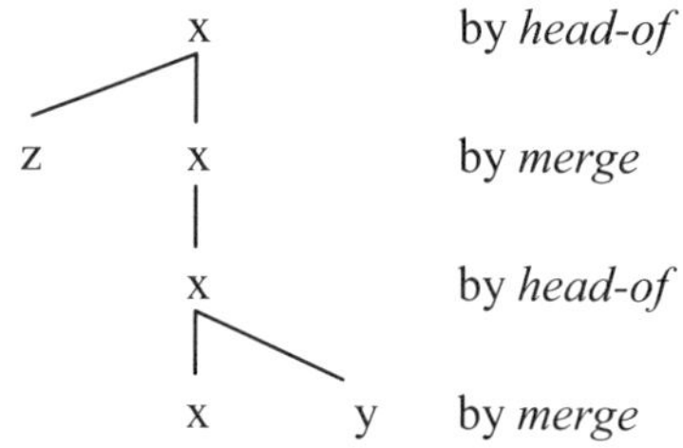

Both configurations are bare structures. They do not incorporate derivationally introduced objects. This is particularly evident in the shell configuration. No light heads are required. Multiple specifiers/shells can be merged as long as the resulting configuration has an interpretation in semantics.

Features of a head can be inherited by the mother node. In the present formalism, the inheritance of features is formalized in terms of non-elimination. Assume an initial array composed of the variables {*x,y,z,g*}. For concreteness, let *z* be a verb, *y* a noun, and *x* a feature F of N that needs to be checked against *g*, a functional head above V. For expository reasons, both the actual derivation, and a translation using more familiar labels will be given.

First *xy*, and then *zxy*, are derived by *merge*. Then *head-of* eliminates *y* as a complement, while leaving *x* unaffected. This designates *zx* (not *z* alone) as head of *zxy* (27a). Traditionally, we would say that an index of feature F has percolated from N to V (27b). Notice that this is an informal way of speaking. Literally, there is no index in the generated structure (27a).

(27) a.

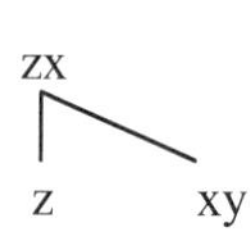

b.

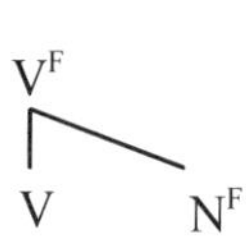

Next, *zx* merges with *g*, forming *gzx*. *Head-of* eliminates *z* as a complement of *gx* (28a). In traditional phrasing, the index of feature F has percolated to the next higher head G (28b).

(28) a.

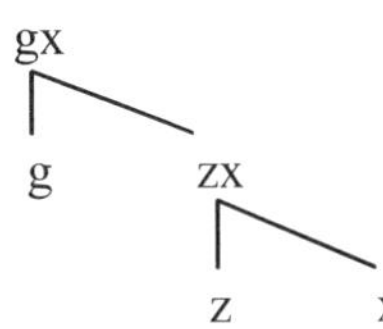

b.

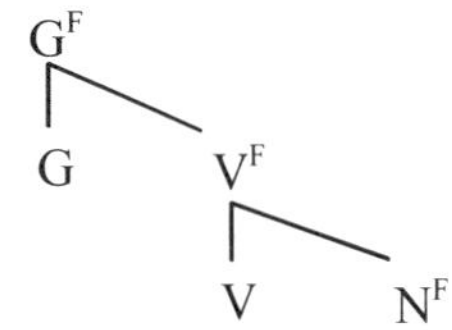

Finally, *head-of* eliminates *x* as a dependent of *g* (29a). This is similar to the deletion of a checked feature (29b). Notice, that the moved feature is not eliminated from the derivation altogether. It is only invisible for further derivational steps.

(29) a.

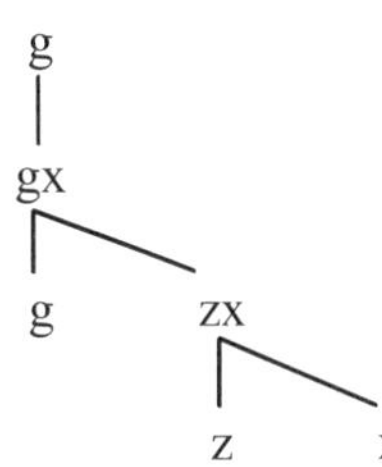

b.

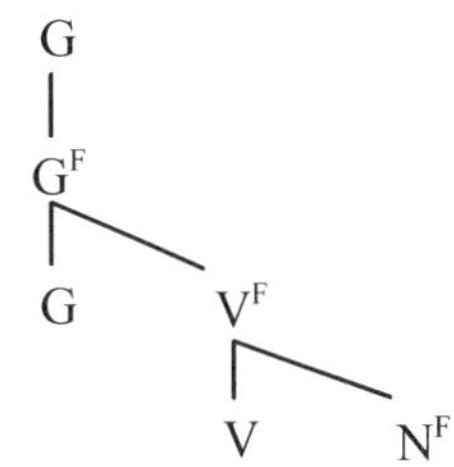

It is one thing to define *interpretation* as a function from A into B. Another thing is whether such a definition accounts for the observed facts. One issue that immediately arises is the question whether all objects in A have an image in B.[5] The way *interpretation* is formalized, we predict that each constituent of prosodic structure has an image in syntax. At face value, this is false. Many constituents of prosodic structure are not exponents of morpho-syntactic features.

The formalism accounts for apparent "lack of interpretation" as mapping on the identity element for *merge*, i.e., the integer 1. The projection principle (13) predicts that mapping on identity is the default case. A grammatical derivation cannot add meaning that is not already present in the lexical items that form part of the derivation. If a derived constituent of prosodic structure is to receive a non-vacuous interpretation, this fact must be part of the respective lexical entry.

1.6. Exemplifying the formalism: stem-derived causatives

There are two major verb classes in German. So-called *strong* verbs inflect by means of stem vowel alternations (Bittner 1996; Grimm 1819; Halle

1953; Ségéral and Scheer 1998). This class is limited to approximately 165 lexically listed verbs. As Bittner (1996) observes, strong inflectional features diachronically tend to be lost. By contrast, *weak* inflection by affixation is fully productive.

In addition to inflection, it was observed in chapter 2 above that stem vowel alternations can mark causativization. Stem-vowel changes can be observed for a wide variety of derived verbs, but let us concentrate here on causatives that are derived from a strong verbal base. Bendjaballah and Haiden (2002, 2003) observe an implicational relation: If a strong verb is causativized by means of a stem-vowel alternation, it must be weak.

Take as an example the strong verb *heben* 'lift' (30a). This verb marks the tense opposition by a change of /e/ in the present tense to /o/ in the past tense. Application of this alternation does not in principle block the application of a further inflectional alternation, the one that marks mood. Past indicative /o/ alternates with /ø/ in the past subjunctive. The same holds for the compatibility of tense and agreement marking. In (30b), the stem vowel /i/ in *tritt* 'he kicks' is a primary marker of (non-past) tense, and a secondary marker of singular agreement.

(30)		inf.	present 3sg	past 3sg	past.subj. 3sg	
	a.	*heb-en*	*heb-t*	***h**o**b***	*h**ö**b-e*	'lift'
	b.	*tret-en*	*tr**i**t-t*	*tr**a**t*	*tr**ä**t-e*	'kick'

Now compare this with the alternation that marks causativization. The verb *springen* 'jump' is strong. Changing /i/ to /e/ derives the causative verb *sprengen* 'detonate', which is weak. It marks the past tense with an affix:

(31) a. strong verb:

infinitive	past 3sg	
*spr**i**ngen*	*spr**a**ng*	'jump'

b. causativized verb:

infinitive	past 3sg	
*spr**e**ngen*	*spr**e**ng-te*	'detonate'

Application of the derivational alternation blocks the inflectional alternation. The same holds for a range of other strong base-verbs under causativization.

(32) a. strong base verb: infinitive

*s**i**tzen*	'sit'
*dr**i**ngen*	'urge/penetrate'
*f**a**llen*	'fall'
*f**a**hren*	'drive'
*fl**ie**ßen*	'flow'

b. causativized verb: infinitive

*s**e**tzen*	'put'
*dr**ä**ngen*	'push'
*f**ä**llen*	'fell'
*f**ü**hren*	'lead'
*ein-fl**ö**ßen*	'fill'

The causativized verbs are all weak: they do not show any vowel alternation between present stem and past stem. Tense is expressed by the suffix -*te*.

(33) a. strong base verb

present 3sg	past 3sg	
*s**i**tzt*	*s**a**ß*	'sit'
*dr**i**ngt*	*dr**a**ng*	'urge'
*f**ä**llt*	*f**ie**l*	'fall'
*f**ä**hrt*	*f**u**hr*	'drive'
*fl**ie**ßt*	*fl**o**ss*	'flow'

b. weak derived causative

setzt	*setz-**te***	'put'
*dr**ä**ngt*	*dr**ä**ng-**te***	'push'
*f**ä**llt*	*f**ä**ll-**te***	'fell'
*f**ü**hrt*	*f**ü**hr-**te***	'lead'
*fl**ö**ßt ein*	*fl**ö**ß-**te** ein*	'fill'

Why should this be the case? Why should causativization block tense-marking by vowel alternation?

It seems we cannot blame phonology. The vowel /e/ of most causativized forms does not block apophonic tense marking, as evidenced in (30) above. We cannot blame causative semantics either. Clearly, there are causative strong verbs, as evidenced again by *heben* 'lift' and *treten* 'kick' in (30).

In sum, a stem vowel can be a marker of more than one morphosyntactic feature (tense and mood; tense and agreement), but it cannot mark causativization and tense at the same time. We might want to invoke the derivational/inflectional distinction to account for this generalization. If a derivational alternation has applied, inflectional alternations are barred.

However, this is just another way of stating the question. Why should derivational alternations block inflectional ones?

The formalization of interpretation in terms of a (uniquely defined) mapping provides an immediate answer to questions of this sort. A constituent *C* in prosodic structure can encode all and only those features that belong to the syntactic head *H* it is mapped on. *C* cannot be the exponent of a feature of a head *H'* distinct from *H*. The compatibility of tense and mood marking in German strong verbs is expected, if tense and mood are features of a single syntactic category. Indeed, it is argued in Iatridou (2000) that they are. Thus, the past subjunctive stem of *höb-* 'lift' must be analyzed as in (34).[6] By contrast, the category of a derived causative is still V, not T. The causativized stem *fäll-* 'fell/cut' must then be represented as in (35). Stem-derived causatives must be weak, because there is no representational space for the interpretation of a tense feature in the stem.

(34) base verb: alternation for tense + mood

C V ~> $T_{[past.subj.]}$
C V C V ~> v
C V C V C V ~> V_{base}
h ø b

(35) derived, weak causative

C V ~> v
C V C V ~> V_{caus}
C V C V C V ~> V_{base}
f ɛ l

1.7. Excursus: Grafts, parallel derivations and expressive power

Let us now turn to a set of problems that is rarely discussed in the minimalist literature, and see what predictions the present formalism makes in that area. Van Riemsdijk (1998a, 2005) discusses a range of data for which the two-dimensional tree-format generated by X'-theory faces problems. His data involve phonological strings, which serve more than one function in syntax, and which cannot be explained by means of syntactic copying, or deletion under identity.

One such configuration is a German free relative as in (36a), where the relative pronoun must satisfy case and selectional requirements in both the matrix and the relative clause. In (36), the superscripts indicate verbal case requirements, the subscripts indicate nominal case features.

Crucially, the relative pronoun can satisfy two distinct case requirements, as in (36b), but it can only do so, if its phonological shape is compatible with the two cases. If the two cases correspond to distinct phonological shapes, this is impossible (36c). The two case requirements must be realized by distinct phonological expressions (36d).

(36) a. *Ich hasse*^{ACC} *wen*$_{ACC}$ *du liebst*^{ACC}.
I hate whom you love
b. *Er hat [was*$_{NOM/ACC}$ *dort passierte*^{NOM}*] gefilmt*^{ACC}.
he has what there happened filmed
c. **Ich hasse*^{ACC} *wen*$_{ACC}$*/wem*$_{DAT}$ *du vertraust*^{DAT}.
I hate whom you trust
d. *Ich hasse*^{ACC} *den*$_{ACC}$ *Mann, dem*$_{DAT}$ *du vertraust*^{DAT}.
I hate the man whom you trust

German free relatives show the possibility that a single phonological string can realize clearly distinct syntactic functions. Van Riemsdijk (1998a) argues that

> "the question as to whether the relative pronoun is in Spec,CP position **or** in the position of the head of the relative clause may well be fundamentally misguided and imposed by the wrong kind of theory about syntactic representations, since in a multidimensional theory [...], the relative pronoun could be **simultaneously** in both positions."

He calls such structures *grafts*

> "in the sense that one tree structure, the scion, is grafted into another tree, the stock. Thereby, a structure is created in which two (or more) tree structures share a portion of terminal and non-terminal material."

The present formalism with its strict separation of phonological and syntactic derivations makes a number of predictions regarding the availability of grafted structures. Since phonological, not syntactic identity is required in the German free relatives above, the scion must be a constituent in prosodic structure. Grafting then consists in the application of two independent syntactic parses for a single phonological string, the scion.

The observation about phonological constituency versus syntactic non-constituency is strengthened by examples like the following, in which the shared string [*dem Essen trinkt*] 'the meal drinks' comprises the DP-complement to an adjunct preposition plus the finite verb, but excludes the preposition:

(37) ... *weil Peter den Pálinka* ***vor*** *und Susi den Tokayer* ***nach*** *[dem Essen trinkt]*
because Peter the pálinka before and Susi the Tokay after the meal drinks
'because Peter drinks the pálinka before and Susi the Tokay after the meal'

(38)

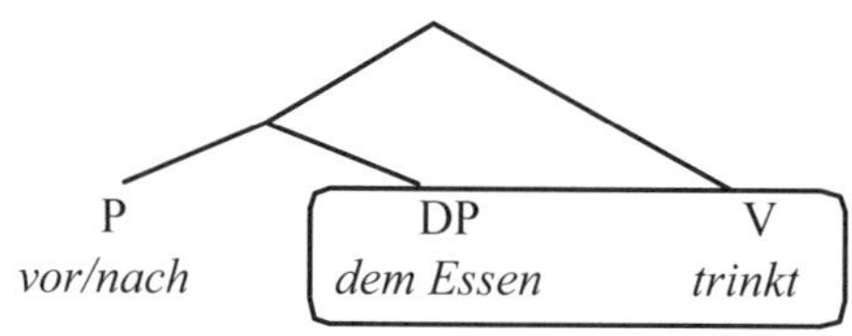

As above, the phonological constituent (and syntactic non-constituent) [*dem Essen trinkt*] 'the meal drinks' is subjected to two distinct syntactic parses. It is interpreted as part of both conjuncts. In van Riemsdijk's multi-dimensional model, the lexical items in the string *dem Essen trinkt* 'the meal drinks' serve as terminal nodes for two syntactic trees.

The desirability of the multi-dimensional analysis is sometimes called into question with reference to its expressive power (cf. van Riemsdijk 1998a for discussion and references). This is where the present formalism can bring some clarification.

Assume for the sake of argument that a given phonological string can only ever correspond to a single syntactic derivation. With this in mind, consider once more the German free relative in (36b) above. Since two case requirements have to be met, we must assume that the relative pronoun has two distinct images in syntax: an accusative and a nominative D.[7]

(39) illicit ambiguous interpretation

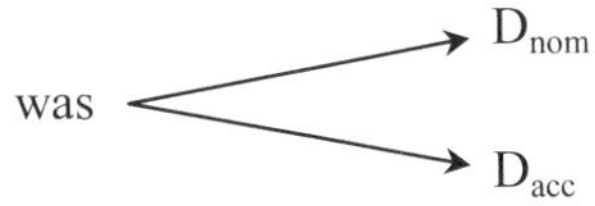

(39) is excluded in the present formalism. Interpretation is formalized as a uniquely defined mapping $f : A \rightarrow B$. As such, it does not allow one-to-many relations like (39). In order to maintain the mono-derivational approach, we must relax the formalization of the interpretation map. Rather than a *many-to-one* mapping, we must allow *many-to-many* relations.

Such a move is serious. It amounts to the claim that grammatical structure is systematically ambiguous in two directions. Arbitrariness is no longer constrained to the lexicon, but a property of grammatical expressions. Under this assumption, we can no longer maintain the research guideline shared by work as diverse as May (1985), Williams (1986), namely that syntactic representations disambiguate potentially ambiguous strings. In sum, if a verdict about the multi-dimensional analysis relies on expressive power, we must conclude that the mono-derivational approach certainly does not fare better.

By contrast, a multi-dimensional analysis allows us to maintain the restrictive definition of *interpretation* as a *many-to-one* mapping. For each derivation, there is a uniquely defined mapping from phonology into syntax. Each parse disambiguates the phonologically ambiguous form.

In addition, the multi-dimensional analysis makes predictions on where we expect apparently contradictory mappings like (39). We find them in exactly those configurations, where multiple parses are well motivated: coordination, parataxis and the like. We never find them in a simple, mono-clausal derivation.

Van Riemsdijk's (1998a) conclusion thus stands: grafting configurations must involve multiple parses. The present formalization of bare phrase structure is not only compatible with this conclusion, but it implies it. This is independent support for the correctness of both. The ground is now prepared to turn back to syntactic argument structure, and to implement the generalizations found in chapter 2.

2. Generating syntactic argument structure

2.1. Subcategorization and formal transitivity

As defined above, the operation *merge* can take any two objects and form a product. In reality, the options are constrained. One type of constraints is related to the categorial features of the respective objects:

> "The idea seems to be that within a projection we have categorial cohesion or attraction between likes, a kind of magnetism in which the positively specified features attract one another internal to a projection but repel each other externally." (van Riemsdijk 1998b:42)

Van Riemsdijk expresses the generalization that the merger of two objects with the same category should be analyzed in terms of a single (extended) projection, while the formation of a head-complement construction requires the merger of a distinct category. A verbal projection is thus formed if a verb merges with a categorially distinct object. Let us state this generalization in the strongest possible way in the form of a subcategorization frame:[8]

(40) Subcategorization of V
V / _N

(40) states that a verb phrase can only be well-formed, if V has merged with N. It does not state that an internal argument must be present in every verb phrase. An intransitive VP is derived with Hale and Keyser (1993) by merging a semantically vacuous, phonologically null N with V. By the same reasoning, (40) forces the merger of a semantically vacuous, silent N for verbs that select a prepositional, but no nominal internal argument, as in (41), and for the aspectual construction with *an* 'at', as illustrated in (42b).

(41) *Johanna sprach über interessante Dinge*
Johanna spoke about interesting things

(42) a. *Johnanna baute ein Haus.*
Johanna built a house

b. *Hans baute an einem Haus (aber es wurde nie fertig).*
Hans build at a house (but it became never ready)
'Hans was working on the construction of a house (but it was never finished).'

The presence of a VP-external subject is required in the same way. A functional head in the extended projection of V subcategorizes for a functional element in the extended projection of N. (43) replaces the extension-clause of the *Extended Projection Principle* (Chomsky 1982).

(43) Subcategorization of v (EPP)
v / _D

The requirement in (43) can be satisfied either by merger of a subject DP, or by raising of D from a VP-internal position. In the latter case, an unaccusative verb is derived. Ignoring for the moment the assignment of thematic roles, the vP of a transitive verb is derived as in (44), an unaccusative vP as in (45). In both cases, let us start with a partial initial array consisting of {V, v, N, D}.

In a transitive derivation, an extended projection of N is formed by merger of N with accusative D. Then, the extended projection of N merges with V, and summation eliminates first N, then D. This leaves V as head of the verb phrase, which finally merges with v. At the vP level, the derivation proceeds analogously.

(44)

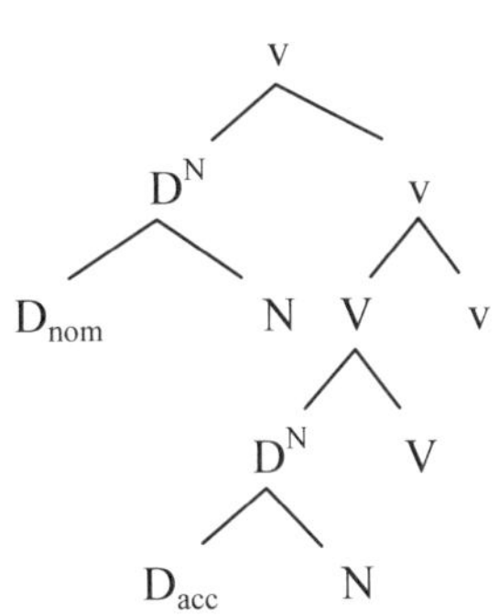

In an unaccusative derivation, D is not eliminated by summation. Instead, v merges with the complex element VD. Summation then eliminates V as a dependent of v, and finally D as a dependent of v. This derivation is comparable with raising of a D feature to v in the framework of Chomsky

(1995), and with raising of a "spirit" in the HPSG approach of Meurers (1999). Crucially, raising of D by means of non-elimination does not preclude phrasal movement of DP with or without VP.

(45)

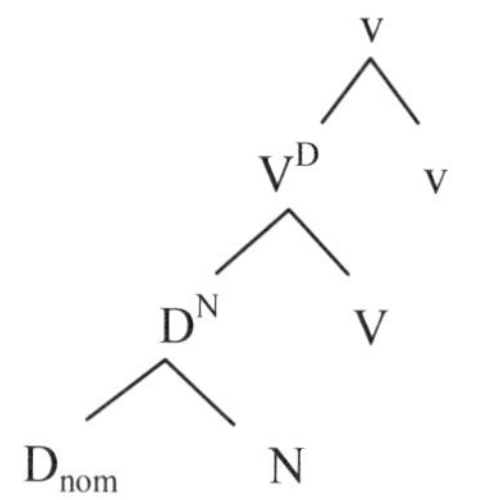

Subcategorization by V and v, respectively, correlates with morphological case. If a noun phrase is morphologically marked with the accusative case, then its lexical head N is visible for a subcategorization relation with V, but its functional head D is invisible for v. A noun phrase in the accusative case is the internal argument of a transitive verb.

By contrast, a noun phrase in the nominative case can be both an internal, and an external argument. With a transitive verb, the nominative D is visible for v; with an unaccusative verb, D is the subject of v, N is the subject of V: the nominative satisfies the subcategorization of both V and v. Let us state this observation as follows:[9]

(46) Structural Case
D_{ACC} is invisible for v.

In the Theta System, the requirement of an internal argument is encoded with reference to an accusative case feature. If a verb is marked with this feature, an internal argument must be present. With (46), the accusative feature can be replaced by a D-feature. The adapted version is given in (50) below. The ACC-feature of V must be checked against the head D of an argument DP. The argument can be either a nominative or an accusative, but only nominative D can move to v to create an unaccusative configuration. Accusative D is invisible for v by condition (46).

2.2. Thematic roles in syntactic structure

It is a very basic, yet mostly implicit assumption in the Theta System that thematic roles are listed in the lexicon as part of verbs. Verbs assign thematic roles to nouns, sometimes through a preposition. Let us make this asymmetry explicit as follows:

(47) Main Thematic Condition
Θ is assigned by [/-N] to [/-V].

The Main Thematic Condition assures that Θ-roles can be assigned by verbs and prepositions, and that they are assigned to nouns and prepositions. Adjectives neither assign, nor receive Θ-roles. Adjectives and nouns can only assign a thematic role through P, or by reanalysis with V. Role assignment through P is exemplified with the nominalization in (48b), role assignment by reanalysis with V will be of primary importance in the analysis of the adjectival passive (49b) in chapter 4.

(48) a. *The Birmingham City Council revitalized the Bull Ring.*
b. *the revitalization *(of) the Bull Ring*

(49) a. *Er hat den Schlüssel verloren.*
he has the key lost
'He lost the key.'
b. *Der Schlüssel ist verloren.*
the key is lost

With this prerequisite, let us now reconsider the generalizations regarding thematic role realization of the *Theta System*, together with the modifications introduced in chapter 2.

In the Theta System, a lexical verb entry is prepared for insertion into a syntactic derivation by a marking procedure. This procedure applies to verbs that select more than one Θ-role, it assigns indices to role clusters, and it marks the verb with an accusative (ACC) feature under certain conditions. (50) gives the modified version defended in chapter 2. Instead of ACC, the verb is marked with a D-feature.

The marking procedure conspires with the merging instructions (51) to generate syntactic argument structures.

(50) Lexicon marking
Given an n-place verb-entry, n>1,
a. Mark a fully specified [-] cluster with index 2.
b. Mark a [+] cluster with index 1.
c. Mark the verb with a D-feature, if its entry includes
(i) both a [+] cluster and a fully specified cluster [/α,/-c], or
(ii) both a [/+c] cluster and a [-] cluster.

(51) CS merging instructions ((29) in Reinhart and Siloni 2005)
a. When nothing rules this out, merge externally.
b. An argument realizing a cluster marked 2 merges internally; an argument with a cluster marked 1 merges externally.

In the Theta System, arity-reducing operations apply to marked lexical entries. The conceptual framework defended in chapter 1 is partly incompatible with this assumption. Since there are no operations in the lexicon, we must reanalyze lexical arity-reducing operations as generalizations over listed pairs of alternants. Such generalizations are typically prone to exception and lexical drift. Indeed this is what we found for reduction in chapter 2 above, and Siloni (2002) argues that it is true at a much wider, universal scale. Lexically reduced forms are only available for a certain subset of verbs, they are often marked morphologically, and they tend to exhibit a slight difference in meaning with respect to their alternant. In what follows, the term *lexical reduction* will be used in the sense of a listed pair of alternants.

In chapter 2, two phenomena have been analyzed in terms of reduction, the causative alternation and anti-causative reflexives. In both cases, we have found substantial lexical restrictions and special meanings. This confirms a prediction in Reinhart and Siloni (2005) to the effect that decausativization (52) applies in the lexicon cross-linguistically. As above, the ACC feature of V is to be replaced by D.

(52) Decausativization: Reduction of a external [+c] role ((67a) in Reinhart and Siloni 2005)
$V_{acc} (\Theta_{1[+c]}, \Theta_2) \rightarrow V (\Theta_2)$

In contrast to decausativization, the application of reflexivization (53) is parametrized. For German, Marelj (2004), Reinhart and Siloni (2005) argue that it applies in syntax. Indeed it was found in chapter 2 that both internal and external Θ roles are syntactically present in German reflexives, and that reflexivization is always possible in principle.

(53) Reflexivization bundling ((24) in Reinhart and Siloni 2005)
$[\Theta_i]$ $[\Theta_j]$ -> $[\Theta_i - \Theta_j]$, where Θ_i is an external role.

True reflexives must be distinguished from reduced forms with reflexive morphology. Reduced reflexives are subject to strong lexical constraints, and they often come with a special meaning. This confirms the assumption that causativization is not a syntactic operation.

If decausativization is not an operation in the strict sense, but a generalization over pairs of listed alternants, then its output should be visible for the marking procedure. This is where clause (50c.ii) becomes relevant. If a verb retains both a [/+c] and a [/-c] cluster after reduction, it must still take an internal argument.

Cases at hand are unaccusative subject-experiencer verbs like *erschrecken* 'get scared' and unaccusative dying verbs that assign underspecified [-c] to their subject. While *erschrecken* 'get scared' is lexically related to causative *erschrecken* 'scare', the unaccusative dying verbs discussed in chapter 2 do not have a causative alternant. Still, they exhibit the same behavior: an unmarked cluster must be assigned VP-internally, and an instrument cluster can be assigned in a selected PP. This pattern is accounted for, if the marking procedure does not see the difference between lexical entries with and without a causative alternant.

Notice in passing that the clusters selected by German *erschrecken* 'scare' are different from the clusters selected by comparable verbs like *worry* in English. While German *erschrecken* 'scare' selects a fully specified subject matter role [+c-m], *worry* selects underspecified [-m]. Thus, the German configuration after reduction {[-c+m], [+c-m]} triggers assignment of a D-feature, the corresponding English configuration {[-c+m], [-m]} does not. Therefore, reduced English *worry* assigns the experiencer role externally, reduced German *erschrecken* 'get scared' assigns it internally.

There is a peculiarity about the marking procedure as stated in (50). It can only affect verbs that select more than one thematic role. Why should that be the case?

The condition is introduced for empirical reasons, the existence of a set of apparent *theme-unergatives*, in Reinhart (2001).

(54) theme-unergatives (Reinhart 2001:15)
glow, shine, beam, glare, glimmer, sparkle, babble, flash, buzz, click, whistle, squeal, stink, bleed, drip, sweat, radiate, [...] shudder, tremble, flower

(54) is a curious set of verbs. A large number of these verbs are emission verbs. According to Levin and Rappaport Hovav (1995), such verbs assign the role *immediate cause*, not *theme*, to their sole argument. Immediate causes cannot be specified as [/-c]. These verbs select either fully specified [+c-m], or underspecified [-m]. If they select [+c-m], no special condition is necessary for monadic lexical entries. If they select underspecified [-m], then the marking procedure must be modified, but there is still no motivation for a special treatment of monadic lexical entries.

Next, there is a sub-class of (54) including *whistle*, which takes either a volitional agent, or an inanimate instrument as its subject. On both uses, one is hard pressed to imagine that the subject realizes a [/-c] role. If there is an object that is affected by a whistling event, then it must be the air that is set in motion by the agent and/or instrument. Neither an agent, nor an instrument can be assigned [/-c]. Other verbs like *stink* denote internally caused events or states. Once more, internal causation is not one of the most natural interpretations of [/-c].

In sum, a careful lexical semantic analysis of the verbs in (54) might well reduce the set of genuine *theme*-unergatives to zero. The set of verbs in (54) is therefore not sufficient evidence against the strong version of the marking procedure in (55):

(55) Lexicon marking (strengthened)
a. Mark a fully specified [-] cluster with index 2.
b. Mark a [+] cluster with index 1.
c. Mark the verb with a D-feature, if its entry includes
(i) both a [+] cluster and a fully specified cluster [/α,/-c], or
(ii) both a [/+c] cluster and a [-] cluster.

In this general form, the independent content of the marking procedure reduces to clause (c). Clauses (a) and (b) can be stated in the merging instructions directly. The residue of the marking procedure in (56) is now exclusively responsible for the designation of verbs that must take an internal argument.

The merging instructions (57) are stated with exclusive reference to thematic roles. They cannot refer to argument noun phrases, because the latter are not part of a lexical verb entry. Only thematic role clusters are.

(56) Lexicon marking (residue)
Mark the verb with a D-feature, if its entry includes
(i) both a [+] cluster and a fully specified cluster [/α,/-c], or
(ii) both a [/+c] cluster and a [-] cluster.

(57) Merging instructions
a. If nothing rules this out, merge Θ externally.
b. Merge a fully specified [-] cluster with V.
c. Merge a [+] cluster with v.

As stated in (57), the merging instructions introduce a fundamental distinction between two classes of thematic role clusters. One class of clusters is recognized by clauses (b) and (c). Such clusters must always be realized in designated syntactic positions. By contrast, the realization of mixed value and underspecified [-] clusters is only indirectly affected by clause (a) of the merging instructions. Taken literally, the merging instructions (57) make a prediction that distinguishes the present theory from Reinhart's version of the Theta System. Since the merging instructions do not refer to mixed value and underspecified [-] clusters, the realization of these clusters should, in principle, be optional. This general kind of optionality must be distinguished from specific conditions of non-realization, which affect [+] clusters. (58a,b) are adapted from the original version of the Theta System in Reinhart (2002), (58c) was added in chapter 2. In contrast to the original versions, the conditions in (58) refer to [+] clusters only.

(58) Non-realization
a. [+c] may remain unrealized, if it is indistinguishable from another cluster in the lexical entry of a verb.[10]
b. [+c]/[+c+m] may remain unrealized, if another [/+c] cluster is selected by a verb.
c. [+m] may remain unrealized, if a verb selects {[+m], [-c-m] [-m]}.

The distinction between two kinds of non-realization is relevant for the derivation of double causatives in the following sections. For the time being, just notice the different phenomenology associated with (57) vs. (58). The merging instructions introduce optionality of realization. By contrast, once a condition of (58) has applied to a [+] cluster, this cluster must not be realized. Consider as an example the double causative *verschmutzen* 'contaminate'. When [+c] is assigned, the realization of [+c-m] is optional (59a). By contrast, once [+c] has been rendered implicit by (58), it cannot be realized in any way (59b).

(59) a. *Die Industrie verschmutzt den Fluss (mit Abwässern).*
the industry contaminates the river (with sewage)
b. *Abwässer verschmutzen den Fluss (*mit/von/... der Industrie).*
sewage contaminates the river (with/by the industry)

Once a Θ-role has been merged, it must be assigned to an argument. This is guaranteed by the Θ-criterion (60):

(60) Θ-criterion ((33) in Reinhart and Siloni (2005)
Every Θ-role must be assigned in the smallest full IP.

2.3. Finite transitives

In order to get acquainted with the formalism, consider a simple agent-patient verb like *bauen* 'build'.

(61) *bauen* 'build': [+c+m], [-c-m]

This entry contains both a [+] cluster and a fully specified [/-c] cluster. Therefore V is marked with D by clause (56.i) of the marking procedure. Now the verb is ready for selection into an initial array. Assume a partial array that incorporates the lexical categories *Bauer* 'farmer', *Stall* 'barn' and the verbal stem *bau-* 'build', and two definite articles. The merging instructions recognize both clusters selected by *bau-* 'build': fully specified [-c-m] must merge with V by clause (57b), fully specified [+c+m] must merge with v by clause (57c). This allows the partial derivation in (63) for sentence (62), represented in the tree (64). To abstract away from the influence of verb-fronting, derivations are exemplified with embedded clauses.

(62) *dass der Bauer den Stall baut*
that the$_{nom}$ farmer the$_{acc}$ barn builds
'that the farmer builds the barn'

(63)

$\mu(V_{bau}, \Theta_{[-c-m]})$	merger of the internal Θ-role
$\mu(D_{den}, N_{Stall})$	creation of internal argument DP
$\mu(V\Theta, DN)$	merger of the internal argument: assignment of internal Θ-role checking of V-subcategorization checking of [+κ]
Σ w.r.t. Θ	elimination of the assigned Θ-role
Σ r.t. N, D	introduction of DP-structure
μ(V, v)	merger of functional v
Σ w.r.t. V	closure of VP
$\mu(v, \Theta_{[+c+m]})$	merger of external Θ-role
$\mu(D_{der}, N_{Bauer})$	creation of external argument DP
$\mu(v\Theta, DN)$	merger of the external argument: assignment of external Θ-role checking of v-subcategorization
Σ w.r.t. Θ	elimination of assigned Θ-role
Σ w.r.t. N, D	introduction of DP-structure

(64)

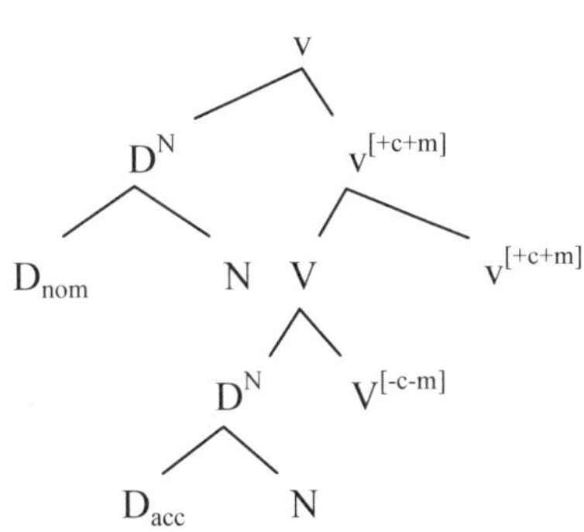

There is one interesting contingency in the derivation of the present initial array. The speaker of (62) chose to realize *der Bauer* 'the farmer' in the nominative case, and *den Stall* 'the barn' in the accusative case. She could have chosen to realize *den Bauern* 'the farmer' in the accusative case, and *der Stall* 'the barn' in the nominative. Since the accusative is invisible for v, *den Bauern* must now merge inside VP. It is assigned the internal Θ-role there. The nominative merges externally, where it is assigned the external Θ-role. The resulting sentence (65) is unacceptable, because the inanimate object *der Stall* 'the barn' is incompatible with the role of a volitional agent.

(65) **dass der Stall den Bauern baut*
that the_{nom} barn the_{acc} farmer builds

2.3.1. Dative and selected P

Consider next the preliminary lexical entry of *mitteilen* 'pass on information', with three thematic role clusters:

(66) *mitteilen* 'pass on information': [+c+m] [-c+m] [-c-m]

The V is again marked with D, because it selects a [+] cluster and fully specified [-c-m]. The merging instructions recognize both the [+] cluster and fully specified [-c-m]. It does not recognize the mixed value cluster [-c+m]. The merger of this cluster is, in principle, free. However, in the present configuration, neither the internal, nor the external argument position is available, because [-c-m] must merge with V, and [+c+m] must merge with v. The realization of the third cluster therefore depends on the availability of a further argument position.

Following the literature on double object constructions (den Dikken 1995; Emonds 1972, 2000; Jackendoff 1990; Larson 1988, 1990) let us assume that this additional argument position is introduced by a preposition. Dative case is thus analyzed as a syntactically complex object composed of a DP under a possibly silent head P.[11] If dative case is indeed the morphological manifestation of a syntactic head P, then the selection of a dative is identical with the selection of an overt preposition: V and P must be listed in the lexicon together, as a V-P idiom (66). The lexical entry of the verb *mitteilen* contains a P_{dat}, which enters the initial array with it.

(67) *mitteilen* 'pass on info': {V, P_{dat}, [+c+m], [-c-m], [-c+m], ...}

The derivation is then straightforward. The fully specified Θ-roles merge as dictated by the merging instructions, [-c+m] merges with P_{dat}. The accusative checks D on V, and it is assigned [-c-m] inside VP. The nominative is assigned [+c+m] as an external argument, and the dative realizes the third role.

(68) *dass Hans den Studenten die Ergebnisse mitteilt.*
that $Hans_{nom}$ the_{dat} students the_{acc} results passes
'that Hans informs the students of the results.'

The realization of the [-c+m] role as a dative in (68) is consistent with assumptions in the event decomposition framework of Rapp (1997) and the lexical decomposition grammar of Wunderlich (1997). In both of these frameworks, the dative realizes a hierarchically intermediate, third argument. In the present theory, [-c+m] could be described as hierarchically intermediate, because the merging instructions do not force this cluster into an internal or external position, respectively. The present theory sides with Rapp, contra Wunderlich, with respect to the analysis of the dative itself. For Wunderlich, a selected dative is a structural argument. For Rapp (1997:58) the dative belongs in a natural class together with the genitive and selected prepositions. All of these are non-structural markers, which must be listed as part of the lexical verb entry together with the thematic role they are associated with.[12] In line with Rapp, the lexical entry (66) must be adapted to (69), where the association of P_{dat} with [-c+m] is encoded as a subset.

(69) *mitteilen* 'pass on info': {V, [+c+m], [-c-m], {P_{dat}, [-c+m]}, ...}

2.3.2. Double causatives

A thematic role may remain unrealized. The present theory allows two types of non-realization. First, mixed-value and underspecified [-] clusters are not recognized by the merging instructions. Their realization is, in principle, optional. Second, special conditions allow the non-realization of [+] clusters. Consider as an example the verb *schmücken* 'decorate':

(70) *schmücken* 'decorate': {V, [+c+m], [-c-m], [+c-m], ...}

Since this lexical entry incorporates both a [+] cluster and a fully specified [/-c] cluster, V is marked with a D-feature. It must take an internal argument. Since there are two [/+c] clusters in the lexical entry, one of them may remain unrealized. Imagine a speaker decides to merge the agent cluster [+c+m]. By the merging instructions, [-c-m] merges with V, [+c+m] with v: the internal argument must be interpreted as a theme, the external argument as an agent. Finally, [+c-m] is not recognized by the merging instructions. Since both V and v assign a designated Θ-role, the realization of [+c-m] depends on the availability of a preposition in the lexical array. It is assumed here with Rapp (1997) that the identity of the preposition is governed by lexical redundancy rules. An optional instrument cluster is usually identified by *mit* 'with' (Rapp 1997:64, 71-73, 79). Notice that *mit* 'with' governs the dative case. Formally, the instrument cluster merges with P_{dat}, rather than the lexical P_{mit}.

(71) *dass Hans den Balkon mit Blumen schmückt*
that Hans the balcony with flowers decorates

(72)

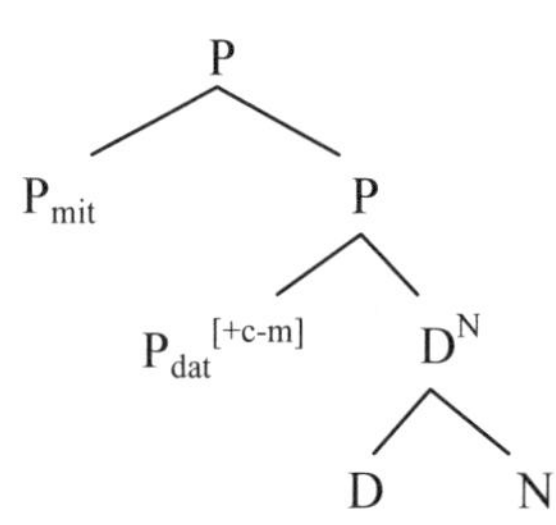

If a speaker decides to leave [+c+m] unrealized by (58b), V remains marked with a D-feature, and [-c-m] must merge internally by the merging instructions. Since there is no designated external Θ-role present in the lexical array, [+c-m] merges with v. The external argument is thus interpreted as an instrument/source argument. The unrealized [+c+m] cluster cannot be identified by a PP.

(73) *dass Blumen den Balkon schmücken*
that flowers the balcony adorn

2.3.3. *Decausativization by non-realization*

Non-realization by clause (a) of (58) is exemplified by the verb *tragen* 'carry'. Either [+c], or [-m] is assigned to the subject.

(74) *tragen* 'carry': {V, [+c], [-c-m], [-m], ...}

(75) a. *dass der Wind den Gleiter trägt*
that the wind the glider carries
'that the wind is carrying the glider'
b. *dass das Dokument das Siegel der Stadt trägt*
that the document the seal of-the city carries
'that the document bears the seal of the city'

In both cases, the derivation is straightforward. Fully specified [-c-m] merges with V by the merging instructions. An internal argument DP satisfies the N-subcategorization of V and checks its D feature. If [+c] is realized, it merges externally. [-m] must then remain implicit, because it is formally indistinguishable from [+c]. If [+c] remains unrealized, then [-m] merges externally.

2.3.4. *Decausativization by role reduction*

Let us now consider some representative examples for the derivation of a decausativized verbal entry. The verb *erhalten* 'keep/receive' retains two clusters after reduction, [-c] and [-c-m]. The verb *rollen* 'roll' retains only one cluster, fully specified [-c-m].

(76) a. erhalten 'keep/receive': {V, [+c], [-c-m], [-c], ...}
b. rollen 'roll': {V, [+c], [-c-m], ...}

(77) a. *dass die Regierung dumme Bräuche erhält*
that the government silly customs keeps
'that the government keeps silly customs alive'
b. *dass er einen Knödel rollt*
that he a dumpling rolls
'that he rolls a dumpling'

In the fully realized cases, the derivations are straightforward. The verb is marked with a D feature, [-c-m] merges internally, [+c] merges externally, and the [-c] cluster of *erhalten* 'keep' is optionally assigned through a P. If no P has been selected into the lexical array as in (77a), [-c] remains implicit.

After decausativization, the lexical entries of the two verbs are quite different. Recall that decausativization eliminates the D feature of V. However, the merging instructions still force internal merger of [-c-m] in both cases. From then on, the two derivations differ. The reduced entry of *erhalten* 'receive/get' still contains a [-c] cluster that can merge externally, resulting in a regular transitive derivation (78a). By contrast, reduced *rollen* 'roll' cannot assign a second Θ-role. Therefore, the D of the internal argument must raise, in order to satisfy the subcategorization of v. Reduced *rollen* 'roll' is unaccusative (78b, 79).

(78) a. *dass die Wand einen Anstrich erhält.*
that the wall a coating receives
'that the wall gets a coating'
b. *dass die Kugel rollt.*
that the ball rolls
'that the ball rolls'

(79) unaccusative

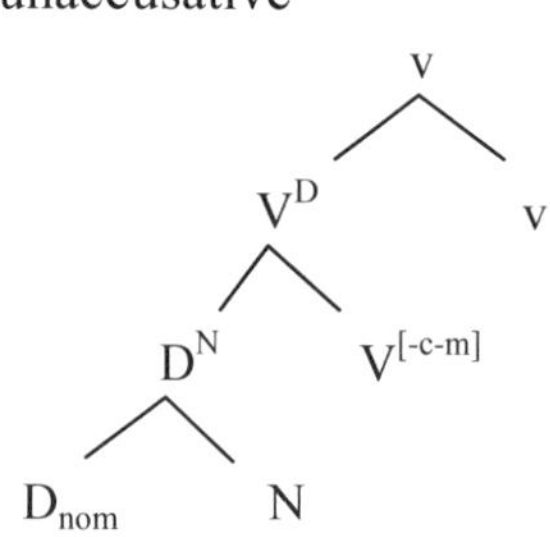

Consider next *erschrecken* 'get scared'. The non-causative alternant of this verb is morphologically marked, so it should be derived by reduction, rather than non-realization. After reduction, this verb seems to retain only a single [-c+m] cluster. Since reduction eliminates the D-feature of V, the remaining [-c+m] cluster should be assigned externally by clause (a) of the merging instructions (57). In chapter 2 it was observed, though, that reduced *erschrecken* 'get scared' is an unaccusative verb.

With the modified formulation of marking conventions and merging instructions, this verb is no longer problematic. Recall that [-c+m] is not the only cluster retained by reduced *erschrecken* 'get scared'. A stimulus role can be assigned through a selected preposition *vor* 'before'. The presence of both a [/+c] and a [/-c] cluster in the reduced entry trigger the assignment of a D feature to V. Therefore, an internal argument must merge. Since this argument is in need of a Θ-role, [-c+m] can only merge internally. External realization of the stimulus role [+c-m] is excluded by the lexical association of this cluster with the preposition *vor* 'before'. The reduced experiencer verb *erschrecken* 'get scared' must be unaccusative.

(80) a. *erschrecken* 'scare': {V, [+c], [-c+m], [+c-m], ...}
b. *erschrecken* 'get scared': [V, [-c+m], (P_{vor}, [+c-m]), ...}

(81) *dass das Kind vor dem Gespenst erschrak.*
that the child before the ghost scared
'that the ghost frightened the child'

2.3.5. Minder verbs

Consider first an emotional verb like *lieben* 'love'. In chapter 2 it was argued that such verbs select two underspecified clusters, [+m] and [-m]. One of these clusters is recognized by the merging instructions: [+m] must merge externally. The other cluster, underspecified [-m], should in principle be optional. In this case, though, formal conditions on syntactic projection force its presence in the following way. First, V subcategorizes for N. Second, the presence of an external Θ-role excludes an unaccusative derivation. Third, the lexical entry of emotional verbs like *lieben* 'love' does not list a silent, semantically vacuous N morpheme. Only unergatives and optional intransitives do. Therefore, an overt direct object must be inserted. Since the direct object requires a Θ-role, [-m] must merge with V.

(82) a. *lieben* 'love': {V, [+m], [-m], ...}
b. [$_{vP}$ DP$_{nom}$ v$^{[+m]}$ [$_{VP}$ DP$_{acc}$ V$^{[-m]}$]
c. *weil sie ihn lieben.*
because they him love
'because they love him.'

Consider by contrast the sensation verb *hören* 'hear/listen'. As for the external Θ-role, this verb is identical with *lieben* 'love'. In contrast to *lieben*, the verb *hören* is optionally intransitive (83). This fact must be represented in the lexical entry (84).

(83) *Hans hört in letzter Zeit nicht mehr sehr gut.*
Hans hears in recent time not more very good
'Hans has recently developed a hearing problem.'

(84) *hören* 'hear/listen': {V, [+m], [-m], [+c-m] ...(N), ...}

When N is selected into the numeration, it satisfies the subcategorization of V, and neither [-m], nor [+c-m] need to be merged. The merging instructions do not refer to these clusters (83). However, both of them may merge, if a preposition supports them. The instrument cluster is supported by *mit* 'with' (85), underspecified [-m] requires *auf* 'on/to' (86). A combination of the two PPs is impossible, because they bias different interpretations of the underspecified external role. The instrument PP biases an experiencer-reading (85), the directional PP forces an agent reading (86).

(85) a. *Er hört mit dem Hörgerät wieder recht gut.*
he hears with the hearing-aid again quite well
'The hearing aid has considerably improved his hearing.'
b. [$_{vP}$ DP$_{nom}$ v$^{[+m]}$ [$_{VP}$ ([$_{PP}$ [P$_{dat}$$^{[+c-m]}$ DP] P$_{mit}$]) N V]]

(86) a. *Er hört auf mich.*
he listens to me
b. [$_{vP}$ DP$_{nom}$ v$^{[+m]}$ [$_{VP}$ ([$_{PP}$ DP P$_{auf}$$^{[-m]}$]) N V]

If silent N is not selected into the lexical array, then an overt DP must merge with V, and this DP requires a Θ-role. In this context, [-m] merges with V.[13]

(87) a. *Er hörte die Neuigkeit.*
he heard the news
b. $[_{vP}$ DP_{nom} $v^{[+m]}$ $[_{VP}$ DP_{acc} $V^{[-m]}$ V]

Finally, it is possible to leave the external role [+m] unrealized. In this case, [+c-m] merges externally.

(88) a. *Alle Ohren hörten einen Laut.*
all ears heard a sound
b. $[_{vP}$ DP_{nom} $v^{[+c\text{-}m]}$ $[_{VP}$ DP_{acc} $V^{[-m]}$ V]

The most interesting class in the set of minder verbs is the one that exhibits an intentional alternation. This class is exemplified by *finden* 'find'. Since the lexical entry includes both a [+] cluster and a fully specified [/-c] cluster, the verb is marked with a D feature. An internal argument is obligatory.

(89) *finden* 'find': {V, [+m], [-c-m], [-m], ...}

The intentional reading is derived by merging [+m] with v and [-c-m] with V. The third role is optional. If it merges, it is assigned through a locational preposition (90).

(90) a. *dass er den Schlüssel (im Bad) fand.*
that he the key in-the bathroom found
'that he found the key in the bathroom.'
b. $[_{vP}$ DP_{nom} $v^{[+m]}$ $[_{VP}$ DP_{acc} $([P_{in}$ $[P_{dat}{}^{[-m]}$ DP]]) $V^{[-c\text{-}m]}$]

A special configuration obtains when *finden* 'find' takes an adjectival small-clause complement as in (91). Recall that adjectives neither assign nor receive thematic roles by the main thematic condition (47). Rather, the adjective reanalyzes with V, and the small-clause subject is assigned [-c-m] by V.

(91) a. *dass er das Buch toll fand*
that he the book great found
'that he found the book great'
b. $[_{vP}$ DP_{nom} $v^{[+m]}$ $[_{VP}$ DP_{acc} A $V^{[-c-m]}$]

Verbs like *finden* 'find' have a dimensional alternant. This alternation is derived by non-realization of [+m] and assignment of [-m] to the external argument.

(92) a. *dass die Beziehung ein Ende fand*
that the relationship a end found
'that the relationship came to an end'
b. $[_{vP}$ DP_{nom} $v^{[-m]}$ $[_{VP}$ DP_{acc} $V^{[-c-m]}$]

2.3.6. *Transitive [-] verbs*

Two sets of lexically basic, transitive [-] verbs were discussed in chapter 2. The first set is exemplified by *enthalten* 'contain', the second one by *bekommen* 'get/receive'.

(93) a. *enthalten* 'contain': {V, [-m], [-c-m], ...}
b. *bekommen* 'receive/get' {V, [-c], [-c-m], ...}

Both verbs were found in chapter 2 to exhibit a clearly transitive behavior. They cannot be analyzed as two-place unaccusatives. This follows from the present formulation of the merging instructions. The behavior of underspecified [-] clusters is free. Since these verbs do not select a [+] cluster, clause (a) of the merging instructions forces external realization of the underspecified [-] cluster. The derivation is nearly identical with the dimensional alternant of minder verbs. The only formal difference is that lexically basic [-] verbs do mark V with a D feature.

(94) a. *dass die Flasche Orangensaft enthält.*
that the bottle orange-juice contains
'that the bottle contains orange juice.'
b. $[_{vP}$ DP_{nom} $v^{[-m]}$ $[_{VP}$ DP_{acc} $V^{[-c-m]}$]

(95) a. *dass die Wand einen neuen Anstrich bekommt.*
that the wall a new coating gets
'that the wall gets a new coating.'
b. [$_{vP}$ DP$_{nom}$ v$^{[-c]}$ [$_{VP}$ DP$_{acc}$ V$^{[-c-m]}$]

2.4. Intransitives

In the set of lexically basic intransitives, chapter two discussed unaccusative dying verbs (96a, b), unaccusative change of state verbs (96c), unergative emission verbs (97a), and unergative statives (97b).

(96) a. *sterben* 'die': {V, (P$_{an}$, [+c-m]), [-c], ...}
b. *verhungern* 'die of starvation': {V, ([+c-m]), [-c], ...}
c. *verwelken* 'wilt': {V, [-c-m], ...}
(97) a. *klappern* 'rattle': {V, [+c+m], [+c-m], ...N, ...}
b. *blühen* 'flower/bloom': {V, [-m], ... N, ...}

Emission verbs like *klappern* 'rattle' have two alternants. If they merge the agent with v, then the instrument can be realized in a *mit*-PP. Otherwise, the instrument merges with v. In both cases, no Θ-role merges with V. The formal requirement of V is satisfied by a silent N-morpheme listed in the lexical entry of these verbs.

(98) a. *dass er (mit seinen Zähnen) klapperte.*
that he (with his teeth) rattled
'that he rattled his teeth.'
b. [$_{vP}$ DP$_{nom}$ v$^{[+c+m]}$ [$_{VP}$ ([P$_{mit}$ [P$_{dat}$$^{[+c-m]}$ DP]]) N V]

(99) a. *dass seine Zähne klapperten.*
that his teeth rattled
'that his teeth were rattling.'
b. [$_{vP}$ DP$_{nom}$ v$^{[+c-m]}$ [$_{VP}$ N V]

Stative verbs like *blühen* 'flower/bloom' were found to be unergative too. Their derivation is again straightforward. The formal N-requirement of V is satisfied by silent N, and underspecified [-m] merges externally by clause (a) of the merging instructions.

(100) a. *dass die Wirtschaft blühte.*
that the economy bloomed
'that the economy was blooming.'
b. $[_{vP}$ DP_{nom} $v^{[-m]}$ $[_{VP}$ N V]

Now consider the unaccusatives in the set. The derivation of *verwelken* 'wilt' is straightforward, if the marking/merging system treats one- and many-place verbs alike. In the present formulation of the merging instructions, [-c-m] must merge with V. Since the lexical entry of the verb does not provide a Θ-role for a second argument, the D of the internal argument must raise to satisfy the formal requirements of v. The verb is unaccusative.

(101) a. *dass die Blume verwelkte.*
that the flower wilted
'that the flower wilted.'

b.

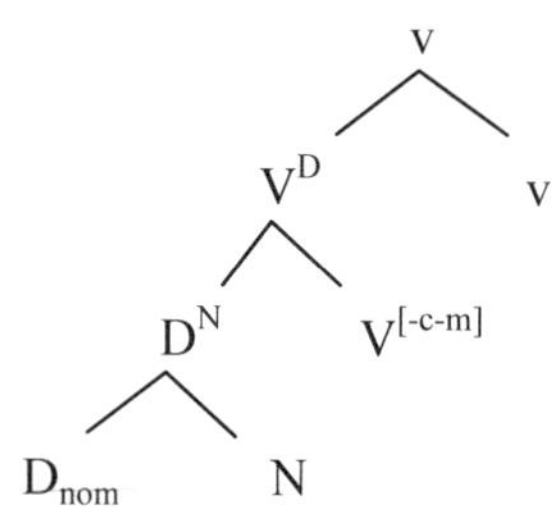

For dying verbs, it was argued in chapter 2 that two clusters are present in the lexical entry: the affected individual is assigned underspecified [-c]. In addition, an immediate cause role (i.e., [+c-m]) may be assigned through a selected preposition. The presence of both a [/+c] and a [/-c] cluster triggers assignment of a D-feature to V. However, the [+c-m] cluster cannot merge with v. In the lexical entry of *sterben* 'die', it is lexically associated with the selected preposition *an* 'at'. With *verhungern* 'die of starvation' it is frozen: this verb is overtly derived from the noun *Hunger* 'hunger', which names the immediate cause of dying. Therefore, the D of the internal argument must raise to satisfy the subcategorization of v.

(102) *dass er (an Krebs) starb.*
that he at cancer died
'that he died of cancer.'

2.5. Reflexives

Let us finally consider reflexives. The Theta System distinguishes between two reflexive configurations. In a true reflexive configurations, an internal and an external Θ-role are bundled. True reflexives must be distinguished from unaccusatives with reflexive morphology. The latter are derived by reduction of an external Θ-role, and they are expected to have unaccusative syntax (Reinhart and Siloni 2005).

Consider first true reflexives. Marelj (2004), Reinhart and Siloni (2005) argue that the locus of reflexivization is parametrized. Some languages, including Hebrew, reflexivize verbal predicates in the lexicon. Others apply reflexivization in syntax. German is of the latter kind. Strong evidence for this distinction can be found in syntactically complex contexts. If reflexivization applies in the lexicon, it cannot affect syntactically complex constructions. If it applies in syntax, it can. Thus, Hebrew (103a) ((12a) in Reinhart and Siloni 2005) is ungrammatical, but German (103b) is fine.

(103) a. **dan mitxaSef intelligenti*
Dan considers(refl) intelligent
b. *Dan hält sich für intelligent.*
Dan considers refl. for intelligent
'Dan considers himself intelligent.'

Reflexivization is formalized in the Theta System as a bundling operation (repeated as (104)) that applies, crucially, to unassigned Θ-roles. This assumption introduces an apparent problem. Consider a standard example in (105):

(104) Reflexivization bundling ((24) in Reinhart and Siloni 2005)
$[\Theta_i]$ $[\Theta_j]$ -> $[\Theta_i - \Theta_j]$, where Θ_i is an external role.

(105) a. *rasieren* 'shave': {V, [+c+m], [-c-m], ...}
b. *dass du dich rasierst.*
that you refl. shave
'that you shave.'

Since the lexical entry of this verb contains both a [+] cluster and a fully specified [/-c] cluster, the verb is marked with a D feature. This feature forces the presence of an internal argument. If an internal argument is merged, though, it is assigned the internal Θ-role. Reflexivization can only apply, if the reflexive pronoun does not count as an argument. In fact, Sæbø (2001), von Stechow (1995) endorse this position. They argue that the German reflexive pronoun is an object expletive. Translated into the present framework, we may assume that the reflexive pronoun checks formal features of V, but it does not have semantic content. The internal Θ-role thus remains unassigned, and reflexive-bundling can apply.

The analysis of the German reflexive pronoun as an object expletive extends to reduced forms with reflexive morphology. Reduced reflexives were found to be problematic in chapter 2, because generalizations over thematic role assignment predict them to be unaccusatives, but in actual fact, German reduced reflexives often fail standard unaccusativity tests.

If the German reflexive pronoun is not an argument, but an object-expletive, then the internal Θ-role remains unassigned. Since there is no external role, reflexive bundling cannot apply. Instead, the internal role is inherited by the DP that binds the reflexive (cf. Sæbø 2001 for a formalization in terms of λ-abstraction). Consider as an example the derivation of *sich verbrennen* 'suffer a burn'.

(106) a. *verbrennen* 'burn': {[V, [+c], [-c-m], ...]}
b. *verbrennen* 'suffer a burn': {[V, [-c-m], ... refl., ...]}

First, the lexical entry of causative *verbrennen* 'burn' undergoes decausativization. This operation applies in the lexicon. Its output is itself a lexical entry. The reduced lexical entry is marked as a reflexive, and it has a special meaning. The only Θ-role retained by the reduced entry is [-c-m]. This cluster must merge with V by the merging instructions The reflexive pronoun merges with V too, and it checks the formal features of V. However, it cannot be assigned a Θ-role. Since there is no external Θ-role, bundling cannot apply, and the internal Θ-role is inherited by the first c-commanding DP. In this derivation, it is irrelevant whether DP merges internal or external to VP. It is therefore expected, rather than problematic, that reduced reflexives exhibit an inconsistent behavior with respect to syntactic argument structure.

(107) and (108) with the structures in (109) and (110), respectively, give two of the most stable examples. Austrian German *sich ausgehen* 'fit in' passes most unaccusativity tests, *sich tragen aus* 'be supported by' fails most of them. The respective structures are as follows.

(107) a. *sich ausgehen* 'fit in': {[V, [-c-m], ... refl., ...]}
b. *dass sich noch eine einzige Prüfung am Vormittag ausgeht.*
the refl still a single exam at-the morning in-fits
'that one more exam can be done in the morning.'

(108) a. *sich tragen aus* 'be supported by': {[V, [-c-m], {P_{aus}, [-m]}, ... refl., ...]}
b. *dass sich die Projekte sich aus Spendengeldern tragen.*
that refl. the projects from donations support
'that the projects are supported by donations.'

(109)

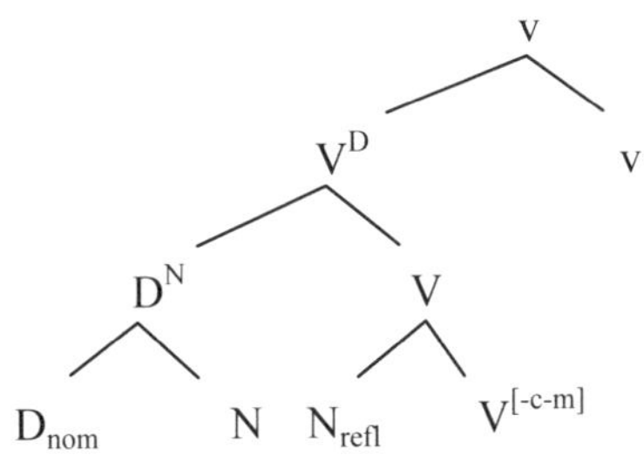

(110)

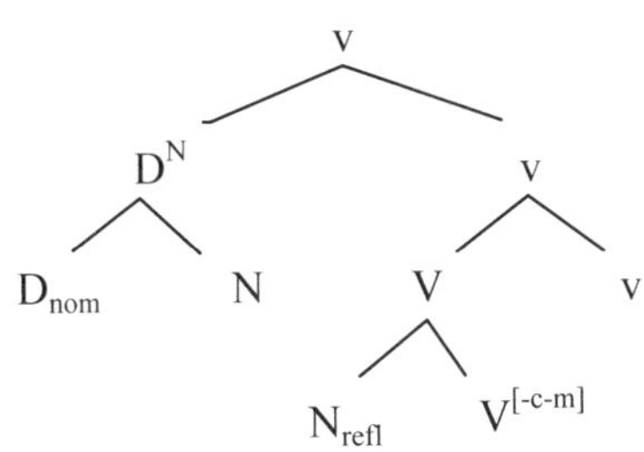

Chapter 2 discussed another set of non-causative reflexives, which cannot be derived by decausativization, because they are related to verbs that select a [/+m] external role. It was argued there that such reflexives must be derived by means of non-realization. Indeed, the verbs found in chapter 2 all satisfied the conditions of non-realization (58) that were observed in non-reflexive contexts too. For example, *sich verraten* 'give oneself away' has a double-causative agentive alternant. It is subject to clause (a) of non-realization. *Sich finden* 'find oneself/appear' has an intentional alternant with two [/-m] clusters. It is subject to clause (c).

Nevertheless, these verbs remain exceptional, because their availability is lexically constrained, and the reflexive verbs of this class come with a (mildly) special meaning. The reflexive forms must be lexically listed as follows:

(111) a. *sich verraten* 'give oneself away':
{[V, [-c-m], [+c-m], ... refl., ...]}
b. *sich finden* 'find oneself/appear in':
{[V, [-c-m], [-m], ... refl., ...]}

3. Conclusion

Starting with a discussion of the phonology-syntax interface, this chapter developed a theory of autonomous syntactic projection. In this theory, thematic roles provided by lexical entries merge with syntactic heads of category [/-N], and they are assigned to [/-V]. Generalizations over argument-linking are formulated in terms of merging instructions, which recognize a certain set of roles, but not others. A fully specified [-] cluster must always merge with V, and [+] clusters must merge with v. The syntactic realization of the other clusters is, in principle, free. The asymmetry between two role-types was held responsible for two distinct phenomena. First, roles that are recognized by the merging instructions are always assigned to a structural argument position. The remaining roles tend to be realized in datives and PPs. Second, roles of the first set are obligatory. Their absence follows a few universal conditions of reduction and non-realization. By contrast, the roles of the second class are systematically optional.

Notes

[1] Borer's argument is slightly adapted here.

[2] For phonological assumptions cf. Lowenstamm (1996).

[3] Notice that prosodically structured utterances are not specific to the human species. What is specific to human language is the ability to assign meanings to complex phonetic expressions. Hauser, Chomsky and Fitch (2002) discuss the hypothesis that the transparency of a small set of modules may be at the core of human language. The availability of (23) can be viewed as an expression of this hypothesis.

[4] A formal proof is less interesting. Assuming phonology is an *abelian monoid* with multiplication, a mapping from phonology into syntax is structure preserving, if syntax is an *abelian monoid* with multiplication, and $fxy=fxfy$. This is our working hypothesis. The question whether it makes sense is a much harder, empirical one. Its answer depends on the linguistic behavior of phonological and syntactic objects, as explored in the main text, especially in chapter 4.

[5] We might also want to ask if all members of the range are images under *interpretation*, i.e., if *interpretation* is *surjective*. The presence of a number of phonologically silent categories in syntactic theory (including silent motion verbs, as in van Riemsdijk 2002) suggests this is not the case.

[6] It is possible to imagine languages in which tense and mood are features of distinct syntactic heads (Cinque 1999). (34) would be unavailable in such a language. Similar considerations hold for tense and agreement. I assume with Chomsky (1995) that there is no independent Agr head.

[7] We do not want to postulate covert elements, (i) because there would be no principled reason why silent relative pronouns are unavailable elsewhere in German, and (ii) because silent syntactic categories are presumably constituents in syntax, and (37) shows that syntactic constituency is not a requirement for grafted configurations. The silent element approach would not carry over to examples like (37).

[8] In the system of van Riemsdijk (1998b), there is an important distinction between positive and negative categorial features. Since P is specified as [-N, -V], it can be both an argument of V, and extend its projection. If P extends the projection of V, it has the grammatical function of a complementizer. If it introduces an argument of V, it often extends the projection of a complement N. The subcategorization frame (40) is preferred here, because it is a stronger condition. The

role of P in the projection of argument structure is constrained by the Main Thematic Condition (47).

[9] (46) makes a strong claim about ECM configurations. If (46) is correct, then the (accusative) ECM subject cannot enter a feature checking relation with the embedded v. Indeed it has been argued (cf. Runner 2002 for an overview) that the ECM subject must be a matrix direct object in surface syntactic structure. The trace of the ECM subject can check the features of the embedded v, if we assume (as it was standard in the LGB framework) that NP-traces are not assigned case.

[10] "Distinctness: Two feature-clusters α, β, are distinct iff. a. they share at least one feature, and b. there is at least one feature or value which they do not share" ((59b) in Reinhart 2002).

[11] Bayer, Bader, and Meng (2001) argue that a German noun phrase in the dative case is embedded in a KP shell, the head of which is usually overt. For Berber, Bendjaballah and Haiden (2005), Guerssel (1987, 1992) argue that K and P are closely related categories. The same reasoning can be applied to German.

[12] "Neben der strukturellen Realisierung eines Arguments ist auch eine nicht-strukturelle Realisierung durch ein Dativ-, Genetiv- oder präpositionales Objekt möglich. Der Lexikoneintrag enthält hier folglich nicht nur die LSS, sondern auch die syntaktische Realisierung des betreffenden Arguments [...]" (Rapp 1997:58).

[13] The instrument cluster cannot merge with V, because its interpretation requires a saturated VP (cf. sections 3.7 – 3.9 in chapter 2).

Chapter 4
Applications and extensions: participial and infinitival constructions

The theory outlined in the previous chapter is applied to a number of constructions in this one. The discussion starts with the present participle, because this form exhibits a number of very stable thematic alternations, which moreover correspond to the presence and absence, respectively, of morphological markers. The discussion is then extended to modal infinitival complements to the auxiliaries *haben* 'have' and *sein* 'be'. It will be argued that the infinitival prefix *zu* triggers arbitrarization of the external Θ-role in the present participle and under *sein* 'be', but not under *haben* 'have'. This asymmetry is attributed to the size of the infinitival constituent: vP in the present participle and under *sein* 'be', but TP under *haben* 'have'. A common property for all three construction types is the presence of the infinitival suffix /*n*/, which checks the formal features of infinitival V and acts as an *alternative realization* of the internal argument in the sense of Emonds (1987, 2000).

The second part of this chapter deals with constructions with the second participle. Starting with observations about the erratic auxiliary selection of intransitive manner of motion verbs, it is argued that the verbs in this class must be analyzed as lexically derived reflexives. This requires a minimal adaptation of the Lexicon-Syntax Parameter of Reinhart and Siloni (2005).

Regarding the status of perfect, passive and adjectival participles, it is argued that many specific properties of the adjectival passive must be attributed to the auxiliary, rather than the adjectival participle, because they disappear, when the adjectival participle is used as an attributive modifier of N. It is argued that a core structure is shared by all types of the second participle. In particular, the participial suffix checks formal features of V, and it alternatively realizes the internal argument, if V assigns an internal Θ-role.

The adjectival passive is analyzed with Horvath and Siloni (2005), Marelj (2004) as a lexically derived form with a neutralized external Θ-role. Lexical neutralization of the external role does not preclude the projection of phrasal adjectival participles, though. It is argued that this option depends on prosodic properties of the participial stem. If the stem is the prosodic head of the word, a phrasal adjectival participle is available. This is why the prefixation of */un/* excludes the phrasal derivation: */un/*, rather than the stem, is the prosodic head. The analysis is shown to extend to notoriously problematic data regarding verb particle constructions.

The discussion of the verbal passive discovers a general constraint on syntactic Θ-role saturation. It seems to be the case that [/-m] is never accessible for saturation. This condition cannot be reduced to arbitrarization, because it applies in the existential environment of the personal passive as well.

The final section turns back to auxiliary selection. Based on the definition of auxiliaries as a-thematic verbs that may assign the external role of their complement, an overall picture of perfect, passive and future constructions is given.

1. The present participle and modal infinitives

1.1. The present participle

1.1.1. Basic facts

The German present participle is used as a nominal modifier (1) and as a clausal adjunct (2). In both cases, an argument of the participial verb is identified by a noun external to the participial phrase. In the case of N-modifying participles (1), this is the modified noun. In the case of clausal adjuncts (2), it is either the subject, or the direct object of the minimal containing clause. The participial affix will be glossed as *ND* throughout.

(1) *ein [schöne Lieder singendes] Kind*
a beautiful songs sing.ND.AGR child
'a child singing beautiful songs'

(2) a. *Er stand singend im Regen.*
he stood sing.ND.AGR in-the rain
'He was standing in the rain, singing.'

b. *Wir haben ihn nur singend zu Gesicht bekommen.*
we have him only sing.ND.AGR to face got
'Whenever we met him, he was singing'
or: 'We only saw him while/because we were singing.'

Morphologically, the present participle is made up of a verbal stem and the suffix */nd/*.[1] When it is used as a modifier of N, the participle agrees with a c-commanding D. The form and distribution of the agreement markers is identical with the agreement of adjectives.

(3) a. *ein sing-end-er Bub*
a sing-ND-AGR boy
'a singing boy/a boy who sings'
b. *ein glücklich-er Bub*
a happy-AGR boy
'a happy boy'

(4) a. *Er stieg sing-end (*-er) in den Zug.*
he stepped sing-ND-AGR into the train
'He boarded the train singing.'
b. *Er stieg glücklich (*-er) in den Zug.*
he stepped happy-AGR into the train
'He boarded the train happy.'

In its basic form, i.e., without the prefix *zu*, the present participle refers to an ongoing or habitual event, and its subject Θ-role is identified by a noun external to the phrase projected by the participle. The interpretation of the unprefixed participle is active (1)-(4).

If the infinitival prefix *zu* 'to' is present as in (5), then the internal Θ-role of the participle is identified by a noun external to the projection of the participle. The reading of a prefixed present participle is thus passive. In addition, the prefixed present participle has an obligatory, yet somewhat vague modal reading. The most natural way to interpret (5a) is as an obligation. In (5b) a possibility-reading is more natural.

(5) a. *das [zu ess-end-e] Fleisch*
the to eat-ND-AGR meat
'the meat that should/must/ought to be eaten'

b. *das [nicht mehr zu ess-end-e] Fleisch*
the not more to eat-ND-AGR meat
'the meat that can/should not be eaten any more'

1.1.2. Verbal properties

In spite of their similarity with respect to agreement, the present participle differs from adjectives in some fundamental respects (cf. Toman 1986; Wunderlich 1987). First, adjectives form comparatives and superlatives (6), participles do not (7). Notice that there are exceptions to this generalization. Truly adjectival participles will be discussed in section 1.1.3.

(6) a. *ält-er als sie*
old-COMP than she
'older than she'
b. *der ält-est-e Mann*
the old-SUP-AGR man
'the oldest man'

(7) a. **alter-nd-er als sie*
age-ND-COMP than she
b. **der alter-nd-st-e Mann*
the age-ND-SUP-AGR man

Second, the present participle takes overt internal arguments in the accusative case (8a), adjectives do not (8b).[2]

(8) a. *Einen Scotch trinkend (stand er am Fenster).*
a.ACC Scotch drink.ND stood he at-the window
b. **Hans ist die Aufgabe fähig*
Hans is the.ACC task able

Wunderlich (1987) takes such facts to indicate the presence of an infinitival verb in the morpho-syntactic structure of the present participle. In addition to the above observations, he points to the following fact as supporting this analysis:

Infinitival verbs undergo a rule of *schwa* epenthesis, which inserts a vowel to the left of the final consonant, the suffix /*n*/ (9a).[3] This rule applies to participles too. However, it does not target the position expected by morphologically blind, phonotactic considerations, i.e., the position to the left of the final consonant (9b). Instead, schwa is inserted to the left of -*n*, exactly as in infinitival verbs (9c).

(9)	a.	*/red/ + /n/*	→	*red-e-n*	'speak.INF'
	b.	*/red/ + /nd/*	→	**red-n-e-d*	
	c.	*/red/ + /n/+/d/*	→	*red-e-nd*	'speak.ND'

This is so, according to Wunderlich (1987), because the morphological structure of the present participle is derived in two steps. First, the infinitival suffix attaches to a verbal stem. Schwa epenthesis targets the infinitival verb. Then, participial -*d* attaches. Attachment of opaque -*nd* to the verb-stem plus subsequent schwa epenthesis would yield ungrammatical (9b).

Similar considerations apply to the prefix *zu*. On the assumption that the present participle incorporates an infinitival verb, the subcategorization of *zu* can be kept simple and consistent: *zu* attaches to an infinitival verb. If -*end* were an opaque participle-marker, we would have to stipulate that *zu* subcategorizes for both infinitival verbs and participles.

(10) a. *(zu) überdach-en*
(to) cover-INF
b. *der zu überdach-en-d-e Hof*
the to cover-INF-D-AGR yard
'The yard that ought to be covered with a roof.'

According to Wunderlich (1987), the correct analysis of the present participle must therefore be (11). The shorthand *ND* will still be used in glosses to indicate the presence of both infinitival /*n*/ and participial /*d*/.

(11) (*zu*)- $[_{\text{Inf}}\,[_{\text{V}}$ *überdach*] -*en*] -*d*-(*e*)
(to)- cover-N-D-(AGR)

1.1.3. Adjectival participles

In sharp contrast to the facts just outlined, the unprefixed participle allows a truly adjectival derivation too. The availability of an adjectival derivation is subject to conditions that go beyond the scope of this book (cf. Haiden 2004; Rapp 2001, 2002). It is enough to notice that the adjectival participle has comparative and superlative forms (12b, c), and it cannot take a direct object in the accusative case. Instead, an implicit internal Θ-role can be identified by a PP (13). Notice that a verbal derivation is available too (14). However, this derivation is incompatible with the comparative in (13a).

(12) a. *Die Vorstellung faszinierte sie.*
the performance impressed them
b. *eine faszinier-end-er-e Vorstellung*
a impress-ND-COMP-AGR performance
'a more impressing performance'
c. *die faszinier-end-st-e Vorstellung*
the impress-ND-SUP-AGR performance
'the most impressive performance'

(13) a. **eine uns alle faszinier-end-er-e Vorstellung...*
a us all impress-ND-COMP-AGR performance
b. *eine für uns alle faszinier-end-er-e Vorstellung...*
a for us all impress-ND-COMP-AGR performance
'a more impressing performance for all of us...'

(14) *eine uns alle faszinier-end-e Vorstellung...*
a us all impress-ND-AGR performance
'a performance that impressed all of us'

An adjectival participle can be used as a predicate together with the copula (15a), a verbal participle cannot. The verbal derivation is evidenced in (15b) by the presence of an accusative direct object.

(15) a. *Die Vorstellung war für das Publikum faszinierend.*
the performance was for the audience impress-ND-AGR
'The performance impressed the audience.'
b. **Die Vorstellung war das Publikum faszinierend.*
the performance was the.ACC audience impress-ND-AGR

In line with Wunderlich's generalization about the distribution of *zu*, the infinitival prefix can only appear, if a verbal derivation is allowed (16a). If an adjectival derivation is forced, as in (16b), then *zu* is ungrammatical.

(16) a. *das zu faszinierende Publikum*
the to impress.ND.AGR audience
'The audience that ought to be impressed'
b. **das zu faszinierend-er-e Publikum*
the to impress.ND-COMP-AGR audience
intended: 'the audience that ought to be more impressed'

1.1.4. Preliminary observations about argument structure

If the (verbal) present participle incorporates a verbal element, we may still wonder if this verb projects phrasal structure or not. Floating quantifiers supply evidence to the effect that an external Θ-role is assigned in the unprefixed participle, and that an internal argument is promoted to subject position in the prefixed participle. Such facts would be hard to reconcile with the assumption that v is absent.

The presence of a syntactic subject position in the unprefixed participle is evidenced by the presence of subject-oriented floating quantifiers. Although the floating quantifiers in (17) can take wide scope, as indicated in the translations, preceding narrow-scope adverbials show that they are constituents of the participle phrase, and not of the containing DP. The distribution of the floating quantifiers with respect to overt accusatives mirrors Burzio's generalization. With transitive (17a) and unergative base verbs (17b), the floating quantifier relates to an external argument. With an unaccusative base verb (17c), it relates to an internal argument.

(17) a. *die [hier* ***alle*** *unablässig Zigaretten rauchenden] Studenten*
the here all incessantly cigarettes smoking students
'all those students who are incessantly smoking cigarettes in this place'
b. *die [jetzt doch wieder* ***alle*** *arbeitenden] Kumpel*
the now AFFIRM again all working miners
'all those miners who are at work again now'

c. *die [jetzt wieder* ***alle*** *sinkenden] Pegel*
the now again all falling indicators
'the indicators, which are all falling again'

Similar observations can be made about the prefixed participle. There, the external Θ-role is absorbed. It can be identified by a *by*-phrase (18). In this configuration, the internal argument is promoted to subject position. As in (17) above, the subject cannot be realized as a full noun phrase, but floating quantifiers bear witness to its presence in syntax (19).

(18) a. *der* ***von ihnen*** *zu überdachende Hof*
the by them to cover-ND-AGR yard
'the yard that ought to be covered by them'
b. *Der Hof wird* ***von ihnen*** *überdacht.*
the yard is by them covered
'The yard is covered with a roof by them.'

(19) *die [bis morgen noch* ***alle*** *zu überdach-end-en] Höfe*
the until tomorrow still all to cover-ND-AGR yards
'all those yards that are to be covered with a roof by tomorrow'

Absorption of the external role is subject to a number of conditions that interact with the content of the Θ-role assigned by a given verb to its external argument, and with the kind of modality of the construction.

1.1.5. Intransitives

A first observation we can make is that monadic verbs do allow the formation of a prefixed participle. This is true for both unaccusative (20a,b) and unergative intransitives (20c,d). In contrast to finite environments, the present participle does not allow an impersonal passive.

(20) a. **der zu sterbende Patient*
the to die.ND.AGR patient
b. **die zu verwelkende Blume*
the to wilt.ND.AGR flower
c. **die zu leuchtende Lampe/Person*
the to shine.ND.AGR torch/person

d. **der zu arbeitende Handwerker*
the to work.ND.AGR craftsman

1.1.6. Agents, causes, and double causation

Agentive transitives appear in the prefixed participle, but notice that the instrumental alternant of double causatives is lost. The implicit Θ-role must be [+c+m], not [+c-m] (21a). The instrument cluster can be assigned as usual in a PP (21b). As for modality, both dispositional (21c) and deontic readings (21b) are available.

(21) a. *der (von uns/*von Blumen) zu schmückende Balkon*
the (by us/by flowers) to decorate.ND.AGR balcony
'the balcony that ought to be decorated by us'
b. *ein unbedingt mit Blumen zu schmückender Balkon*
a absolutely with flowers to decorate.ND.AGR balcony
'a balcony that should absolutely be decorated with flowers'
c. *ein leicht zu schmückender Balkon*
a easy to decorate.ND.AGR balcony
'a balcony that is easy to decorate'

Verbs that select underspecified [+c] exhibit a similar behavior. While [+c] easily allows inanimate cause subjects in a finite sentence, the implicit argument of the participle can only be interpreted as a volitional agent (22a). (22b, c) show that both deontic and dispositional readings are available.

(22) a. *das zu verbrennende Dokument*
the to burn.ND.AGR document
'the document that ought to be burned'
b. *ein unbedingt zu verbrennendes Dokument*
a absolutely to burn.ND.AGR document
'a document that must be burned'
c. *eine leicht zu verbrennende Plastiktüte*
a easy to burn.ND.AGR plastic-bag
'a plastic bag that is easy to burn'

In contrast to dispositional and deontic readings, epistemic readings are not so easy to find. Admittedly, epistemic possibility is a very weak reading that includes most others. An impression of epistemic possibility is therefore not considered sufficient evidence for epistemic readings. Epistemic possibility is a stronger reading. A strongly supporting context is given in (23). The epistemic reading *it is inevitable that the skin gets burned* is not available.

(23) ??*die beim exzessiven Sonnenbad notwendig zu verbrennende Haut*
the at-the excessive sun-bathing necessarily to burn.ND.AGR skin

1.1.7. Underspecified [-m] and cluster distinctness

Consider next verbs that assign either [+c] or [-m] to their subject. In a full clause, the two configurations can easily be distinguished in the translation, because they are expressed by different verbs in English. With a [+c] subject, *tragen* translates as *carry*, with a [-m] subject it translates as *bear*.

The requirement of volitionality seems much weaker for these verbs (24b) than it was for the double causatives like (21a) above. In terms of argument realization, though, (24b) should be compared with (21b), rather than (21a). (24b) expresses an obligation for some intentional individual to acquire the seal, or to stamp it onto the document. The *von*-PP is thus a source-argument, not a true *by*-phrase in (24b). It seems to be the case that the cluster distinctness condition fails to apply in this configuration. The reason for this seems to be that deontic modality forces an intentional interpretation for underspecified [+c]. In contexts where human intervention is excluded, as in (24c), the construction is indeed unacceptable.

(24) a. *die zu tragende Tasche*
the to carry.ND.AGR bag
'the bag that ought to be carried'

b. (?) *das (von dem Dokument) zu tragende Siegel*
the by-the document to carry.ND.AGR seal
'the seal that ought to be born by the document'

c. ??*der vom Wind zu tragende Gleiter*
the by-the wind to carry.ND.AGR glider

While deontic modality exceptionally allows the co-occurrence of [+c] and [-m], dispositional modality does not. If the dispositional reading is forced, only the agentive *carry*-reading is available for the participle, and the *von*-PP must refer to an agent, rather than a source.

(25) *das (vom Sekretär/*vom Dokument) leicht zu tragende Siegel*
the (by-the clerk/by-the document) easily to carry.ND.AGR seal
'the seal that is easy to carry for the clerk'

A similar behavior can be observed with non-alternating verbs that assign [-m] to the subject. The verb *enthalten* 'contain' allows the formation of a participle on a reading that attributes an obligation to the producer of a consumer product (26a). This suggests that the lexical representation of *enthalten* 'contain' in fact contains a frozen [+c] cluster that can be accessed in the participle under a deontic reading, where it remains distinct from [-m]. A possibility reading is excluded (26b). Notice that examples like (26a) are rejected by some speakers (including the author), but they seem to be acceptable for many others. Inter-speaker variation is expected, if access to a frozen [+c] cluster is a lexical idiosyncrasy of *enthalten* 'contain'.[4]

(26) a. %*die (von der Packung) zu enthaltenden Nudeln*
the (by the package) to contain.ND.AGR pasta
'the pasta that ought to be in the package'
b. ??*die relativ leicht zu enthaltenden Nudeln*
the relatively easily to contain.ND.AGR pasta

Epistemic necessity is excluded in all cases. The only reading available for (27a) is a deontic one. Since a deontic reading is impossible in (27b), the example is unacceptable. In (27c), the contrast between *notwendig* 'necessarily' and *unbedingt* 'absolutely' illustrates the same observation. *Unbedingt* 'absolutely' is fully acceptable, because it supports a deontic reading; *notwendig* 'necessarily' supports an epistemic reading, and it is much less acceptable.

(27) a. *der notwendig zu tragende Gleiter*
the necessarily to carry.ND.AGR glider
'the glider that must be carried'

b. ??*das notwendig zu tragende Siegel*
the necessarily to carry.ND.AGR pasta
c. *die (unbedingt/??notwendig) zu enthaltenden Nudeln*
the absolutely/necessarily to carry.ND.AGR pasta
'the pasta that must be contained'

1.1.8. Underspecified [-c]

Consider next *erhalten* 'keep/get', which assigns either [+c] or [-c] to the subject. Again, the two alternants can be distinguished by a different translation. The causative alternant translates as *keep/maintain*, the non-causative one as *get*. If the implicit role is [+c], then both deontic and dispositional readings are easily available, and volitionality is implied (28). The non-causative alternant is more interesting. Its most natural interpretation is dispositional (29a). However, it is possible at least for some speakers to force what looks like a deontic reading. This reading is comparable with the performative use of the verb in (29c). In both cases, the option of interpreting [/+m] with underspecified [-c] makes intentional contribution to the causation of the event possible. Some speakers seem to consider this sufficient to license a deontic reading.

(28) *das unbedingt/schwierig zu erhaltende Monument*
the absolutely/easily to keep.ND.AGR monument

(29) a. *das leicht zu erhaltende Stipendium*
the easy to get.ND.AGR grant
'the grant that is easy to get'
b. ?*das unbedingt zu erhaltende Stipendium*
the absolutely to get.ND.AGR grant
'the grant that you must get'
c. *Ich erhalte noch 2 Cent zurück!*
I get still 2 cent back
'I'm still waiting for 2 cents change!'

Non-alternating verbs that assign [-c] to the subject behave more or less the same. (31) shows that the availability of a deontic reading disappears even for those speakers who would otherwise allow it, if intentional contribution by a [-c+m] argument is excluded.

(30) a. *das leicht zu bekommende Stipendium*
the easy to get.ND.AGR grant
'the grant that is easy to get'
b. ?*das unbedingt zu bekommende Stipendium*
the absolutely to get.ND.AGR grant
'the grant that you must get'
c. *Ich bekomme das Steak mit Pommes!*
I get the steak with fries
'I would like to have the steak with fries!'

(31) ??*die unbedingt vor 10 zu bekommende Kinderkrankheit*
the absolutely before age-10 to get ND.AGR children's-disease

While the interpretation of [/+m] allows an obligation reading for some speakers, the participle is altogether ungrammatical, if an intentional interpretation is unavailable. This holds equally for alternating *erhalten* 'keep/get' and for non-alternating *bekommen* 'get'.

(32) **die (von der Wand) zu erhaltende/bekommende Farbe*
the (by the wall) to get.ND.AGR/get.ND.AGR color
'the color that the wall should be painted with'

Epistemic necessity is generally unavailable. If no deontic reading is easily available to save the construction, as in (33a), examples that bias a necessity reading are unacceptable.

(33) a. *das notwendig zu erhaltende Monument*
the necessarily to keep.ND.AGR monument
'the monument that must be kept'
b. ??*das notwendig zu erhaltende Stipendium*
the necessarily to get.ND.AGR grant
c. ??*das notwendig zu bekommende Stipendium*
the necessarily to get.ND.AGR grant
d. ??*die notwendig zu erhaltende/bekommende Farbe*
the necessarily to get.ND.AGR/get.ND.AGR color

1.1.9. Underspecified [+m]

Underspecified [+m] allows both readings with verbs of emotion (34). With verbs of sensation (35), the implicit argument must be [+m], not [+c-m]. The instrument cluster can only be assigned through an instrumental *mit*-PP.

(34) a. *eine schwer zu liebende Person*
a difficult to love.ND.AGR person
'a person who is difficult to love'
b. *eine zu liebende Person*
the to love.ND.AGR person
'a person who ought to be loved'

(35) a. *eine unbedingt zu hörende Sendung*
a absolutely to hear.ND.AGR program
'a program one absolutely has to listen to'
b. *ein schwer zu hörender, relativ leiser Ton*
a difficult to hear.ND.AGR relatively silent sound
'a rather silent sound that is difficult to hear'
b. *ein (mit/*von den Ohren) schwer zu hörender Ton*
a with/by the ears difficult to hear.ND.AGR sound
'a sound that is difficult to hear with bare ears'

With verbs that exhibit an intentional alternation the participle excludes the non-intentional alternant (36b).

(36) a. *die unbedingt/leicht zu findende Lösung*
a absolutely/easily to find.ND.AGR solution
'a solution that is easy to find/that must be found'
b. **das (vom Krieg) zu findende Ende*
the (by-the war) to find.ND.AGR end

Epistemic readings seem somewhat less marginal with underspecified [+m] as implicit subject than they are otherwise. Nevertheless, the examples in (37) are still far from perfect under the intended reading.

(37) a. ?*eine notwendig zu liebende Person*
a necessarily to love.ND.AGR person

b. ?*ein notwendig zu hörender Ton*
   a necessary to hear.ND.AGR sound
c. ?*die notwendig zu findende Lösung*
   a necessarily to find.ND.AGR solution

1.1.10. Mixed value clusters

Verbs that select fully specified [-c+m] as a subject behave like those that select [-c]. A dispositional reading is always easily available, a deontic one is very marginal at best. Notice that the acceptability of (38b) is comparable with (31), rather than with (30b). If the implicit argument is specified as [/-c], a deontic reading is not available, unless specific conditions apply. In the *bekommen* 'get' example (30b) above, the deontic reading was supported by the performative use of the verb. Such a strategy is not available for *erblicken* 'catch sight of'.

(38) a. *der leicht zu erblickende Schaden*
   the easily to catch-sight.ND.AGR damage
   'the damage that can easily be detected'
b. ??*der unbedingt zu erblickende Schaden*
   the absolutely to catch-sight.ND.AGR damage

The verb *faszinieren* 'impress', which selects [+c-m], has a dispositional reading in the participle. A deontic reading is marginal. Notice that a *von*-PP is completely impossible with this verb (40a). Instead, it is possible to realize a stimulus in a *mit*-PP (40b). This scenario is comparable with what we found for frozen [+c] with *enthalten* 'contain'. In the prefixed participle, it is possible to access frozen [+c] for saturation, and realize [/-m] in a PP.

(39) a. *das leicht zu faszinierende Publikum*
   the easily to impress.ND.AGR audience
   'the audience that is easy to impress'
b. ??*das unbedingt zu faszinierende Publikum*
   the absolutely to impress.ND.AGR audience

(40) a. **das vom Sänger/von der Vorstellung leicht zu faszinierende Publikum*
the (by-the singer/by the performance) easily to impress.ND.AGR audience
b. *das mit dummen Witzen leicht zu faszinierende Publikum*
the with silly jokes easily to impress ND.AGR audience
'the audience that is easy to impress with silly jokes'

With respect to epistemic readings, implicit [-c+m] patterns with [+m] in that the necessity reading is somewhat less marginal than it is with other implicit roles. Epistemic necessity is unavailable with implicit [+c-m].

(41) a. *?der notwendig zu erblickende Schaden*
the necessarily to catch-sight.ND.AGR damage
b. *??das notwendig zu faszinierende Publikum*
the necessarily to impress.ND.AGR audience

1.1.11. Summary

We have made the following observations so far.

First, the implicit Θ-role of the present participle must be compatible with an interpretation as [/+m]. A [/-m] cluster cannot be the implicit subject of a prefixed participle.

Second, dispositional readings are generally possible. Deontic readings are generally impossible, if the implicit argument is specified as [/-c]. This generalization allows for exceptions, though. In some contexts, and for some speakers, the availability of [/+m] saves a deontic reading. Epistemic necessity is unavailable, or at least significantly marginal.

Third, role-absorption can access the lexically frozen [+c] cluster of some verbs, for some speakers.

Forth, in some contexts, the cluster distinctness condition fails to apply. A [+c] cluster (interpreted as [+c+m]) can co-occur with [-m] in a single predicate. Similar observations have been made for the middle by Marelj (2004:195-198).

Fifth, no conclusive evidence has been found for or against a syntactic analysis of Θ-role absorption. A lexical analysis would be supported by the fact that some lexically frozen roles are accessible. A syntactic analysis is supported by the fact that the overt prefix *zu* triggers absorption. Syntactic, but not lexical role absorption is consistent with Marelj (2004), who argues that Θ-role absorption is always a syntactic operation in German.

1.2. Modal Infinitives under *sein* 'be'

1.2.1. Basic facts

The prefixed participle is closely related to another construction, modal infinitival complements to the auxiliary *sein* 'be'. The similarity between the two constructions has long been noticed (Gelhaus 1977; Haider 1984; Toman 1986; Wunderlich 1987; for an extensive comparative and historical discussion cf. Demske-Neumann 1994). First, the infinitive under *sein* 'be' has a somewhat vague, modal meaning. Second, its interpretation is passive, although there is no uncontroversial evidence for passive morphology in the construction; notice the contrast in English between the gloss and the translation of (42).

The two constructions differ in two obvious ways. First, the internal argument is overtly realized as a (raised) DP in the modal infinitive, but it is apparently silent with the participle. Second, the participle is marked with an affix */d/*, the infinitive is not. This clustering of properties is summarized in (43).

(42) a. *der zu rasierende Kunde*
the to shave.ND.AGR client
'the client who ought to be shaved'
b. *Der Kunde ist zu rasieren.*
the client is to shave
'There is a client to be shaved.'

(43) - infinitive under *sein* 'be':
raising of the internal argument
absence of */d/*
- prefixed participle:
covertness of the internal argument
presence of */d/*
- presence of *zu* correlates with passive argument structure

Toman (1986) observes that the infinitival prefix *zu* must play a role in the passivization of both the modal infinitive and the participle. The reasoning is that *zu* is the only overt marker that distinguishes the active participle in (44) from the passive one in (42). Of course, Toman's observation is in conflict with the fact that *zu* is likewise present in controlled infinitival clauses (45a), and in modal infinitives under the auxiliary *haben* (45b), and these are both active Haider (1984).

(44) *der einen Kunden rasierende Friseur*
the a client shave.ND.AGR barber
'the barber who is shaving a client'

(45) a. *Der Friseur vergaß, seinen Kunden zu rasieren.*
the barber forgot his client to shave
'The barber forgot to shave his client.'
b. *Der Friseur hat einen Kunden zu rasieren.*
the barber has a client to shave
'The barber ought to shave a client.'

The analysis to be developed will side with Toman. Before that, a more detailed study of modal infinitives is in order.

1.2.2. Intransitives

Intransitives usually do not appear in the modal construction with *sein* (46). However, unergatives allow an impersonal construction (47c, d). An impersonal construction is impossible for the prefixed participle in (20).

(46) a. **Der Patient ist zu sterben*
the patient is to die
b. **Die Blume ist zu verwelken*
the flower is to wilt
c. **Die Lampe/die Person ist zu leuchten.*
the lamp/the person is to shine
d. **Der Handwerker ist zu arbeiten.*
the craftsman is to work

(47) a. ??*Es ist zu sterben*
it is to die
b. ??*Es ist zu verwelken*
it is to wilt
c. *Es ist zu leuchten.*
it is to shine
'It is obligatory to light the way.'
d. *Es ist (am Montag) zu arbeiten.*
it is (on Monday) to work
'It is obligatory to work (on Monday).'

In the impersonal construction, the reading is usually deontic (47). A dispositional reading can be forced (48a), an epistemic one cannot (48b).

(48) a. *Mit dieser Lampe ist (es) leicht zu leuchten/zu arbeiten.*
with this torch is (it) easy to shine/to work
'This torch is easy to light the way with/to work with.'
b. ??*Mit dieser Lampe ist (es) notwendig zu leuchten/zu arbeiten.*
with this torch is (it) necessary to shine/to work

1.2.3. Agents, causes, and double causation

With agentive and causative verbs, the internal argument appears as an overt subject, and the external role remains implicit. The instrument cluster of double causatives cannot be the implicit argument (49a). This is identical with what we have found for the prefixed participle.

(49) a. *Der Balkon ist (von uns/*von Blumen) zu schmücken.*
the balcony is (by us/by flowers) to decorate
'The balcony is to be decorated (by us).'
b. *Der Balkon ist unbedingt (mit Blumen) zu schmücken.*
the balcony is absolutely (with flowers) to decorate
'The balcony must be decorated (with flowers).'
c. *Der Balkon ist leicht zu schmücken.*
the balcony is easy to decorate
'The balcony is easy to decorate.'

(50) a. *Das Dokument ist zu verbrennen*
the document is to burn
'The document ought to be burned.'
b. *Die Plastiktüte ist kaum zu verbrennen.*
the plastic bag is hardly to burn
'The plastic bag is hardly inflammable.'

Both dispositional and deontic modality is available in (49b, c) and (50). Epistemic necessity is once more excluded. (51a) is only saved by the availability of a deontic reading. Such a reading is less readily available in (51b), which is therefore unacceptable.

(51) a. *Der Balkon war unter diesen Umständen notwendig zu schmücken.*
the balcony was under these circumstances necessarily to decorate
'Under these circumstances, the balcony had to be decorated.'
b. ??*Bei exzessivem Sonnenbaden ist die Haut zu verbrennen.*
at excessive sun-bathing is the skin to burn

1.2.4. Underspecified [-m] and cluster distinctness

In the prefixed participle, a lexically frozen [+c] cluster can be accessible as an implicit external argument, and it can co-occur with [-m] in a *von* 'by' phrase. (52a) is interpreted as an obligation for the producer of a consumer product. This is not so easily possible in the auxiliary construction (52b).

(52) a. *das (vom Salz) zu enthaltende Jod*
the (by salt) to contain.ND.AGR iodine
'the level of iodine to be contained by salt'
b. ??*Jod ist (von Salz) zu enthalten.*
iodine is (by-salt) to contain

The same holds for *tragen* 'carry'. The implicit [+c] cluster receives an intentional interpretation. The *von* 'by' phrase can only refer back to the implicit argument (53b). In contrast to what we observe for the participle (53c), it cannot introduce an additional [-m] cluster.

(53) a. *Die Tasche ist zu tragen.*
the bag is to carry
'The bag ought to be carried.'
b. *Das Siegel ist (vom Sekretär/??vom Dokument) zu tragen.*
the seal is (by-the clerk/by the document) to carry
'The seal ought to be carried (by the clerk).'
c. *das (vom Dokument) zu tragende Siegel*
the (by-the document) to carry.ND.AGR seal
'the seal that ought to be born by the document'

With respect to modality, the auxiliary construction behaves exactly like the participle. Dispositional (54a) and deontic readings (54b) are possible, epistemic necessity is excluded (54c).

(54) a. *Die Tasche ist leicht zu tragen.*
the bag is easy to carry
'The bag is easy to carry.'
b. *Die Tasche ist unbedingt zu tragen.*
the bag is absolutely to carry
'The bag must be carried.'
b. ??*Die Tasche ist notwendig zu tragen.*
the bag is necessarily to carry

1.2.5. Underspecified [-c]

Verbs that assign either a cause or a goal role to their subject retain both alternants in the modal *ist zu tun* construction. (55) exemplifies an implicit cause, (56) an implicit goal. With [-c] as implicit external argument, the deontic reading is at best marginal (56b). Exactly as in the participle, the deontic reading is incompatible with [/-c] for most speakers. The same is true for non-alternating verbs that select a goal subject (57). If the context forces a non-intentional interpretation of [/-c], the construction is unacceptable (58).

(55) *Das Monument ist unbedingt/schwierig zu erhalten.*
the monument is absolutely/easy to keep
'The monument must be/is easy to be kept in good shape.'

(56) a. *Das Stipendium ist leicht zu erhalten.*
the grant is easy to get
'The grant is easily available.'
b. ??*Das Stipendium ist unbedingt zu erhalten!*
the grant is absolutely to get

(57) a. *Das Stipendium ist leicht zu bekommen.*
the grant is easy to get
'The grant is easy to get.'
b. ??*Das Stipendium ist unbedingt zu bekommen.*
the grant is absolutely to get

(58) ??*Diese Farbe ist von der Wand zu erhalten/bekommen.*
this color is by the wall to get/get

Epistemic necessity is once more excluded:

(59) a. ??*Das Monument war notwendig zu erhalten.*
the monument was necessarily to keep
b. ??*Das Stipendium war notwendig zu erhalten/bekommen.*
the grant was necessarily to get/get
c. **Die Farbe ist von der Wand notwendig zu erhalten/bekommen*
the color is by the wall necessarily to get/get

1.2.6. Underspecified [+m]

Emotion verbs (60) behave exactly as they did in the prefixed participle. The [+m] role remains implicit, and the deontic reading is a bit unnatural, but possible. With sensation verbs (61), [+c-m] cannot be the implicit external argument. The implicit role must be [+m].

(60) a. *Diese Person ist nicht leicht zu lieben.*
this person is not easy to love
'This person is hard to love.'

b. *Diese Person ist zu lieben.*
this person is to love
'This person ought to be loved.'

(61) a. *Diese Sendung ist zu hören.*
this program is to hear
'This program ought to be heard.'
b. *Dieser Ton ist kaum zu hören.*
this sound is hardly to hear
'This sound is hardly audible.'
c. *Der Ton ist (mit/*von den Ohren) zu hören.*
the sound is (with/by the ears) to hear
'The sound can be heard (with one's ears).'

The verbs in the intentional alternation once more exemplify the generalization that [/-m] cannot be an implicit argument. Only the intentional reading (62a) is available in the modal infinitive.

(62) a. *Eine Lösung ist unbedingt/leicht zu finden.*
a solution is absolutely/easy to find
'A solution ought to be/is hard to be found.'
b. **Ein Ende ist (vom Krieg) zu finden.*
an end is (by-the war) to find

With respect to epistemic modality, we find exactly the same pattern as with the participle: it is less deviant than in other cases, but still far from perfect.

(63) ?*Eine Lösung war notwendig zu finden.*
a solution was necessary to find
'A solution ought to be found/is hard to find.'

1.2.7. Mixed value clusters

Verbs that select an experiencer subject appear in the modal infinitive, but they exclude a deontic reading (64b). As with goal subject verbs above, the absence of the deontic reading seems to be related to the specification of the implicit role as [/-c].

(64) a. (?)*Der Schaden ist leicht zu erblicken.*
the damage is easy to catch-sight
'The damage is well visible.'
b. **Der Schaden ist unbedingt zu erblicken.*
the damage is absolutely to catch-sight

Verbs that select [+c-m] together with lexically frozen [+c] differ markedly from those that select underspecified [-m]. With *faszinieren* 'impress', the lexically frozen [+c] cluster can be accessed, and it easily co-occurs with [+c-m] in the *von* 'by'-PP in (65b). With verbs like *enthalten* 'contain' in (52) above, co-occurrence of saturated [+c] with [-m] is restricted to the present participle.

(65) a. *Das Publikum ist leicht zu faszinieren.*
the audience is easy to impress
'The audience is easy to impress.'
b. *Das Publikum ist mit dummen Witzen leicht zu faszinieren.*
the audience is with silly jokes easy to impress
'It is easy to impress the audience with silly jokes.'
c. ??*Das Publikum ist unbedingt zu faszinieren.*
the audience is absolutely to impress

Epistemic necessity is again excluded, if [+c-m] is the external argument (66a), and marginal with [-c+m] (66b).

(66) a. ??*Das Publikum war notwendig zu faszinieren.*
the audience was necessarily to impress
b. ?*Der Schaden war notwendig zu erblicken.*
the damage is necessarily to catch-sight

1.2.8. Summary

The following observations have been made about the infinitive under *sein* 'be'.

First, the implicit Θ-role must be compatible with an interpretation as [/+m]. The same holds for the prefixed participle.

Second, dispositional readings are generally possible. Deontic readings are generally impossible, if the implicit argument is specified as [/-c]. Epistemic necessity is unavailable, or at least significantly marginal. The same holds for the prefixed participle.

Third, role-absorption can sometimes access a lexically frozen [+c] cluster. Here we find a difference with respect to the prefixed participle. Lexically frozen [+c] can be the implicit argument of *faszinieren* 'impress', but not of *enthalten* 'contain'.

Forth, the locus of role absorption is equally uncertain as it was for the prefixed participle. Accessibility of some lexically frozen roles would support a lexical analysis, but a syntactic analysis seems preferable because of the overt trigger of absorption, the prefix *zu*.

Fifth, cluster distinctness applies. [+c] cannot be realized together with [-m], even if [+c] remains implicit. This property distinguishes the prefixed participle from the modal infinitive under *sein* 'be'.

1.3. Modal infinitives under *haben* ‚have'

The modal infinitive under *haben* 'have' differs significantly from its counterpart under *sein* 'be' in two respects. First, there is no role-blocking/absorption involved in the construction with *haben*. The infinitival verb retains its full role-assignment potential. Second, a dispositional reading is never available.

The infinitival prefix *zu* is present in all three constructions. This fact is potentially problematic for Toman's analysis, according to which *zu* is a marker of passivization (Toman 1986). If *zu* has the same syntactic status in all three constructions, Toman's analysis cannot be correct.

1.3.1. Intransitives

In contrast to both infinitives under *sein* 'be' and the prefixed participle, infinitives under *haben* 'have' are grammatical with unaccusative verbs.

(67) a. *Der Patient hat zu sterben.*
the patient has to die
'The patient must die.'
b. *Die Blume hat zu verwelken.*
the flower has to wilt
'The flower must wilt.'
c. *Die Lampe/die Person hat zu leuchten.*
the lamp/the person has to shine
'The torch must shine/the person must light the way.'
d. *Der Handwerker hat zu arbeiten.*
the craftsman is to work
'The craftsman must work.'

Epistemic readings are relatively easily available too (68). By contrast, none of the examples in (67) gives rise to anything like a dispositional reading.

(68) a. *Früher oder später hat jeder Mensch zu sterben.*
sooner or later has each human-being to die
'Sooner or later everybody must die.'
b. *Die Blume hatte bei dieser Hitze einfach zu verwelken.*
the flower had at that heat simply to wilt
'With that heat, it was inevitable that the flower wilted.'

1.3.2. Agents, causes, double causation, and the causative alternation

Agentive double causatives retain their full argument realization potential (69). Both [+c+m] and [+c-m] can be assigned to the subject. Likewise, causatives with an unaccusative alternant retain both uses under *haben* (70).

(69) a. *Wir haben den Balkon zu schmücken.*
we have the balcony to decorate
'We must decorate the balcony.'
b. *Blumen haben den Balkon zu schmücken.*
flowers have the balcony to decorate
'The balcony must be decorated with flowers.'

(70) a. *Wir haben das Dokument zu verbrennen.*
we have the document to burn
'We must burn the document.'
b. *Das Dokument hat zu verbrennen.*
the document has to burn
'The document must burn.'

It is interesting to observe that even the agentive use of *schmücken* 'decorate' allows an epistemic necessity reading, if such a reading is supported by the context (71a). With a reduced unaccusative, the epistemic reading is very natural (71b). By contrast, the dispositional reading has disappeared.

(71) a. *Der Nachbar hatte seinen Balkon einfach zu schmücken, das liegt so in seiner Natur.*
the neighbor had his balcony simply to decorate, this lies in his nature
'It was inevitable that the neighbor would decorate his balcony. That's in his nature.'
b. *Das Streichholz hatte wohl zu verbrennen.*
the match had well to burn
'It was inevitable that the match should burn.'

1.3.3. Underspecified [-m] and cluster distinctness

The alternation between [+c] and [-m] is fully retained under *haben*.

(72) a. *Er hat die Tasche zu tragen.*
he has the bag to carry
'He must carry the bag.'
b. *Das Dokument hat ein Siegel zu tragen.*
the document has a seal to bear
'The document must bear a seal.'

The modality of the construction is deontic, as in the examples above, or epistemic, as below. Dispositional readings are once more excluded.

(73) a. *Die Queen hatte einfach eine Tasche zu tragen – das macht sie immer.*
the queen had simply a bag to carry – that does she always
'It is inevitable that the queen would carry a bag – she always does.'
b. *Das Dokument hatte einfach ein Siegel zu tragen – das ist hier für alle so.*
the document had simply a seal to carry – that is here for all so
'It was inevitable that the document would bear a seal – all of them do.'
c. *Meerwasser hat einfach Salz zu enthalten.*
sea-water has simply salt to contain
'Sea-water must contain salt."

1.3.4. Underspecified [-c]

The alternating verb *erhalten* 'keep/get' can be used both in its causative (74), and in its non-causative form (75). Notice about the non-causative form that an intentional interpretation is not forced (75b). Once more, epistemic readings are available, and dispositional ones are not.

(74) *Das Institut hat das Monument zu erhalten.*
the institute has the monument to keep
'The institute must keep the monument in good shape.'

(75) a. *Er hat das Stipendium zu erhalten/bekommen.*
he has the grant to get/get
'He must get the grant.'
b. *Die Wand hat einen neuen Anstrich zu erhalten/bekommen.*
the wall has a new coating to get/get
'The wall must get a new coating.'

1.3.5. Underspecified [+m]

The same can be observed in the class that selects [+m]. Under *haben*, these verbs retain their full role realization potential. In particular, sensation verbs can (marginally) assign [+c-m] to the subject (76), and the verbs in the intentional alternation can assign [-m] (77). Once more, epistemic readings are available, dispositional ones are not.

(76) a. *Er hatte die Sendung zu hören.*
he had the program to hear
'He had to listen to the program.'
b. ?*Alle Ohren hatten das zu hören.*
all ears had that to hear
'That had to be generally audible.'

(77) a. *Sie haben eine Lösung zu finden.*
they have a solution to find
'They must find a solution.'
b. *Der Krieg hat ein Ende zu finden.*
the war has an end to find
'The war must come to an end.'

1.3.6. Mixed value clusters

Likewise for mixed value clusters. The verbs behave exactly as they do as finite main verbs. There are no additional restrictions with respect to the availability of roles. Once more, epistemic readings are available, dispositional ones are not.

(78) a. *Er hatte den Schaden zu erblicken.*
he had the damage to catch-sight
'He had to become aware of the damage.'
b. *Sie hatten das Publikum zu faszinieren.*
they had the audience to impress
'They had to impress the audience.'

1.3.7. Summary

The following observations have been made about the infinitive under *haben* 'have'. First, the external Θ-role is assigned, not absorbed. Second, dispositional readings are generally impossible. Deontic and epistemic readings are available. We can now extend the initial observations (43) as follows:

(79)
- prefixed participle:
  covertness of the internal argument
  presence of /*d*/
  absorption of the external Θ-role
  dispositional/deontic modality
- infinitive under *sein* 'be':
  raising of the internal argument
  absence of /*d*/
  absorption of the external Θ-role
  dispositional/deontic modality
- infinitive under *haben* 'have':
  raising of the subject (internal or external)
  absence of /*d*/
  no role absorption
  deontic/epistemic modality
- argument-blocking *zu* correlates with dispositional/deontic modality
- non-blocking *zu* correlates with deontic/epistemic modality

1.4. Morphology, syntax and ARB-interpretation

Toman (1986) argues that the infinitival prefix *zu* is responsible for the reduced argument assignment potential of the prefixed participle and of the infinitive under *sein* 'be'. It is a passivizing affix. This analysis implies that *zu* has a different status in infinitives under *haben* 'have'. Indeed there is independent evidence regarding the presence of a syntactic tense head in support of such a distinction. Neither the present participle, nor infinitives under *sein* 'be' show any convincing sign of T. Infinitives under *haben* 'have', by contrast, do. It will be argued that *zu* merges with T, if T is present. If T is absent, *zu* merges with v.

1.4.1. Against T in the participle, and under sein *'be'*

The present participle does not tolerate any overt tense marker. Absence of T thus seems to be the null hypothesis. However, one might want to argue that the presence of temporal modifiers in examples like (80) supports the presence of T.

(80) a. *der **seit gestern** malende Anstreicher*
the since yesterday paint.ND.AGR painter
'the painter who has been working since yesterday'
b. *der **heute** wiederum sinkende Kontostand*
the today again fall.ND.AGR account-balance
'the account balance that is falling again today'
c. *der **nächste Woche** voraussichtlich sterbende Patient*
the next week presumably die.ND.AGR patient
'the patient who will presumably pass away during the coming week'

This is not conclusive evidence, though, because similar modifiers are equally well possible in noun phrases, and with underived adjectives. Unless one is prepared to posit a T node in DP and AP, (80) does not tell us anything about the presence of tense in the present participle.

(81) a. *der **seit gestern** stolze Vater Gordon*
the since yesterday proud.AGR father Gordon
'Gordon – since yesterday the proud father of a child –'
b. *die **morgige** Zeitung*
the tomorrow.AGR paper
'tomorrow's newspaper'
c. *eine **heute** vollkommen wertlose Münze*
a today completely worthless.AGR coin
'a coin that is absolutely worthless today'

If the presence of temporal modifiers does not show the presence of T in the present participle, then maybe temporal reference does. After all, the temporal reference of the participle is not determined by the containing clause. In (82a), a simultaneous reading is most natural. In (82b), the event denoted by the participle precedes, and in (82c) it follows the matrix event. One could argue that independent temporal reference entails the presence of T.

(82) a. *Der schwer leidende Patient wurde ins Spital gebracht.*
the heavily suffering patient was to-the hospital taken
b. *Der gestern noch schwer leidende Student wurde heute schon wieder in einer Disco gesichtet.*
the yesterday still heavily suffering student was today already again in a disco seen
c. *Die im Nachhinein sicher wieder weinende Person intrigiert gerade eben noch fröhlich.*
the in-the aftermath certainly again crying person plots now still happily
'The person who, for sure, will by crying again later, is still plotting happily at the moment.'

Once more though, these facts are not conclusive evidence for the postulation of a T head. The same effects of temporal ordering can be observed with underived adjectives, as long as the adjective denotes a stage level property (Carlson 1977). The stage at which the property is true of the modified noun may vary with context: in (83a) the simultaneous reading is most natural. In (83b) the state *worthless* precedes the matrix event, and in (83c) it follows.

(83) a. *Eine müde Katze liegt am Weg.*
a tired cat lies on-the road
'A tired cat is lying on the road.'
b. *Das gestern noch wertlose Grundstück wurde heute um 3 Millionen verkauft.*
the yesterday still worthless estate was today for 3 million sold
'The estate that had been worthless yesterday was sold for 3 million today.'

c. *Die morgen wertlose Münze ist heute noch gesetzliches Zahlungsmittel.*
the tomorrow worthless coin is today still legal tender
'The coin that will be worthless tomorrow is still legal tender today.'

In the absence of further evidence, we must stick to the null hypothesis and conclude that the German present participle is untensed.[5]

Conclusive evidence can be found for the absence of tense. Recall that epistemic necessity is systematically excluded in the prefixed participle. Under *sein* 'be' there are some less offending examples, but they are still far from perfect. This initially puzzling observation finds an immediate explanation, once we adopt the claim that different types of modal operators are located in different syntactic positions. If it is true that epistemic operators are located at a high position in the functional/inflectional domain of the clause (Erb 2001; Kratzer 1991; Wurmbrand 2001), then the absence of a syntactic T node predicts the absence of epistemic readings.

1.4.2. Infinitives under haben *'have' are tensed*

The availability of epistemic readings in turn entails the presence of T. The fact that infinitives under *haben* 'have' systematically allow epistemic readings is thus evidence for the presence of T.

In addition to modal readings, the presence of T is supported by an observation in Haider (1984): while the nominative in the modal *sein*-construction must correspond to the internal argument of the infinitival verb, the nominative in the *haben*-construction corresponds to the syntactic subject of the infinitival verb. This can be either an external (84a), or an internal argument (84b). Even passivization is possible (84c).

(84) a. *Die Regierung hat zu arbeiten.*
the government has to work
'The government must work.'

b. *Die Blume hat zu verwelken.*
the flower has to wilt
'The flower must wilt.'

c. *Der Kunde hat rasiert zu werden.*
the client has shaved to be
'The client must be shaved.'

If the subject of the *haben*-construction raises from [Spec, T], then these facts follow immediately, and the analysis is additionally compatible with general assumptions about the syntax of modality.

1.4.3. The position of zu*, and its role in role-absorption*

To summarize, we have so far found a correlation between the presence of T, and thematic role absorption. If T is present, a prefixed infinitival verb retains its full role assignment potential. If T is absent, the external role remains implicit, and a number of additional conditions apply. With this correlation in mind, let us re-consider Toman's (1986) analysis of the prefix *zu* as a passivizing morpheme.

Notice first that *zu* always attaches to the highest infinitival verb in a given cluster. This distribution is accounted for on the assumption that *zu* merges with T, if T is present (Haiden 1997). If *zu* merges with T, then it does not interfere with the assignment of thematic roles. It marks infinitival tense.

(85) a. *Er verspricht, den Knödel zu essen.*
he promises the dumpling to eat
'He promises to eat the dumpling.'
b. *Er gibt an, den Knödel essen zu wollen.*
he claims PRT the dumpling eat to want
'He claims he wants to eat the dumpling.'
c. *Er gibt an, den Knödel gegessen zu haben.*
he claims PRT the dumpling eaten to have
'He claims he has eaten the dumpling.'
d. *Er gibt an, den Knödel essen wollen zu haben.*
he claims PRT the dumpling eat want to have
'He claims he wanted to eat the dumpling.'

If T is absent, *zu* merges with the highest available head, i.e., with v. Now recall the Main Thematic Condition, repeated as (86).

(86) Main Thematic Condition
Θ is assigned to [/-V] by [/-N].

This condition assigns a special status to the category P. Specified as [-V, -N] it can act as a role assignor, but it can likewise be an assignee. In the discussion of chapter 3, we have only come across prepositions as role-assignors. What would happen if an intransitive P like the infinitival prefix receives a Θ-role? The preposition itself cannot be interpreted as an argument, because it does not refer. On the standard assumptions that Θ-role assignment is strictly local, i.e., that Θ-roles do not move, the only option is saturation.

(87) Saturation Corollary
If Θ_i is assigned to intransitive P, then saturation must apply to Θ_i.

If *zu* merges with v, this is exactly the configuration that obtains. The external Θ-role is assigned to P and must be bound by an operator. This requirement in turn allows us to understand the correlation between argument-blocking *zu* and modal readings. The modal operator serves to bind the Θ-role assigned to *zu*.

1.4.4. Arbitrarization and the interpretation of implicit roles

Saturation of thematic roles is subject to a number of additional conditions. Building on Chierchia (1995), Marelj (2004) argues that the implicit thematic role in middle constructions is subject to an operation of *arbitrarization*:

> [U]nlike the variable introduced by ordinary saturation - the variable introduced by Arbitrarization (here either existential or generic) comes in with a built-in domain restriction, indicated by a special subscript 'arb'. With the application of ARB-saturation, the set of individuals is restricted pragmatically and contextually – as it is in the case of passive saturation– with the special properties of *arb* being that a) it cannot be made referential and b) it ranges over groups of humans (+human). [...] Thus, the ARB-saturation (either generic or existential) introduces a special type of variable – x_{arb} or index *arb*, which ranges over groups of humans (Marelj 2004:202).

Marelj's implementation of arbitrarization differs from Chierchia's in that it does not make reference to the reflexive clitic. It thus generalizes to the

German infinitival constructions discussed here. The only relevant difference is that the implicit role is bound by a modal operator in the constructions discussed here. (88) is adapted from (131) in Marelj (2004:202).

(88) Arbitrarization
OP x_{arb} [P (x_{arb})]

If the implicit thematic role of the prefixed participle and the infinitive under *sein* 'be' is subject to arbitrarization, then it is immediately clear why [/-m] is excluded as an implicit role. The sortal restriction to groups of humans is incompatible with [/-m].

The sortal restriction introduced by arbitrarization is relevant in another respect. Recall that the present participle allows the simultaneous realization of indistinguishable clusters [+c] and [-m]. The following example is interpreted as an obligation for some intentional agent to acquire or award seals for each document. The *von* 'by' phrase does not identify the agent, but the [-m] argument.

(89) *das von jedem Dokument zu tragende Siegel*
the by each document to carry.ND-AGR seal
'the seal that must be born by each document'

Because of the sortal restriction it introduces, arbitrarization renders [+c] distinct from [-m]. For this reasoning to apply, it is necessary to assume, though, that the condition of cluster distinctness applies to a full predicate, after arbitrarization. Cluster distinctness is then comparable in its status to the Θ-criterion. Let us assume that this is the case.

1.4.5. On the morpho-syntactic status of /n/ *and* /d/

Recall another correlation we have found between the affix */d/* and the presence of overt arguments. In the presence of */d/*, the highest (non arbitrized) argument of V remains covert. In the absence of */d/*, the argument is realized by an overt DP. The generalization is illustrated in (90). In (90a), an external role is assigned, but no overt subject is present. In (90b), only an internal role is assigned, but no overt internal argument is present. In (90c), */d/* is absent, and the internal argument shows up as a nominative DP.

(90) a. *ein [Häuser bauen**d**er] Bauer*
a houses build.ND-AGR farmer
'a farmer who is building houses'
b. *ein [zu bauen**d**es] Haus*
a to build.ND-AGR house
'a house that ought to be built'
c. ***Das Haus*** *ist zu bauen.*
the house is to build
'The house ought to be built.'

This distribution suggests that the suffix */d/* in fact realizes the apparently covert argument. In other words, the morpheme */d/* does not only look like, it is a relative pronoun (on the morpho-syntax of German determiners and relative pronouns, cf. Giusti 1995; Löbel 1990; Wiltschko 1998). The present participle is then analyzed as a reduced relative clause (on participial relative clauses of various sizes in French and Hebrew, cf. Siloni 1995). Now, the alternation of */d/* with overt DP can be related to the formal requirements of verbs, i.e., subcategorization. The D-feature of v is checked against the D-head */d/* in the present participle. If raising into the matrix licenses an overt DP, then */d/* remains absent (90c).

A similar reasoning applies to the infinitival suffix */n/* too. Let us assume that infinitival */n/* is an *alternative realization* of an internal argument in the sense of Emonds (1987, 2000). Its category is N. If a Θ-role is assigned to */n/*, then it must be referentially identified by a locally c-commanding DP.[6]

1.4.6. Derivations

In an unprefixed present participle, the derivation is now straightforward. The internal Θ-role is assigned to an accusative DP via its alternative realization */n/*. If V is marked with a D-feature by the marking conventions, then the overt D-head of the accusative must check this feature. The external role is assigned to */d/*.

(91) present participle: transitive, unprefixed

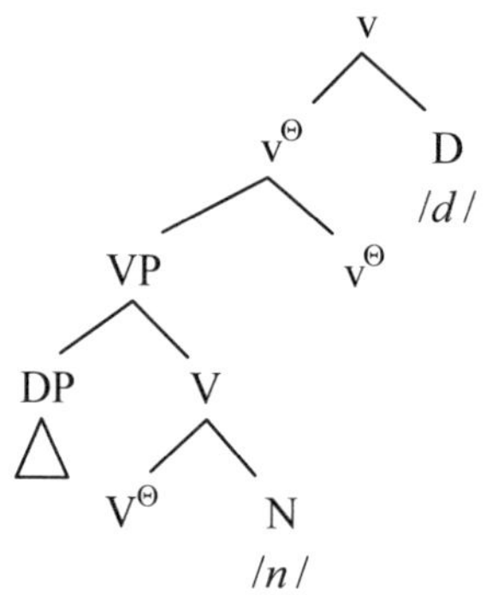

If the base verb is unaccusative, then /*d*/ acts as an identifier of /*n*/. D then raises to v, exactly as it does in a finite environment.

(92) present participle: unaccusative, unprefixed

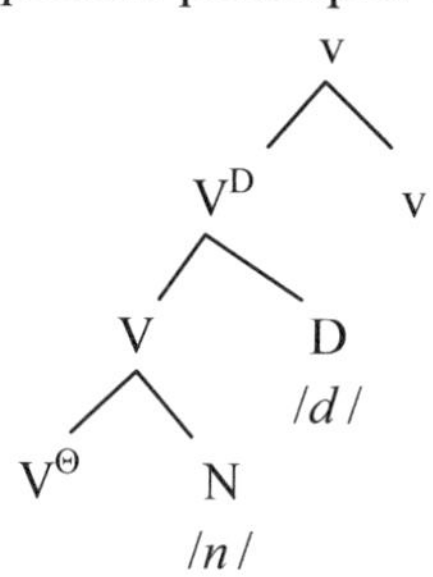

Now imagine that the /*d*/ identifies /*n*/ as its alternative realization, but the base verb is transitive. Since /*d*/ cannot be assigned two Θ-roles at a time, the external Θ-role must be saturated, and this is accomplished by the insertion of the prefix *zu*. Notice that P must merge with v before D raises from V. Otherwise, the external Θ-role would be assigned to D, rather than P. Notice also that v linearly precedes V in the tree below. This is a mere artifact of the two-dimensional tree format. As an interpretation of the verbal stem, v occupies the same linear position as the stem.

The analysis of /*d*/ as a relative pronoun predicts the contrast between the prefixed participle and the infinitive under *sein* 'be' with respect to impersonal constructions. An impersonal construction is impossible for the participle, because the suffix /*d*/ is a (referential) relative pronoun, not an expletive.

(93) present participle: transitive, prefixed

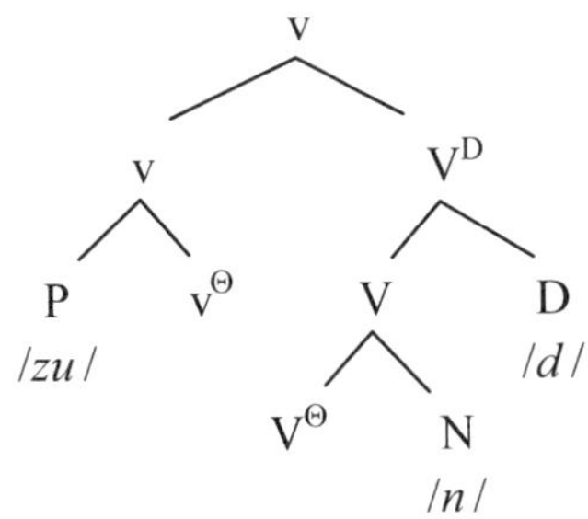

An infinitive under *sein* 'be' projects exactly the same structure, with the minimal difference that an overt DP identifies the infinitival suffix /*n*/ as its alternative realization. After checking the D-feature of the embedded v, DP raises into the matrix subject position.

(94) infinitive under *sein* 'be'

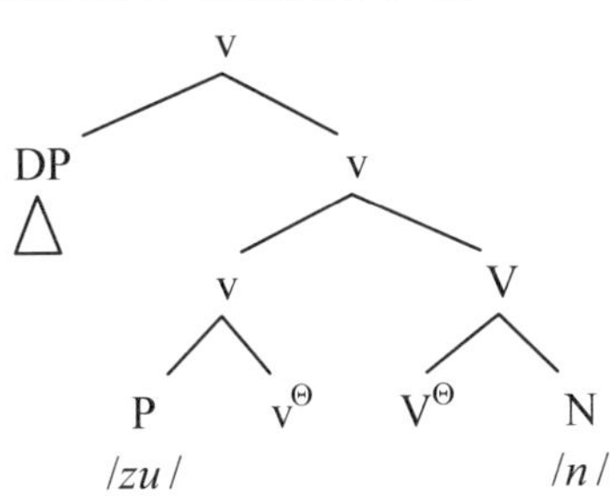

An infinitive under *haben* 'have' projects T, and the specifier of embedded T raises into the matrix clause. Consider as an example an unaccusative verb. The overt DP receives an internal Θ-role via its alternative realization /*n*/. It checks the D-feature of v (raised to T), then moves into [Spec, T]. From there, it raises further on, into the matrix subject position. With a transitive infinitive, the accusative DP (invisible for v) identifies the infinitival suffix as its alternative realization, and v (raised to T) assigns an external Θ-role to the nominative.

(95) Unaccusative infinitive under *haben* 'have'

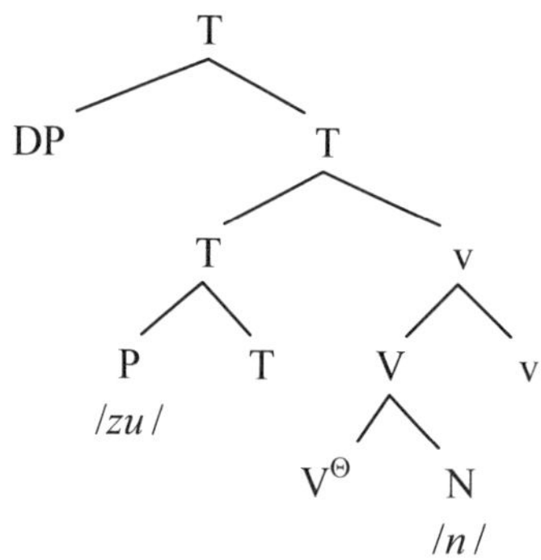

Notice that the preposition *zu* is not assigned a Θ-role in this configuration. However, it still marks the scope of the modal operator. On the standard assumption (Erb 2001; Kratzer 1991) that epistemic operators are located in the functional/inflectional domain of the clause, and that dispositional operators are located in the lexical domain, the structural difference between (95) and (93), (94) predicts that (95) has an epistemic reading and lacks a dispositional one, and that (93), (94) have dispositional readings, but disallow an epistemic one.

1.5. Intermediate conclusion

This concludes the first part of this chapter. In a nutshell, it has been argued that the present participle projects vP, and that its formal features are checked by the suffixes /*n*/ and /*d*/, respectively. The prefixed present participle was analyzed in parallel with modal infinitives under *sein* 'be'. In both constructions, the infinitival prefix /*zu*/ merges with v and triggers arbitrarization of the external Θ-role. Constraints on the availability of specific modalities were attributed to the size of the infinitival/participial projection. In the absence of T, epistemic readings are excluded. Modal *haben* 'have' was analyzed as a raising verb that takes a TP complement.

2. Constructions with the second participle

2.1. Auxiliary selection, intransitive motion and lexical reflexivization

Recall the causative alternation discussed in chapters 2 and 3, with a standard example like the following:

(96) a. *Hans rollt den Ball ins Tor.*
Hans rolls the ball in-the goal
b. *Der Ball rollt ins Tor.*
the ball rolls in-the goal

A consequence of decausativization that has been noted, but not discussed so far is the selection of the auxiliary *sein* 'be' in the perfect tense. A transitive causative selects *haben* 'have'.

(97) a. *Hans hat den Ball ins Tor gerollt.*
Hans has the ball in-the goal rolled
b. *Der Ball ist ins Tor gerollt.*
the ball is in-the goal rolled

This effect on auxiliary selection is fully regular, and therefore interesting. It is exemplified here with a thematically alternating [+c] verb in (98), a morphologically alternating [+c] verb in (99), and with a psychological predicate in (100).

(98) a. *Hans hat seinen Bauernhof verbrannt.*
Hans has his farm-house burned
'Hans burned down his farm-house.'

b. *Der Bauernhof ist verbrannt.*
the farm-house is burned
'The farm-house burned down.'

(99) a. *Hans hat die Ausgaben gesenkt.*
Hans has the expenses lowered
'Hans lowered the expenses.'
b. *Die Ausgaben sind gesunken.*
the expenses are lowered
'The expenses fell.'

(100) a. *Helene hat Hans erschreckt.*
Helene has Hans scared
'Helene scared Hans.'
b. *Hans ist erschrocken.*
Hans is scared
'Hans got scared.'

Anti-causative unaccusatives select *sein* 'be'. The same holds for underived unaccusatives. The verb *verdursten* 'die of thirst' assigns underspecified [-c]. It is unaccusative because of a D-feature triggered by the presence of lexically frozen [+c-m] cluster, *verwelken* 'wilt' is unaccusative, because its single Θ-role is fully specified [-c-m]. Both verbs select the auxiliary *sein* 'be'.

(101) a. *Der Wanderer ist verdurstet.*
the rambler is died-of-thirst
'The rambler died of thirst.'
b. *Die Blume ist verwelkt.*
the flower is wilted
'The flower wilted.'

The following generalization emerges from these facts:

(102) Select *sein* 'be' as a perfect tense auxiliary, if
- the verb requires an internal argument, and
- it assigns no more than one structural role.

2.1.1. Motion verbs and lexical reflexivization

This generalization is widely accepted (den Besten 1989; Diedrichsen 2002; Grewendorf 1989; Haider 1993), and indeed the selection of *sein* 'be' is often considered a test for unaccusativity. Unfortunately, (102) is challenged by the behavior of manner of motion verbs (Levin and Rappaport Hovav 1995). Consider the following contrast:

(103) a. *Hans ist nach Paris gefahren.*
Hans is to Paris driven
'Hans went to Paris.'
b. *Hans hat seinen Wagen an die Wand gefahren.*
Hans has his car at the wall driven
'Hans drove his car against the wall.'

The verb *fahren* 'drive/go' in (103b) is a completely regular transitive verb. It takes an external argument that is in volitional control of the event, and an internal argument that is affected by the event. Notice that the subject does not need to be affected by the event. If *Hans* drove his car against the wall very slowly, then only the car hits the wall, but *Hans* does not. If the direct object is a remotely controlled toy car, then the subject is not even affected by the motion that precedes the impact.

(103a) is very different. The sentence asserts that the subject *Hans* actually was in Paris. The subject is affected by a change of location. This suggests that the subject of (103a) realizes the role that is assigned to the object in (103b). At the same time, the subject of (103a) exhibits features that are otherwise typical of a volitional agent. For example, an imperative is very natural (104), but even then, the agent must be affected by a change of location too. The intransitive manner of motion verb *fahren* 'drive' assigns both a agent, and a theme-role to its subject.

(104) *Fahr nach Paris!*
drive to Paris
'Go to Paris!'

The observation that manner of motion verbs can assign two roles in conjunction is, of course, not new. It goes back at least to Gruber (1965), Jackendoff (1972). In the Theta System, the assignment of two roles to a single argument requires reflexivization. Two clusters can only be assigned to a single argument, if they have been bundled.

The locus of reflexivization is parametrized. Marelj (2004), Reinhart and Siloni (2005) argue that it is a syntactic operation in German. Their analysis is supported by the evidence discussed in chapters 2 and 3 above. Unfortunately, it does not extend to manner of motion verbs. The reason is that syntactic reflexivization must be marked by a reflexive clitic, which checks the formal features of V. The absence of a reflexive clitic with manner of motion verbs shows that these verbs are not reflexivized in syntax. Reflexivization must have applied in the lexicon.

(105) The Lex-Syn Parameter ((4) in Reinhart and Siloni 2005)
UG allows thematic arity operations to apply in the lexicon or in syntax.

Both Marelj (2004) and Reinhart and Siloni (2005) argue that languages make a global choice between lexical vs. syntactic application of arity operations. If this is true, then exceptional lexical application of reflexivization of manner of motion verbs is impossible. There is evidence, though, that the strong claim of a global parameter must be adapted. I suggest a separation into an option provided by UG, and a global parameter as follows:

(106) The Lex-Syn Parameter
UG allows thematic arity operations to apply in the lexicon or in syntax.
Language L allows arity operations to apply in syntax (yes/no).

A modification along the lines of (106) is necessary in the first place, because the Projection Principle (the Lexicon Interface Guideline in Reinhart and Siloni 2005) excludes syntactic reduction. If a thematic role is eliminated altogether, this operation must take place in the lexicon even in those languages that reflexivize their predicates in syntax. Similar considerations apply with respect to the adjectival passive, which must be derived in the lexicon (cf. Horvath and Siloni 2005; Wasow 1977, and section 2.2.4 below).

In addition, there is specific evidence to the effect that the reflexivization of German manner of motion verbs is a lexical operation. First, the set of verbs affected by reflexivization is lexically constrained. Verbs like *fahren* 'drive' and many verbs of bodily motion have a reflexive alternant, but others like *pilotieren* 'to pilot' do not.

(107) a. *Hans pilotierte den Airbus.*
Hans piloted the Airbus
'Hans piloted the Airbus.'
b. ??*Hans pilotierte (nach Paris).*
Hans piloted to Paris

Second, reflexive manner of motion verbs are subject to semantic drive. In some cases, the reflexive alternant has a slightly different meaning than the transitive one. In the case of *fahren* 'drive', this is already obvious in the translation. The transitive alternant corresponds to English *drive*, the reflexive one can mean both *drive* and *go*. I conclude that German manner of motion verbs are lexical reflexives.

2.1.2. Formal vs. thematic features: deriving dialectal variation in auxiliary selection

Reinhart and Siloni (2005) assume that lexical reflexivization eliminates the accusative feature of V (here, the D-feature of V). This assumption is necessary to derive the unergative syntax of lexically derived reflexives like English *shave*, *wash*, etc. The bundled roles of these verbs must be assigned to an external argument. If this assumption exhausts the facts, then German intransitive manner of motion verbs must be unergative, and select the auxiliary *haben* 'have'. This is wrong.

Fortunately, the elimination of the D-feature of V does not exhaust the facts. In section 7 of Reinhart and Siloni (2005), a distinction is introduced between thematic and formal case features. In the framework developed in chapter 3 above, this distinction corresponds to the difference between formal subcategorization features (N for V, D for v) and the thematically determined D-feature of V. By its very nature, lexical reflexivization can only eliminate the thematically determined D-feature of V. The formal features of verbal heads cannot be affected by a lexical operation. Chapter 3 furthermore adopted Hale and Keyser's (1992, 1993) analysis of unergatives as formally transitive verbs. A verb can only be unergative in this theory, if its lexical entry contains an N-morpheme to check the N-feature of V. The distinction between formal vs. thematic subcategorization features accounts for the auxiliary selection of German intransitive manner of motion verbs in the following way.

Reflexivization applies in the lexicon. It bundles the two Θ-roles of the verb, and its eliminates its D-feature. Now recall that the present theory differs from the standard model of the Theta System in one crucial respect. Lexical operations are not operations in the strict sense. They are generalizations over pairs of lexical entries. The "output" of a lexicon operation is still listed. In fact, lexically derived alternants regularly differ from the base in a number of respects (Siloni 2002). For example, chapters 2 and 3 discussed cases where the reduced alternant selects a different preposition for its stimulus role than the base verb (108).

(108) a. *Hans erschrak **vor** dem Gespenst.*
Hans scared before the ghost
'Hans got scared by the ghost.'
b. *Helene erschreckte Hans **mit** einem lauten Schrei.*
Helene scared Hans with a loud scream
'Helene scared Hans by screaming out loud.'

The same may apply to expletive N. If a lexically reflexivized verb lists expletive N, then it is syntactically realized as an unergative verb. If it does not list expletive N, then it must be unaccusative, because its only argument must check the formal N-feature of V.

If the syntactic realization of a lexically derived German reflexive depends on a lexical choice, the presence vs. absence of expletive N in the entry of a given verb, then we predict the existence of inter-speaker variation. As a matter of fact, such variation does not only exist: it has been noted as a long-standing problem for the theory of auxiliary selection (Diedrichsen 2002). Consider the following examples:

(109) a. *%Hans ist geklettert.*
Hans is climbed
b. *%Hans hat geklettert.*
Hans has climbed
'Hans climbed.'

In some varieties of German, reflexivized motion verbs must select *sein* 'be'. In other varieties, *haben* 'have' is preferred. The choice is sometimes determined by aspectual properties (Hoekstra and Mulder 1990). Speakers who prefer *haben* 'have' in (109) would rather use *sein* 'be' in the presence of a directional PP. In other words, speakers who can use *klettern* 'climb' as an unergative have the option of realizing it as an unaccusative too.

(110) *Das Kind ist auf den Stuhl geklettert.*
the child is on the chair climbed
'The child climbed onto the chair.'

By contrast, the speakers who use *sein* 'be' (109) do not have an aspectually determined choice. Even in a non-terminative context, *sein* 'be' must be used:

(111) *Hans ist wochenlang im Velebit geklettert.*
Hans is weeks-long in-the Velebit climbed
'Hans has been climbing for weeks in the Velebit area.'

If the unergative use, and consequently the selction of *haben* 'have' depends on lexical specification, the presence of expletive N, then the restricted options in the *sein* 'be'-dialect are expected. In this dialect, the argument of intransitive manner of motion verbs must merge VP-internally to check the formal N-feature of V. Generalization (102) is no longer challenged, but rather supported by the behavior of intransitive manner of motion verbs.

2.2. The second participle

Syntactically, at least three different participles are distinguished in the literature (Kratzer 1994; Rapp 1997): an active perfect participle (112a), a passive participle (112b), and an adjectival participle (112c).

(112) a. *Der Nachbar hat seinen Hof überdacht.*
the neighbor has his yard covered
'The neighbor built a roof over his yard.'
b. *Der Hof wurde überdacht.*
the yard was covered
'The yard was covered with a roof.'

c. *Der Hof ist überdacht.*
the yard is covered
'The yard is covered with a roof.'

The empirical basis for such a distinction is not conclusive, though. The different properties of perfect tense, verbal passive and adjectival passive could just as well follow from properties of the auxiliary (for discussion cf. Müller 2002). This approach is preferable for two major reasons. First, there is no morphological difference between perfect, passive and adjectival participles (cf. section 2.2.3). Second, the set of verbs that allows verbal participles is different from the set that allows adjectival participles. In particular, some verb classes do not have a verbal passive participle, but they do have an adjectival participle. The adjectival participle therefore cannot be derived from the verbal passive participle (cf. section 2.2.1). Third, the three participle-types have inconsistent properties depending on their syntactic environment. In particular, the attributive pre-nominal participle has the morpho-syntactic distribution of an adjective, but it obeys lexical-semantic and aspectual conditions that are typical of a verbal participle (cf. section 2.2.2). It will therefore be argued that the three participle-types are essentially the same object morphologically. For German, this position goes back at least to Toman (1986); cf. Müller (2002) for a review of the literature.

2.2.1. Verb sets

If there is a grammatically significant distinction between an adjectival and a verbal participle, then it makes sense to assume that the adjectival participle is derived from the verbal one (Kratzer 1994). This approach suggests that the set of verbs that appear as adjectival participles is a subset of the verbs that appear as verbal participles (Müller 2002). Incidentally, this is a wrong generalization. Certain, thematically definable sets of verbs appear in the adjectival passive, but they do not have a well-formed verbal passive (Haiden to appear); on a similar argument for English and Hebrew cf. Horvath and Siloni (2005). Consider the following contrasts. The (a) examples illustrate the adjectival passive, the (b) examples illustrate the verbal passive, which requires the auxiliary *werden* 'become/be'.

(113) a. *In der Kanne ist Wasser enthalten.*
in the jar is water contained
'The jar contains water.'
b. **Wasser wird (in/von der Kanne) enthalten.*
water is in/by the jar contained

(114) a. *Das Publikum ist fasziniert.*
the audience is impressed
b. ??*Das Publikum wird (gerade) fasziniert.*
the audience is (at-the-moment) impressed

The generalization (to be discussed in section 2.3.2) is that the implicit argument of a verbal passive cannot be [/-m]. In an adjectival passive, this is possible.

2.2.2. *Verbal participles with an adjectival distribution*

A number of constraints that apply in the adjectival, as opposed to the verbal passive have been attributed to the adjectival nature of the participle (Emonds 2000; Kratzer 2000; Wasow 1977). If this reasoning is correct, then the same constraints should apply, when the adjectival participle is used as an attributive modifier of N. However, Rapp (1997) observes that this is not the case. In several respects, the attributive participle patterns with the verbal, rather than the adjectival passive. For example, activity verbs do not form an adjectival passive (115a), but they appear as prenominal modifiers (115b), and in the verbal passive (115c); examples (a-b) from Rapp (1997:222), gloss and translation by MH.

(115) a. **Der Wagen war von einem jungen Mann geschoben.*
the cart was by a young man pushed
b. *der von einem jungen Mann geschobene Wagen*
the by a young man pushed cart
'the cart that was pushed by a young man'
c. *Der Wagen wurde von einem jungen Mann geschoben.*
the cart was by a young man pushed
'The cart was pushed by a young man.'

The same holds for sensation (116), emotions (117), cognitive states (118) and non-causative psychological change of state verbs (119). They do not allow an adjectival passive (a), but they appear as prenominal modifiers (b), and in the verbal passive (c); all (a/b) examples (excl. gloss and translation) from Rapp (1997:222-223).

(116) a. **Das Lied war von den Zuschauern gehört.*
the song was by the audience heard
b. *das von den Zuschauern gehörte Lied*
the by the audience heard song
'the song that was heard by the audience'
c. *Das Lied wurde von den Zuschauern gehört.*
the song was by the audience heard
'The song was heard by the audience.'

(117) a. **Sie war von allen gehasst.*
she was by all hated
b. *die von allen gehasste Frau*
the by all hated woman
'the woman whom everybody hated'
c. *Die Frau wurde von allen gehasst.*
the woman was by all hated
'The woman was hated by everybody.'

(118) a. **Die Frau ist von allen gekannt.*
the woman is by all known
b. *die von allen gekannte Frau*
the by all known woman
'the woman whom everybody knows'
c. *Die Frau wird von allen gekannt.*
the woman is by everybody known
'The woman is known by/to everybody.'

(119) a. **Die Berge sind von den Reisenden erblickt.*
the mountains are by the tourists caught-sight
b. *die von den Reisenden erblickten Berge*
the by the tourists caught-sight mountains
'the mountains the tourists caught sight of'

c. *Die Berge wurden von den Reisenden erblickt.*
the mountains were by the tourists caught-sight
'The mountains were seen by the tourists.'

Rapp (1997:331-339) concludes that the pre-nominal participle cannot be an adjective. Following Toman (1986), she assumes it is a feature-neutralized category [+V]. This rather non-standard assumption can be avoided, if the more limited distribution of the adjectival passive is attributed to properties of the copula, rather than the adjectival participle. It would then be possible to keep the properties of the participle relatively constant. The fact that different participle-types do not exhibit a morphological opposition underlines the desirability of this goal.

2.2.3. Morphology

Morphologically, these three participles cannot be distinguished. The second participle generally consists of three morpho-phonological constituents: a prefix, a stem and a suffix. The prefix is usually /g/ (120a), but it can be any other unstressed verbal prefix (120b), including incorporated prepositions like *über-* 'over/above' in *über-setzen* 'translate' (120c). It can even be a non-morphemic pre-stress string, as in *trom-peten* 'to trumpet' in (120d). Word stress is indicated by bold-face.

(120)		infinitive	participle	
	a.	*schr**ei**ben*	*ge-schr**ie**ben*	'write'
	b.	*ver-schr**ei**ben*	*ver-schr**ie**ben*	'mis-spell/ prescribe'
	c.	*über-s**e**tzen*	*über-s**e**tzt*	'translate'
	d.	*trom-p**e**ten*	*trom-p**e**tet*	'trumpet'

The crucial generalization is that there must be at least one pronounced vowel to the left of the main stress of the verbal stem. This generalization is due to Kiparsky (1966), although it is stated in the opposite direction there. Kiparsky is interested in the rules governing the presence (or absence) of /g/ and states that the prefix must immediately precede the syllable that bears word stress. In the second participle, the position to the left of word-stress is occupied either by /g/, or by any other string. It is never phonologically empty. In both the infinitive and the past tense stem, the stressed syllable does not require a prosodic constituent to its left. Following among others Abraham (2004), Bok-Bennema (1994), I assume the prosodic prefix is interpreted as an element of category P that is involved in the derivation of participial aspect (Kratzer 2000).

Regarding the stem, the question is whether it supports the projection of v. If v is projected by the participle, then the participle itself assigns an external Θ-role. However, a large body of literature converges to the conclusion that the second participle cannot independently assign an external Θ-role (Broekhuis and van Dijk 1995; Emonds 2000, 2003; Hoekstra 1984; Kratzer 1996; Roberts 1985). I therefore conclude that v is not present in the second participle.

If the second participle projects V, but not v, then it must check a formal N-feature. It does not need to check a D-feature. Therefore, an overt internal argument does not need to be present, if a semantically vacuous N-morpheme is available. Let us assume with Emonds (2000, 2003) that "the entry for *-en* stipulates (only) that it 'alternatively realises' ϕ-features of objects" (Emonds 2003).

(121) second participle

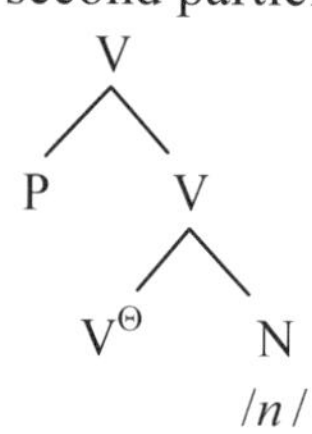

The structure in (121) immediately contradicts the standard analysis of the second participle in Baker, Johnson and Roberts (1989), according to which the participial suffix *en* is an element in Infl that absorbs the external Θ-role. Without going into detail here, notice that the main arguments endorsed by Baker, Johnson and Roberts are based on the presence of an external Θ-role in syntax, not on a morphological analysis of *en*. Morphologically, *en* is clearly an affix of V. With respect to the external Θ-role, the following section defends an account that is compatible with the data in Baker, Johnson and Roberts (1989), but extends to prenominal adjectival participles, where neither Infl, nor an external Θ-role is present, but the suffix *en* is.

2.2.4. Verbal vs. adjectival participles

The biggest asset of Emonds' (2000, 2003) theory is that it derives all uses of the second participle from a single morphological object, a verbal adjective. This means that the adjectival participle is in fact the underlying form. A verbal participle is derived by deletion of the adjectival suffix in syntax.

In the present framework, morphological uniformity can be maintained without the deletion of the suffix. Instead, let us assume that the prosodic head of the participle can be interpreted directly as A. The projection principle dictates that such an option must be lexically licensed. It is therefore necessary to adopt the approach of Horvath and Siloni (2005), Wasow (1977), who argue that the adjectival participle is formed in the lexicon.

To be precise, something is called a "lexical derivation" in the present framework, if the output is listed as a lexical entry. This assumption does not exclude the existence of phrasal adjectival participles. It is well known from idioms (Nunberg, Sag and Wasow 1994) that the lexicon can list complex objects. The only thing that the lexical entry of an adjectival participle must specify is the fact that its prosodic head is interpreted as A. The actual derivation is then left to syntax.

The "lexical" derivation of the adjectival participle is supported by the fact that adjectival participles are subject to semantic drift. They can acquire a meaning that is absent from their verbal base. The following examples illustrate this observation (cf. Horvath and Siloni 2005; Wasow 1977 on similar evidence in English and Hebrew). In the (a) examples below, an idiomatic reading of the adjectival participle is available. This reading is unavailable for the verbal participle in the (b) examples. With the literal verb-meaning, the examples are nonsense.

(122) a. *eine gesalzene Strafe* (adjectival participle)
a salted fine
'a heavy fine'
b. ??*Die Strafe wird gesalzen.* (verbal passive)
the fine is salted

(123) a. *ein abgebrühter Verbrecher* (adjectival participle)
a blanched criminal
'a hardened criminal'
b. ??*Der Verbrecher wird abgebrüht.* (verbal passive)
the criminal is blanched

The syntactic structure of the adjectival participle is now straightforward:

(124) adjectival participle

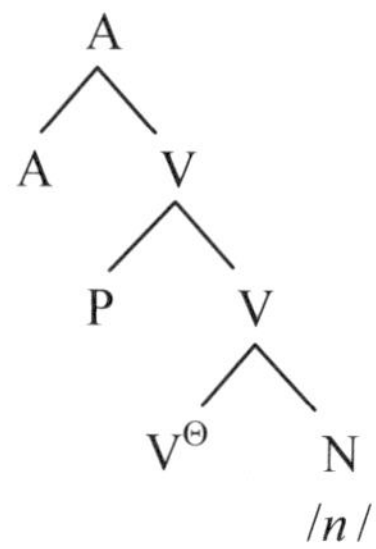

Notice that the suffix /*n*/ is not a projecting head, but a dependent of V. The A-head of the adjectival participle is an interpretation of the stem. The peripheral position of A in (124) corresponds to its prosodic position in a hierarchical, not a linear way. Prosodic, rather than linear prominence of the head A of adjectival participles supplies a straightforward explanation of a number of facts about phrasal constructions, to which we turn next.

2.2.5. Phrasal vs. lexical participles

Consider a so-called phrasal adjectival participle, as discussed in Kratzer (1994). (125) exhibits a bracketing paradox. Linearly, the adverb is adjacent to the adjectival participle, but it modifies the verb, which is embedded under A.

This relation is broken up by an intervening *un*-prefix (125b). The standard explanation for this blocking effect is that *un* attaches to a "lexical" participle, which does not tolerate verbal modifiers.

(125) a. *Sein Hemd ist schlampig gebügelt.*
his shirt is carelessly ironed
b. *Sein Hemd ist (*schlampig) ungebügelt.*
his shirt is carelessly un-ironed

In the present framework, the lexical-phrasal distinction does not derive this contrast. Both phrasal and "lexical" adjectival participles are lexically listed. The difference between (125a vs. b) must follow from the actual derivations.

Consider first the participle in isolation. In this configuration, the participial stem receives primary stress. If A is an interpretation of the maximal prosodic projection of the participle, then its interpretation may actually be delayed, until after a full VP has been projected.

(126) phrasal adjectival participle

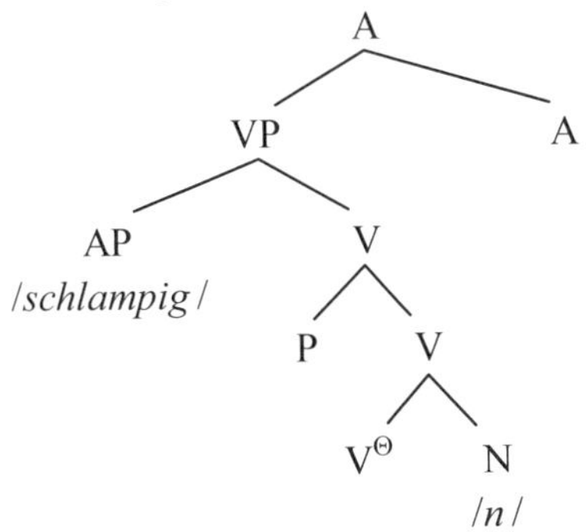

The prefixation of *un* changes this configuration. Notice first that *un* receives primary stress. It is thus the prosodic head of the adjectival participle,[7] and its prosodic dependent, the verb stem, must be interpreted immediately. After A has merged, V is eliminated as its dependent. In the presence of *un*, the projection of V cannot be extended to include VP-adverbs like *schlampig* 'carelessly'.

(127)

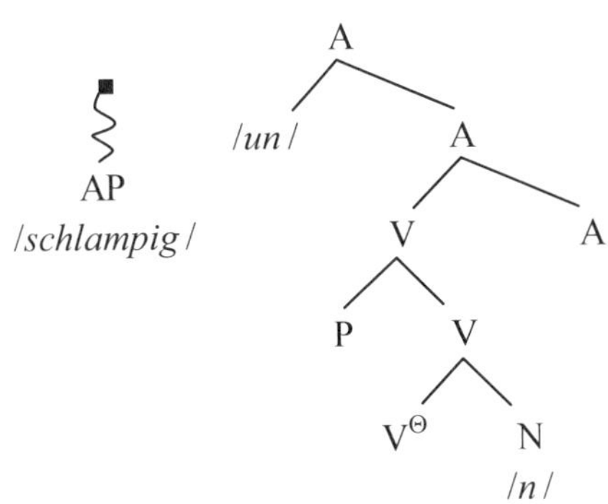

The analysis in terms of prosodic headedness, rather than a lexical/phrasal distinction is corroborated by the behavior of verbal particles (Haiden, 2001).

Consider an example from Kratzer (1994). In (128), the meaning of the two participles is virtually identical. Nonetheless, *un-* can only attach to *abschicken* 'send off' in (128a). It is ungrammatical with *wegschicken* 'send off' in (128b). Kratzer (1994) attributes this contrast to the observation that *weg* is a semantically stable verbal particle, which heads its own phrasal projection, while *ab* does not need to head its own projection.

(128) a. *Der Brief ist unabgeschickt.*
the letter is un-off-sent
'The letter remains unsent.'
b. **Der Brief ist unweggeschickt.*
the letter is un-away-sent
c. *Der Brief ist weggeschickt.*
the letter is away sent
'The letter is sent.'

Kratzer's account in terms of semantic stability has been challenged from various perspectives. The most thorough criticism is developed in Lüdeling (2001), who observes that *un-* can only attach to a listed particle-verb. The verb *ab-waschen* can mean 'wash/clean' (129a) but it can also have an idiomatic reading, on which it applies exclusively to dishes (129b). An adjectival passive is available on both readings of (129), but *un*-prefixation excludes the literal one (130a vs. b). Only the idiomatic (and therefore listed) reading survives *un*-prefixation.

(129) a. *Das Auto ist abgewaschen.*
the car is PRT-washed
'The car has been cleaned.'
b. *Der Teller ist abgewaschen.*
the plate is PRT-washed
'The plate has been cleaned.'

(130) a. ??*das Auto/Gesicht ist unabgewaschen*
the car/face is un-PRT-washed

b. *Der Teller ist unabgewaschen.*
the plate is un-PRT-washed
'The plate remains un-cleaned.'

Lüdeling's data can be complemented with an observation about stress. In a particle-verb combination, the particle receives primary stress. This is true even in adjectival passives (131a). By contrast, the particle is unstressed in the presence of *un* (131b).

(131) a.

*		
*		*
*	*	*
ab	*ge*	*schickt*

b.

*			
*			(*)
*	*	*	*
un	*ab*	*ge*	*schickt*

Combined, the two observations yield a new generalization: Only idiomatic verb-particle combinations allow prosodic demotion of the particle.

Now consider a further property of verb particle combinations. (Stiebels and Wunderlich 1994; Stiebels 1996) argue that the particle is a morphologically maximal, syntactically visible object. This assumption is necessary to account for the fact that the particle is stranded under verb movement (Koster 1975). It surfaces in an even bolder form in non-lexical analyses of verb particle constructions like den Dikken (1995). In the adjectival participle, the particle must therefore be analyzed as a dependent of A, rather than V. Wunderlich (1987:352) analyzes (132a) as (132b).

(132) a. *ein- ge- spar- t- es*
PRT PREF save SUFF AGR
'something that has been saved'

b.

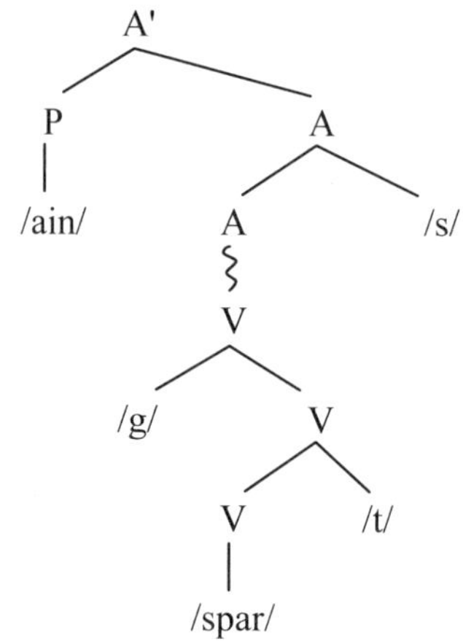

(132b) is exactly the mirror image of (126). In (126), the adverb is linearly external to the adjectival participle, but it is syntactically embedded under VP. In (132b), the particle lexically depends on the head V, but in morphosyntactic structure, it is external to the projection of V.

Externalization crucially depends on stress. The interpretation of P can be delayed until after the projection of A, because P is the head of the prosodic word. The affixation of *un* changes this configuration. By prosodically weakening the particle, it blocks externalization. A particle that follows *un* is no longer a morphologically maximal, syntactically visible object, but a syntactically invisible affix.

(133)

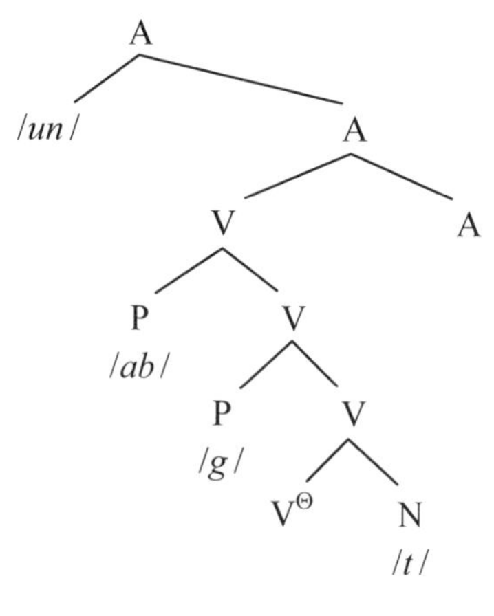

(133) is confirmed by independent syntactic evidence. Consider the verb *flüstern* 'whisper' as discussed in Kratzer (1994). (134) shows that *flüstern* 'whisper' does not license a dative. (135) shows that the idiomatic particle-verb *einflüstern* 'insinuate/prompt' takes a dative, and it allows the formation of an adjectival passive.

(134) a. *weil sie die Antwort flüsterten.*
since they the_{ACC} answer whispered
'because they whispered the answer.'
b. **weil sie ihm die Antwort flüsterten*
since they $them_{DAT}$ the_{ACC} answer whispered.

(135) a. *Ich habe ihm das eingeflüstert.*
I have him_{DAT} $that_{ACC}$ in-whispered
'I prompted him to do that.'
b. *Die Dummheit ist ihm eingeflüstert.*
the silly-idea is him_{DAT} in-whispered
'The silly idea has been passed on to him.'

(Kratzer 1994) argues that *un*-prefixation is ungrammatical (136a), because the particle cannot license a dative complement in this configuration. This observation supports (136). In addition, (133) predicts that acceptability should increase, if the incorporated particle does not license a dative. This seems to be true (136b).

(136) a. **Die Dummheit ist ihm noch uneingeflüstert.*
the silly-idea is him still un-in-whispered
b. (?)*Die Dummheit blieb uneingeflüstert.*
the answer remained un-in-whispered
'The silly idea remained secret/uninsinuated.'

I conclude that the analysis of the passive participle in terms of prosodic prominence is correct. The A-head of the adjectival participle is an interpretation of the stem itself. The participial suffix is an alternative realization of the internal argument.

2.3. The verbal passive

German overtly distinguishes the verbal from the adjectival passive. The auxiliary *werden* 'become' is used in the verbal passive, while *sein* 'be' is used in the adjectival passive. It is therefore very easy to individuate properties of the verbal, as opposed to the adjectival passive. Rapp (1997) summarizes the properties of the verbal passive as follows:

(137) Passivization of transitives (Rapp's generalization)[8]
  a. The predicate must denote a process that develops through time.
  b. If the denotation of a predicate involves an activity-component, the agent must be demoted in the passive.

2.3.1. Aspectual constraints

It is evident that (137) mainly relies on the aspectual condition (137a). The thematic statement (137b) affects a proper subset of those predicates that pass condition (137a). It is an instruction on how to deal with this subset. Let us therefore concentrate on the aspectual condition first.

In Rapp's (1997) framework, the opposition between temporally extended and punctual events is mirrored by the opposition between the base predicates DEV and BECOME. DEV denotes a gradual change of state, BECOME denotes an instantaneous one. This opposition is naturally applied in condition (137a), and it derives the contrast between (138) and (139).

(138) a. DEV (LOC (~~x~~,y))
  b. *Der Berg wurde bestiegen.*
  the mountain was climbed

(139) a. BECOME (PSYCH (~~x~~,y))
  b. **Plötzlich wurden von ihm die Berge erblickt.*
  suddenly were by him the mountains spotted

Unfortunately, the facts are more complex than (137) suggests them to be. Take as an example the verb *finden* 'find', which denotes an instantaneous event, and nevertheless forms a verbal passive:

(140) *Der Schlüssel wurde im Bad gefunden.*
the key was in-the bathroom found
'The key was found in the bathroom.'

Rapp (1997) argues that this is due to an optional preparatory activity associated with the lexical representation of *finden* 'find'. In a passive, the preparatory activity is obligatorily realized:

(141) a. [CAUSE (DO (~~x~~),] BECOME (PSYCH (~~x~~,y))[)]
b. *Der Schlüssel wurde nach langer Suche gefunden.*
the key was after long search found
'The key was found after having been searched for a long time.'

However, this does not seem to be an accurate description of the facts. The finding-event referred to in the passive can occur coincidentally, without any preparatory activity:

(142) *Der Schlüssel wurde zufällig von einem Passanten gefunden.*
the key was coincidentally by a passer-by found
'The key was found accidentally by a passer-by.'

It is correct that the passive in (142) refers to a temporally extended change of state that stretches from some point in time, when the key is already lost, to the moment it is found. If we add context that forces an instantaneous reading, the passive is much less acceptable:

(143) ??*Das Licht ging an, und der Schlüssel wurde in demselben Moment gefunden.*
the light turned on and the key was in the very moment found

(143) differs from (142) aspectually, but not thematically. In both sentences, the implicit argument ends up in possession of a key without having contributed to the causation of the event. The presence of a preparatory activity is not a requirement in the verbal passive. In sum, Rapp's (1997) aspectual condition on the verbal passive is correct, but it is not contingent on thematic interpretation. In lumping together thematic and aspectual information in unanalyzable base predicates, Rapp (1997) and comparable

theories make incorrect predictions about the grammaticality of the verbal passive.

A similar observation can be made about psychological predicates. In Rapp's (1997) framework, emotions, sensations, cognitive states and possession are all represented as PSYCH(x,y). Since PSYCH is a stative predicate, the prediction is that all of these verb classes exclude the passive. Nevertheless, emotions and sensations form a passive.

(144) a. *Du wirst von deinen Eltern geliebt/bewundert/verachtet.*
you are by your parents loved/admired/despised
'You are being loved/admired/despised by your parents.'
b. *Der Dieb wurde von allen gesehen.*
the thief was by everybody seen
'The thief was seen by everybody.'
c. **Die Antwort wurde von ihm gewusst.*
the answer was by him known
d. **Der Täter wird von der Polizei gekannt.*
the criminal is by the police known
e. **Das Auto wird von ihm besessen/gehabt.*
the car is by him owned/had

To account for this behavior, Rapp (1997) sub-classifies psychological predicates into activities and states. One class comprises emotions and sensations. It is represented by the predicate PSYCH-DO. Cognitive states and possession are represented by PSYCH-BE. If aspectual conditions on the verbal passive are separated from thematic ones, then the ad-hoc distinction between two types of the predicate PSYCH would not be necessary.

2.3.2. *Thematic constraints*

Turn back to the verb *finden* 'find'. As discussed in chapters 2, 3, this verb exhibits the intentional alternation. Its subject can be either a sentient individual, or a (temporally) delineated object:

(145) a. *Hans fand den Schlüssel.*
Hans found the key

b. *Die Suche fand ein Ende.*
the search found an end

In the passive, only the sentient subject reading is available:

(146) a. *Der Schlüssel wurde gefunden.*
the key was found
b. **Ein Ende wurde gefunden.*
an end was found

If the intentional alternation is correctly represented in chapter 2, then the generalization must be that [-m] does not make a good implicit argument in the verbal passive. The same holds for the other [/-m] cluster, fully specified [+c-m]. With verbs that alternate between a agentive/causative and an instrumental reading in active sentences, only the agentive/causative reading survives under passivization.

(147) *umgeben* 'surround': {[+c+m], [+c-m], [-c-m]}

(148) a. *Hans umgibt das Dorf mit einer Mauer.*
Hans surrounds the village with a wall
b. *Eine Mauer umgibt das Dorf*
a wall surrounds the village

(149) a. *Das Dorf wird (von Hans) mit einer Mauer umgeben.*
the village is (by Hans) with a wall surrounded
'The village is surrounded with a wall (by Hans).'
b. **Das Dorf wird von einer Mauer umgeben*
the village is by a wall surrounded

The generalization that [/-m] is unavailable as an implicit role is by now familiar. Exactly the same constraint was observed for the prefixed present participle, and for the modal infinitive under *sein* 'be'. In those contexts, it was attributed to *arbitrarization*. The sortal restriction to humans cannot be invoked in the verbal passive, though, because verbs that select underspecified [+c] as an external argument do allow inanimates in the by-phrase (150). The ban against [/-m] must be a general condition for syntactic saturation.

(150) *Der Patient wird von Instrumenten am Leben erhalten.*
the patient is by instruments at-the life kept
'The patient is kept alive by instruments.'

(151) Condition on saturation in syntax
[/-m] cannot be saturated.

Now recall from section 2.2.1 that the adjectival passive is not constrained in this way. (149b) contrasts with (152).

(152) *Das Dorf ist von einer Mauer umgeben.*
the village is by a wall surrounded
'The village is surrounded by a wall.'

This contrast supported a lexical derivation of the adjectival participle. Apart from introducing the category A as an interpretation of the stem, lexical participle formation affects the status of the external Θ-role. In contrast to syntactic saturation, a lexical formation of the participle manipulates the content of Θ-role clusters. For middles, Marelj (2004) posits the following rule, which neutralizes the content of a cluster.

(153) LMF (Lexical Middle Formation; Marelj 2004:190)
a. Target a verbal entry with a [/+c] cluster and delete its content.
b. The implicit role in middles is an empty list i.e. a [ ] cluster.

Since the formation of the German adjectival participle applies in the lexicon too, it is reasonable to assume that it consists in the neutralization of the external cluster. After LPF has neutralized [/-m], saturation can apply. Verbs with a [/-m] external argument are grammatical in the lexically derived adjectival passive, but ungrammatical in the syntactically derived verbal passive.

(154) Lexical Participle Formation (LPF)
Target an external cluster and delete its content.

2.3.3. Impersonal passives

German allows an impersonal passive construction without an overt subject. The impersonal construction is available both for the verbal (155a), and for the adjectival passive (155b):

(155) a. *Hier wird fleißig gearbeitet.*
here is busily worked
'People are busily at work here.'
b. *Im Büro ist meistens gut geheizt.*
in-the office is usually well heated
'The office us usually well heated.'

As opposed to the personal construction, the impersonal construction forces a volitional interpretation for the implicit argument, at least in the verbal passive. This condition is noted in Rapp (1997), and discussed in great detail in Cabredo Hofherr (2000). It is well illustrated for the verbal passive with emission verbs that alternate between an agentive and an instrumental reading. In the impersonal construction, only the agentive reading is available (156).

(156) a. *Bei der Kälte wird oft mit den Zähnen geklappert.*
at the cold is often with the teeth rattled
'People are are likely to rattle their teeth in the cold.'
b. **Bei der Kälte wird oft von den Zähnen geklappert.*
at the cold is often by the teeth rattled

The adjectival passive is less acceptable with the verbs of this class, because they do not support the interpretation of a stable resultant state. The verb *heizen* 'heat' of (155b) seems to be a better example. In the active voice, its subject can be either an agent (157a), or an instrument (157b).

(157) a. *Hans heizt sein Büro selbst.*
Hans heats his office self
'Hans operates the heating of his office himself.'
b. *Ein Ölofen im Keller heizt das ganze Gebäude.*
an oil-burner in the basement heats the entire building
'The building is centrally heated by an oil-burner in the basement.'

In the impersonal adjectival passive, the agentive reading is fully acceptable (158a). The non-agentive reading is attempted in (158b). Although the sentence still seems inappropriate in a situation where no human agent operates the burner, the effect is much weaker than it is in the verbal impersonal passive (156). The data are thus not conclusive, and the impersonal adjectival passive must be left for further research.

(158) a. *Wenn er das Büro betritt, ist schon gut geheizt.*
when he the office enters is already well heated
'When he enters the office, it has already been heated up well.'
b. *Seitdem wir den neuen Ofen haben, ist hier immer gut geheizt.*
since we the new burner have is here always well heated
'Since we have the new burner, the house has always been well heated.'

For the impersonal verbal passive, the facts are clear. Since they exhibit exactly the same interpretational constraint as the prefixed present participle and the modal infinitive under *sein* 'be' it must be derived by the same operation. This operation has been identified in section 1.4.4 as *arbitrarization.*

2.4. Auxiliary and participle: the overall picture

We can now turn back to the initial question of auxiliary selection. Auxiliaries have been analyzed on various occasions as semi-lexical, or defective elements (Corver and Riemsdijk 2001). It is widely agreed (Kenesei 2001) that one of the most interesting properties distinguishing auxiliaries from main verbs is their inability to assign Θ-roles, or, more specifically, Θ-roles of their own. This agreement can be implemented in the present framework without technical complications:

(159) Auxiliaries, Definition
An auxiliary is a verb that does not have a Θ-role in its lexical entry.

(159) does not mean that auxiliaries could not assign Θ-roles. In fact they do, by merging with the roles of other verbal elements. Apart from their

dependence on embedded infinitival verbs for Θ-role assignment, auxiliaries are like all other verbs. In particular, they must check formal features.

2.4.1. Sein *'be'*

The auxiliary *sein* 'be' is selected if its complement verb has an internal, but no external role to assign. This generalization was argued in section 2.1 to extend to intransitive manner of motion verbs. These verbs were analyzed as lexical reflexives, which lack an expletive N-morpheme to check the N-feature of V. Therefore, their subject must merge VP-internally.

The auxiliary *sein* 'be' itself is an unaccusative verb that allows checking of the D-feature of v by means of feature movement. Taken together with the analysis of the participle suffix as an alternative realization of the internal argument, the derivation is straightforward. In order to identify the suffix as its alternative realization, DP must merge with the participial VP. It then raises into the auxiliary VP, where it checks the N-feature of V, and then D raises to check the D-feature of v. With intransitive manner of motion verbs, the derivation is identical. The lexically bundled Θ-roles are assigned to the subject via its alternative realization, the participial suffix. DP then raises into the VP of the auxiliary and checks formal features there. The trees in this section abstract away from the aspectual prefix /*g*/ of the participle.

(160) *sein* 'be' with unaccusatives

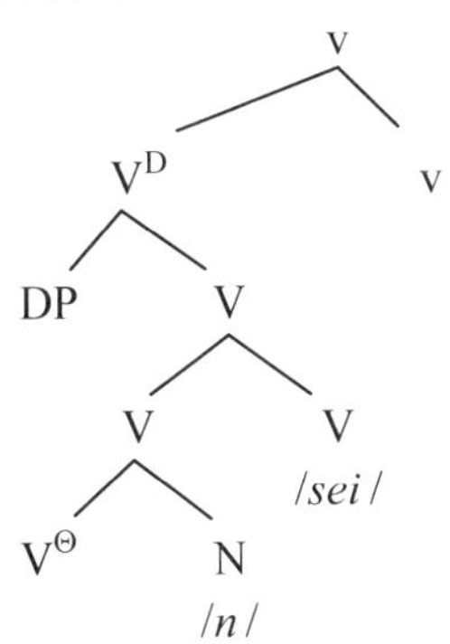

2.4.2. Haben *'have'*

The auxiliary *haben* 'have' is a formally transitive predicate. It does not allow checking of the D-feature of v by means of feature movement. Therefore, an N-morpheme distinct from the subject must be present, if *haben* 'have' is to be selected. In a transitive context, this is the direct object, which raises from the participial VP, where it receives a Θ-role through its alternative realization, the participial suffix. The external Θ-role of the participial verb cannot be assigned by the participle, because the participle does not contain v. It must merge with the auxiliary v, which assigns it to the subject.

(161) *haben* 'have' with transitives

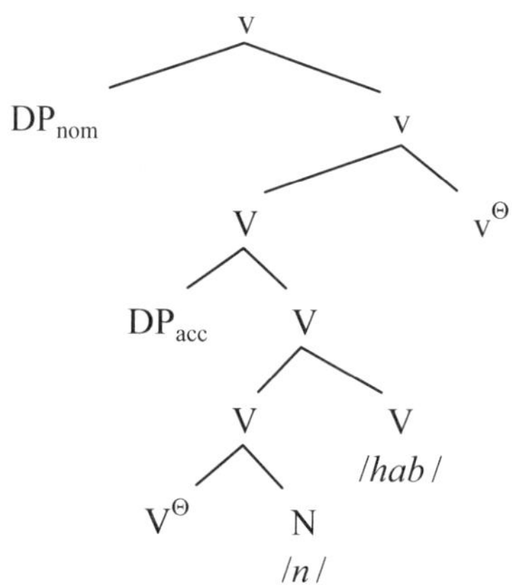

Unergatives were assigned with Hale and Keyser (1992, 1993) as formal transitives with an expletive N-morpheme that checks the N-feature of V. In the participle, the N-feature of V is checked by the participial suffix. Expletive N merges with auxiliary V instead. The external Θ-role merges with auxiliary v exactly as in full transitives. The same derivation is available for intransitive manner of motion verbs in certain dialects.

(162) *haben* 'have' with unergatives

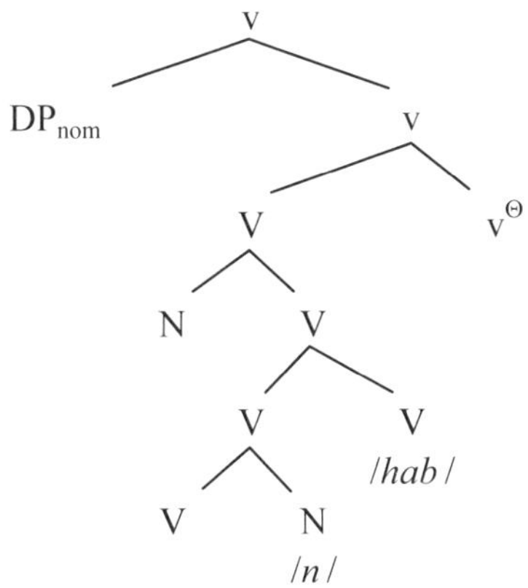

2.4.3. Werden *'become/be'*

The auxiliary *werden* 'be/become' behaves syntactically like the verbs in the causative alternation. Consider first future *werden*. When its complement is a VP projected by a transitive V, the direct object receives an internal Θ-role via its alternative realization, the infinitival suffix. It then checks the N-feature of the auxiliary V. The subject receives its external Θ-role directly from the auxiliary v. When future *werden* takes an unaccusative complement, the internal argument receives a Θ-role via its alternative realization, the infinitival suffix, and it checks both formal features in the auxiliary vP.

As far as formal feature checking is concerned, passive *werden* behaves exactly like future *werden* with an unaccusative complement. Since the external role of the participle is saturated, rather than assigned, the internal argument checks the features of both V and v in the auxiliary vP.

(163) future *werden* with transitive infinitive

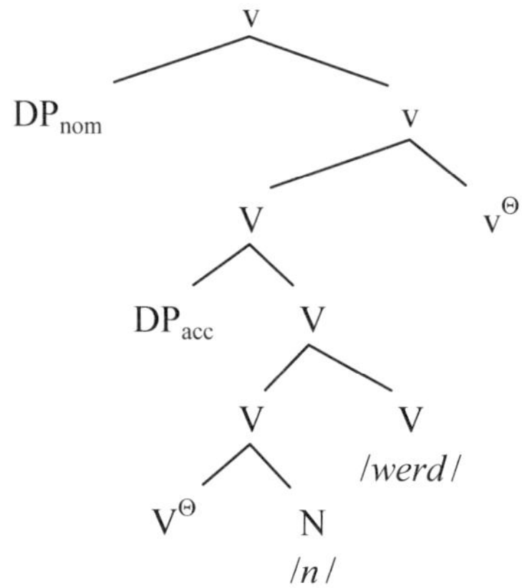

For the impersonal passive, Cabredo Hofherr (2000) assumes that an expletive pro is present in direct object position. Cabredo Hofherr (2000) supports this assumption mainly with semantic observations related to arbitrary interpretation. The argument from arbitrary interpretation is not conclusive, though; because middles trigger the same arbitrary interpretation as the impersonal passive, and there is arguably no silent expletive present in middles. The formal features are checked by the overt subject and the reflexive, and arbitrary interpretation is introduced by arbitrarization of the external Θ-role (Marelj 2004). Cabredo Hofherr's analysis of the impersonal passive is adopted here for purely formal reasons: a silent expletive must check the formal features of the auxiliary vP.

(164) *werden* in the personal passive

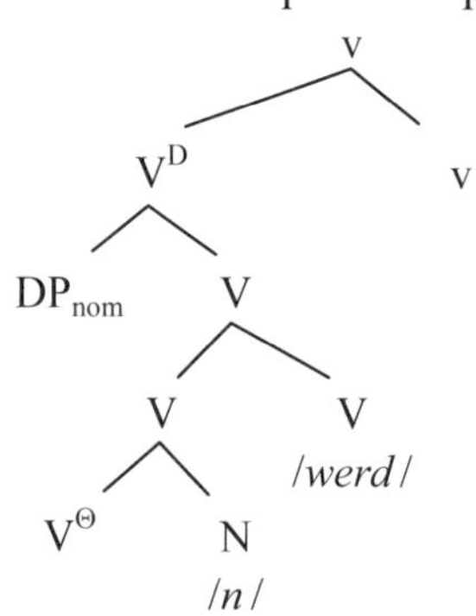

(165) *werden* in the impersonal passive

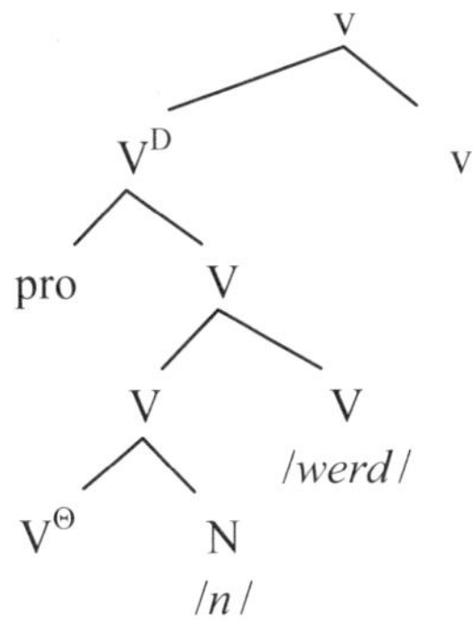

3. Conclusion

In this chapter, the scope of the analysis developed in chapter 3 was extended to infinitival constructions of various types. The goal of this extension was a better understanding of the interaction between morphophonological marking, lexical specification, syntactic projection, and semantic interpretation.

Starting with the present participle and modal infinitival complements to *haben* 'have' and *sein* 'be', it was argued that the infinitival suffix /*n*/ checks the formal features of V, and it alternatively realized the internal argument, if V assigns an internal Θ-role. If the prepositional prefix *zu* merges with v, it triggers aribitrarization of the external Θ-role. Constraints on the availability of specific modalities were attributed to the size of the infinitival/participial projection. In the absence of T, epistemic readings are excluded. Modal *haben* 'have' was analyzed as a raising verb that takes a TP complement.

The second part of chapter 4 discussed constructions with the second participle. The erratic auxiliary selection of intransitive manner of motion verbs was argued to follow from their status as lexically derived reflexives. Regarding the status of perfect, passive and adjectival participles, it was argued that a core structure is shared by all types of the second participle. In particular, the participial suffix checks formal features of V, and it alternatively realizes the internal argument, if V assigns an internal Θ-role.

The adjectival passive was analyzed with Horvath and Siloni (2005), Marelj (2004) as a lexically derived form with a neutralized external Θ-role. However, lexical neutralization of the external role does not preclude the projection of phrasal adjectival participles. It is argued that this option depends on prosodic properties of the participial stem. If the stem is the prosodic head of the word, a phrasal adjectival participle is available. This is why the prefixation of /*un*/ excludes the phrasal derivation: /*un*/, rather than the stem, is the prosodic head. The analysis was shown to extend to notoriously problematic data regarding verb particle constructions.

The discussion of the verbal passive turned back to a more explicit comparison between the Theta System approach defended in this book, and event-decomposition. It was argued that some of the most robust generalizations of Rapp (1997) are partly lost by the combination of aspectual and thematic information in base predicates. The separation of thematic and aspectual information in the Theta System is thus supported.

The final section turned back to auxiliary selection. It gave an overall picture of perfect, passive and future constructions based on the assumption that the second participle cannot independently assign an external Θ-role provided by its lexical entry. If an external Θ-role is present, then it must be assigned through the auxiliary. The perfect, passive and future auxiliaries, respectively, were argued to differ only with respect to their formal feature checking requirements. The transitive perfect auxiliary *haben* 'have' requires checking of N- and D-features by independent noun phrases, *sein* 'be' requires checking of its D-feature by means of D-raising from within VP, and *werden* 'become/be' allows both options.

Notes

[1] An epenthetic vowel, *schwa*, spelled as 'e', is inserted in most cases, according to the phonological context; cf. the discussion of example (9) below.

[2] Some dimensional adjectives like *wert* 'worth', *breit* 'wide' etc. behave exceptionally. They select quantities in the accusative case, as in (i). I claim we are dealing with adverbial, not structural accusative here, comparable to the accusative in (ii).

(i) *Der Graben ist einen Meter breit*
the trench is one.ACC meter wide

(ii) *Wir haben diesen Weg immer lustige Lieder gesungen*
we have this route.ACC always funny songs sung

[3] *Schwa*-epenthesis does not apply in casual speech. This (and the phonological implementation of the rule) is irrelevant for the present purposes.

[4] A similar behavior can be observed with unaccusative *erscheinen* 'appear'. Some speakers consistently accept examples like (i), provided a volitional agent can be inferred. (ii) is severely ungrammatical for all speakers.

(i) *%der bis Montag zu erscheinende Artikel*
the by Monday to appear.ND.AGR article
'the article that must be published by Monday'

(ii) **die jeden Morgen im Osten zu erscheinende Sonne*
the each morning in-the east to appear.ND.AGR sun

[5] Wurmbrand (pc) points out (cf. also Müller 2002) that the presence of nominative case in (i) could be construed as evidence for the presence of T. In (i), the case on the reciprocal phrase *einer nach dem anderen* 'one after the other' is nominative; cf. already Wunderlich (1987:361) for criticism of this test. In the present framework, the nominative on the reciprocal phrase is evidence for the projection of v. It tells us nothing about T.

(i) *die, einer nach dem anderen verwelkenden Büsche*
the one.NOM after the other wilt.ND.AGR bushes
'the bushes that are wilting one after the other'

[6] The claim that participial suffixes satisfy subcategorization requirements of a head to their left violates the *Right Hand Head Rule* of Williams (1981). In the present theoretical framework, this is not problematic, because headedness is defined in a hierarchical, rather than a linear way. For discussion cf. chapter 3, and sections 2.2.3. - 2.2.5.

[7] Roland Noske (p.c.) points out that Dutch *un* is unstressed, but it behaves like German stressed *un* in all other relevant respects. Pending a morpho-phonological analysis of the Dutch participle, this observation must be put aside as a problem. A possible solution would be analyzing Dutch *un* as a phrasal affix at the edge of AP. Constituents to the left of *un* then cannot be included in a VP embedded under AP.

[8] „Alle Fälle des persönlichen Vorgangspassivs lassen sich durch die Bedingung erfassen, daß e-strukturell hier stets zeitlich ausgedehnte Vorgänge vorliegen müssen, und daß beim Vorliegen eines DO-Prädikats immer dessen erstes Argument blockiert wird“ (Rapp 1997:151). Earlier in her book, she argues that the first argument of DEV must be blocked in the verbal passive.

Conclusion

The topic of this book was the investigation of the realization of thematic roles in the syntactic structure of a given language. Starting with the assumption that syntactic argument structure is projected as a function of individual lexical entries, chapter 1 attempted to find the most appropriate formalization of lexical-semantic information. A first question was whether such information should be generated by a system of rules and wellformedness conditions as in Pustejovsky (1995), or whether the lexicon is better understood as an arbitrary list (Fodor and Lepore 1998). It was argued that questions of this kind cannot be answered strictly within the domain of linguistics. Chapter 1 therefore undertook a brief excursion into cognitive psychology, to argue that lexical representations should encode the core features of event interpretation in two components of the mind, understood as *commonsense theories* (Hirschfeld and Gelman 1994): *folk physics* and *folk psychology*. It was assumed with Leslie (1994) that the main explanatory constructs of these commonsense theories are *force* and *sentience*, respectively. The lexicon should distinguish between agents and patients with respect to both *force* and *sentience*. Such a distinction is encoded by the binary features *c* (*force*) and *m* (*sentience*) of Reinhart (2000). Chapter 1 thus supplied psychological support for Reinhart's feature system.

Chapter two presented a case study of the lexical representation of German verbs, formulated in terms of Reinhart's feature system. The lexical information was then compared with the syntactic distribution of arguments in transitive, anti-causative and reflexive constructions. While the data supplied strong general support for the mapping/merging component of the Theta System, a few minor adjustments were defended. First, underspecified [-] clusters can be assigned to external arguments. Second, the presence of both a [/+c] and a [/-c] cluster triggers the assignment of an accusative feature to V, and third, non-realization of a [+m] cluster is possible in the configuration {[+m], [-c-m], [-m]}. Chapter 2 ended with a discussion of anti-causative reflexives. The distribution of the syntactic properties of the construction was found to be rather erratic.

Chapter 3 developed a new architecture of syntactic projection, which allows the formulation of robust generalizations over thematic role assignment on the one hand, but at the same time acknowledges the relevance of other components, in particular morpho-phonology and narrow syntax. It was proposed that the Θ-roles provided by a lexical entry are semi-independent objects that merge with syntactic heads, through which they are assigned.

Together with the elimination of the problematic set of *theme-unergatives*, this approach made it possible to formulate a conceptually streamlined version of the marking/merging system. The only residue of the marking system is the assignment of interpretable subcategorization features. All generalizations related to internal/external or oblique/prepositional role assignment are incorporated into the merging instructions. The derivations were then exemplified with simple, finite sentences.

Chapter 4 extended the scope of the analysis to infinitival constructions of various types, exploring the interaction between lexical specification, morpho-phonological marking, syntactic projection, and semantic interpretation.

The main empirical conclusion reached in this book is that the lexical-semantic properties of verbs do indeed determine a large part of syntactic argument structure. In particular, a wide variety of German data can be accounted for in a unified manner, once we adopt the Theta System approach developed in Reinhart (2000) and subsequent work. Apart from lexical semantics, it was shown that overt morphology and formal syntactic requirements play a crucial role in the projection of syntactic argument structure. Thus, at a conceptual level, the conclusion of this book is that even a strongly modular theory of grammatical knowledge cannot afford ignoring evidence from neighboring domains. An explicit theory was therefore proposed for the interface between phonology and syntax, and for lexical access.

References

Abraham, Werner
2004 The grammaticalization of the infinitival preposition - toward a theory of 'grammaticalizing reanalysis'. *Journal of Comparative Germanic Linguistics* 7:111-170.

Baker, Mark C.
1988 *Incorporation: A theory of Grammatical Function Changing*. Chikago: University of Chikago Press.
1989 Object sharing in serial verb constructions. *Linguistic Inquiry* 20:513-553.

Baker, Mark C., Kyle Johnson, and Ian Roberts
1989 Passive arguments raised. *Linguistic Inquiry* 20:219-251.

Bayer, Josef, Markus Bader, and Michael Meng
2001 Morphological underspecification meets oblique case: syntactic and processing effects in German. *Lingua* 111:465-514.

Belletti, Adriana, and Luigi Rizzi
1988 Psych-Verbs and Θ-Theory. *Natural Language and Linguistic Theory* 6:291-352.

Bendjaballah, Sabrina, and Martin Haiden
2002 Meaningful Vowels. Paper presented at *IGG*, Lecce.
2003 Templatic Architecture. *Recherches Linguistiques de Vincennes* 32:157-168.
2005 Berber Prepositions, Templates, and the PF Interface. Paper presented at *GLOW*, Geneva.

Besten, Hans B. den
1981 On the interaction of root transformations and lexical deletive rules. *Groninger Arbeiten zur Germanistischen Linguistik* 20:1-78.
1989 *Studies in West Germanic Syntax*. Amsterdam: Rodopi.

Besten, Hans B. den, and Gert Webelhuth
1987 Stranding. In *Scrambling and Barriers*, Günther Grewendorf and Wolfgang Sternefeld (eds.), 77-92. Amsterdam: Benjamins.

Bittner, Andreas
1996 *Starke 'schwache' Verben - schwache 'starke' Verben: deutsche Verbflexion und Natürlichkeit*. Tübingen: Stauffenberg (Studien zur deutschen Grammatik 51).

Bok-Bennema, Reineke
1994 Dutch verbalization and the theory of morphology. In *Language and Cognition*, Ale de Boer, Helen de Hoop, and Hans de Swarts (eds.), 13-26. Groningen: Groningen University.

Booij, Geert
to appear Morphology and the tripartite parallel architecture of the grammar. In *La formazione delle parole*, Maria Grossman and Anna-Maria Thornton (eds.). Roma: Bulzoni.

Borer, Hagit
1991 The causative-inchoative alternation: a case study in parallel morphology. *The Linguistic Review* 8:119-158.
1994 The Projection of arguments. In *University of Massachusetts Occasional Papers in Linguistics* 17, Elena Benedicto, and Jeff Runner (eds.), 19-47.
1997 The morphology-syntax interface: A study of autonomy. In *Advances in Morphology*, Wolfgang U. Dressler, Martin Prinzhorn; and John R. Rennison (eds.), 5-30. Berlin, New York: Mouton de Gruyter.
1998 Deriving the passive without theta grids. In *Morphology and Its Relation to Phonology and Syntax*, Stephen G. Lapointe, Diane K. Brentari, and Patrick M. Rarrell (eds.), 60-99: CSLI Publications.
2000 Exo-skeletal vs. endo-skeletal explanations: syntactic projections and the lexicon. Ms., USC (published as Borer 2003).
2003 Exo-skeletal vs. endo-skeletal explanations: syntactic projections and the lexicon. *The Nature of Explanation in Linguistic Theory*, Maria Polinsky and John Moore (eds.), 31-68. Stanford: CSLI and Chikago: University of Chikago Press.

Brandt, Patrick
2003 Cipient predication: Unifying double object, dative experiencer and existential/presentational constructions. Ph.D. diss., Utrecht University.

Bresnan, Joan, and Jonni M. Kanerva
1989 Locative inversion in Chicheva: A case study of facturization in grammar. *Linguistic Inquiry* 20:1-50.

Broekhuis, Hans
1992 Chain-government: issues in Dutch syntax, Ph.D. diss., University of Amsterdam.

Broekhuis, Hans, and Kees van Dijk
1995 The syntactic function of the auxiliaries of time. In *Linguistics in the Netherlands*, Karcel den Dikken, and Kees Hengeveld (eds.), 37-48. Amsterdam: John Benjamins.

Burzio, Luigi
1986 *Italian Syntax*. Dordrecht: Reidel.
Cabredo Hofherr, Patricia
2000 La passivation des intransitifs en allemand et le statut des explétifs. Ph.D. diss., Université Paris 7.
Carey, Susan, and Elizabeth Spelke
1994 Domain-specific knowledge and conceptual change. In *Mapping the Mind*, Lawrence A. Hirschfeld, and Susan A. Gelman (eds.), 169-200. Cambridge: Cambridge University Press.
Carlson, Greg
1977 Reference to kinds in English. Ph.D. diss., UMass., Amherst.
Carrier-Duncan, Jill
1985 Linking of thematic roles in derivational word formation. *Linguistic Inquiry* 16:1-34.
Castañeda, Hector-Neri
1967 Comments on Donald Davidson's 'The logical form of action sentences'. In *The Logic of Decision and Action*, Nicholas Rescher (ed.), 104-112. Pittsburgh: University of Pittsburgh Press.
Chierchia, Gennaro
1989 A semantics for unaccusatives and its syntactic consequences. Ms., Cornell University (published as Chierchia 2004).
2004 A semantics for unaccusatives and its syntactic consequences. In *The Unaccusativity Puzzle. Explorations at the Syntax-Lexicon Interface*, Artemis Alexiadou, Elena Anagnostopoulou, and Martin Everaert (eds.), 22-59. Oxford, Oxford University Press.
1995 The variability of impersonal subjects. In *Quantification in Natural Languages*, Emmon Bach (ed.), 107-143. Dordrecht: Kluwer.
Chomsky, Noam
1955 *The Logical Structure of Linguistic Theory*. New York: Plenum.
1981 *Lectures on Government and Binding*. Berlin: de Gruyter.
1982 *Some Concepts and Consequences of the Theory of Government and Binding*. Cambridge, Mass.: MIT Press.
1986 *Barriers*. Cambridge, Massachusetts: MIT Press.
1995 *The Minimalist Program*. Cambridge, Mass.: MIT Press.
2001 Beyond explanatory adequacy. Ms., MIT.
Cinque, Guglielmo
1999 *Adverbs and Functional Heads: A Cross-Linguistic Perspective*. Oxford: Oxford University Press.
Clark, Eve V., and Kathie L. Carpenter
1989 The notion of source in language acquisition. *Language* 65:1-30.

Corver, Norbert, and Henk C. van Riemsdijk (eds.)
2001 *Semi-Lexical Categories. The Content of Function Words and the Function of Content Words*. Berlin: Mouton de Gruyter.
Croft, William
1990 *Typology and Universals*. Cambridge: Cambridge University Press.
1991 *Syntactic Categories and Grammatical Relations*. Chikago: University of Chikago Press.
1998 Event structure in argument linking. In *The Projection of Arguments. Lexical and Compositional Factors*, Miriam Butt, and Wilhelm Geuder (eds.), 21-64. Stanford: CSLI Publications.
Csibra, Gergely, György Gergely, Szilvia Bíró, Koós Orsolya, and Margaret Brockbank
1999 Goal attribution without agency cues: the perception of 'pure reason' in infancy. *Cognition* 72:237-167.
Demske-Neumann, Ulrike
1994 *Modales Passiv und Tough Movement. Zur strukturellen Kausalität eines syntaktischen Wandels im Deutschen und Englischen*. Tübingen: Niemeyer.
Diedrichsen, Elke
2002 Zu einer semantischen Klassifikation der intransitiven *haben-* und *sein-*Verben im Deutschen. Paper presented at *Sinn und Bedeutung VI*, University of Osnabrück.
Dikken, Marcel den
1995 *Particles. On the Syntax of Verb-Particle, Triadic, and Causative Constructions*. Oxford, New York: Oxford University Press.
Doron, Edit
2003a Transitivity alternations in the Semitic template system. In *Research in Afroasiatic Grammar II*, Jacqueline Lecarme (ed.), 127-150. Amsterdam, Philadelphia: Benjamins.
2003b Agency and voice: the semantics of the semitic templates. *Natural Language Semantics* 11:1-67.
Dowty, David
1991 Thematic proto-roles and argument selection. *Language* 67:547-619.
Eckardt, Regine
2001 Reanalysing *selbst*. *Natural Language Semantics* 9:371-412.
Emonds, Joseph E;
1972 Evidence that indirect object movement is a structure-preserving rule. *Foundations of Language* 8:546-561.
1987 The invisible category principle. *Linguistic Inquiry* 18:613-631.

2000 *Lexicon and Grammar: The English Syntacticon*. Berlin, New York: Mouton de Gruyter.
2003 Adjectival passives: The construction in the iron mask. In *SYN-COM*, Martin Everaert, and Henk C. van Riemsdijk (eds.).

Engelberg, Stefan
2000 *Verben, Ereignisse und das Lexikon*. Tübingen: Niemeyer.

Erb, Marie Christine
2001 Finite auxiliaries in German. Ph.D. diss., Tilburg University.

Erteshik-Shir, Nomi, and Tova R. Rapoport
1995 A theory of verbal projection. Ms. Ben Gurion University.

Fillmore, Charles J.
1968 The case for case. In *Universals in Linguistic Theory*, Emmon Bach, and Robert T. Harms (eds.), 1-88. New York: Holt, Reinhart and Winston.
1970 The grammar of *hitting* and *breaking*. In *Readings in English Transformational Grammar*, Roderick Jacobs, and Peter Rosenbaum (eds.), 120-133. Waltham, Mass.: Ginn.

Fodor, Jerry A.
1970 Three Reasons for not deriving "kill" from "cause to die". *Linguistic Inquiry* 1:429-438.
1983 *The Modularity of Mind*. Cambridge, Massachusetts: MIT Press.
1987 *Psychosemantics*. Cambridge, Mass.: MIT Press/Bradford Books.

Fodor, Jerry A., and Ernie Lepore
1998 The emptiness of the lexicon: Reflections on James Pustejovsky's *The Generative Lexicon*. *Linguistic Inquiry* 29:269-288.

Frege, Gottlob
1879 *Begriffsschrift, eine der arithmetischen nachgebildete Formelsprache des reinen Denkens*. Halle.
1892 Über Sinn und Bedeutung. *Zeitschrift für Philosophie und philosophische Kritik* 100:25-50.

Frey, Werner
1993 *Syntaktische Bedingungen für die semantische Interpretation*. Berlin: Akademieverlag.

Gelhaus, Hermann
1977 *Der modale Infinitiv*. Tübingen: Narr (Forschungsberichte des IdS Mannheim 35).

Gergely, Gyorgy, Zoltan Nadasdy, Gergely Csibra, and Szilvia Biro
1995 Taking the intentional stance at 12 months of age. *Cognition* 56:165-193.

Gergely, Gyorgy, and Gergely Csibra
1997 Teleological reasoning in infancy: The infant's naive theory of rational action: A reply to Premack and Premack. *Cognition* 63:227-233.
Ghomeshi, Jila, and Diane Massam
1995 Lexical/Syntactic relations without projection. *Linguistic Analysis* 24:175-217.
Giusti, Giuliana
1995 A unified structural representation of (abstract) case and article. Evidence from Germanic. In *Studies in Comparative Germanic Syntax*, Hubert Haider, Susan Olsen, and Sten Vikner (eds.), 77-93. Dordrecht: Kluwer.
Givón, Talmy
1984 *Syntax: A Functional-Typological Introduction.* Amsterdam: Benjamins.
Goldberg, Adele E.
1995 *Constructions: A Construction Grammar Approach to Argument Structure*. Chikago: University of Chikago Press.
Goldsmith, John
1990 *Autosegmental and Metrical Phonology*. Oxford, Cambridge: Blackwell.
Gopnik, Alison, and Henry M. Wellmann
1994 The theory theory. In *Mapping the Mind,* Lawrence A. Hirschfeld, and Susan A. Gelman (eds.), 257-293. Cambridge: Cambridge University Press.
Grewendorf, Günther
1989 *Ergativity in German*. Dordrecht: Foris.
Grimm, Jakob
1819 *Deutsche Grammatik. 4 Theile*. Göttingen [Reprinted in 1837].
Grimshaw, Jane
1982 On the lexical representation of Romance reflexive clitics. In *The Mental Representation of Grammatical Relations*, Joan Bresnan (ed.). Cambridge, Mass: MIT Press.
1990 *Argument Structure*. Cambridge, Massachusetts: MIT Press.
Gruber, Jeffrey S.
1965 Studies in lexical relations, Ph.D. diss., MIT.
Guerssel, Mohamed
1987 The status of the lexical category preposition in Berber: Implications for the nature of the Construct State. In *Studies in Berber Syntax*, Ken Hale (ed.), 159-190. Cambridge, Mass.: Center for Cognitive Science, MIT.

1992 On the case system of Berber. *Canadian Journal of Linguistics* 37:175-195.

Guerssel, Mohamed, and Jean Lowenstamm

1990 The derivational morphology of the Classical Arabic verbal system. Ms., UQAM and Paris 7.

1996 Ablaut in Classical Arabic measure I active verbal forms. In *Studies in Afroasiatic Grammar*, Jaqueline Lecarme, Jean Lowenstamm, and Ur Shlonsky (eds.), 123-134. The Hague: HAG.

Haiden, Martin

1995 On the semantic evaluation of NP syntax, MA. thesis, University of Vienna.

1997 Verbal inflection and the structure of IP in German. *Groninger Arbeiten zur Germanistischen Linguistik* 41:77-106.

2001 Verb particle constructions. In *Syncom*, Martin Everaert, and Henk C. van Riemsdijk (eds.).

2004 Theta theory. Ph.D. diss., Tilburg University.

to appear Review of *Stefan Müller (2002): Complex Predicates*. *Journal of Comparative Germanic Linguistics*.

Haider, Hubert

1984 Was zu haben ist und was zu sein hat. Bemerkungen zum Infinitiv. *Papiere zur Linguistik* 30:23-36.

1993 *Deutsche Syntax - generativ: Vorstudien zur Theorie einer projektiven Grammatik*. Tübingen: Narr.

Hale, Ken, and Samuel Jay Keyser

1992 The syntactic character of thematic structure. In *Thematic Structure: Its Role in Grammar*, Iggy M. Roca (ed.), 107-144. Berlin: Foris.

1993 On argument structure and the lexical expression of syntactic relations. In *The View from Building 20: A Festschrift for Sylvain Bromberger*, Ken Hale, and Samuel Jay Keyser (ed.), 53-108. Cambridge, Massachusetts: MIT Press.

1999 Bound features, merge, and transitivity alternations. In *Papers from the UPenn/MIT Roundtable on the Lexicon*, Liina Pylkkänen, Heidi Harley, and Angeliek van Hout (eds.), 49-72. Cambridge, Massachusetts: MIT.

Halle, Morris

1953 The German conjugation. *Word* 9:45-53.

Hauser, Marc D., Noam Chomsky, and W. Tecumseh Fitch

2002 The faculty of language: What is it, who has it, and how did it evolve? *Science* 298:1569-1579.

Hirschfeld, Lawrence A., and Susan A. Gelman
1994 Toward a topography of mind: An introduction to domain specificity. In *Mapping the Mind*, Lawrence A. Hirschfeld, and Susan A. Gelman (eds.), 3-36. Cambridge: Cambridge University Press.
Hirschfeld, Lawrence A., and Susan A Gelman (eds.)
1994 *Mapping the Mind. Domain Specificity in Cognition and Culture*. Cambridge: Cambridge University Press.
Hoekstra, Teun
1984 *Transitivity*. Dordrecht: Foris.
1992 Aspect and theta theory. In *Thematic Structure: Its Role in Grammar*, Iggy M. Roca (ed.), 145-174. Berlin: Foris.
Hoekstra, Teun, and Rene Mulder
1990 Unergatives as copular verbs: locational and existential predication. *The Linguistic Review* 7:1-79.
Hole, Daniel
2002 Agentive *selbst* in German. In *Sinn und Bedeutung*, Graham Katz, Sabine Reinhard, and Philip Reuter (eds.), 133-150. Osnabrück: Gesellschaft für Semantik.
Hoof, Hanneke van
2004 Split topicalization. In *Syncom*, Martin Everaert, and Henk C. van Riemsdijk (eds.).
Hoop, Helen de, and Wim Kosmeijer
1995 Case and scrambling: D-Structure versus S-Structure. In *Studies in Comparative Germanic Syntax*, Hubert Haider, Susan Olsen, and Sten Vikner (eds.), 139-158. Dordrecht: Kluwer.
Horvath, Julia, and Tal Siloni
2005 Active lexicon: Adjectival passives. Paper presented at *GLOW*, Geneva.
Iatridou, Sabine
2000 The grammatical ingredients of counterfactuality. *Linguistic Inquiry* 31:231-270.
Jackendoff, Ray
1972 *Semantic Interpretation in Generative Grammar*. Cambridge, Massachusetts: MIT Press.
1983 *Semantics and Cognition*. Cambridge, Massachusetts: MIT Press.
1990 *Semantic Structures*. Cambridge, Mass.: MIT Press.
1990 On Larson's treatment of double object constructions. *Linguistic Inquiry* 21:93-129.
1996 The proper treatment of measuring out, telicity, and perhaps even quantification in English. *Natural Language and Linguistic Theory* 14:305-354.
2002 *Foundations of Language*. Oxford: Oxford University Press.

Kaye, Jonathan, Jean Lowenstamm, and Jean-Roger Vergnaud
1985 The internal structure of phonological elements: A theory of charm and government. *Phonology Yearbook* 2:305-328.

Kenesei, István
2001 Criteria for auxiliaries in Hungarian. In *Argument Structure in Hungarian*, István Kenesei (ed.), 79-111. Budapest: Akadémiai Kiadó.

Kiparsky, Paul
1966 Über den deutschen Akzent. *Studia Grammatica* 7:69-98.
1985 Morphology and grammatical relations. Ms., Stanford University.

Koster, Jan
1975 Dutch as an SOV language. *Linguistic Analysis* 1:111-136.

König, Ekkehard
1992 *The Meaning of Focus Particles: A Comparative Perspective.* London; New York: Routledge.

König, Ekkehard, and Peter Siemund
1996 Emphatische Reflexiva und Fokusstruktur: Zur Syntax und Bedeutung von "selbst". In *Sprache und Pragmatik*, Inger Rosengren (ed.), 1-42. Lund: Gleerup.
2000 Intensifiers as sources and targets of semantic change. In *Meaning Change - Meaning Variation*, Klaus von Heusinger, and Regine Eckardt (eds.), 97-110. Konstanz: Fachbereich Sprachwissenschaft.

Kratzer, Angelika
1991 Modality. In *Semantics: An International Handbook of Contemporary Research*, Dieter Wunderlich (ed.), 639-650. Berlin: de Gruyter.
1994 Adjectival passives. Ms. UMass, Amherst.
1996 Severing the external argument from its verb. In *Phrase Structure and the Lexicon*, Johan Rooryck, and Laurie Zaring (eds.), 109-137.
2000 Building statives. Ms., UMass., Amherst.

Larson, Richard
1988 On the double object construction. *Linguistic Inquiry* 19:335-391.
1990 Double objects revisited: Reply to Jackendoff. *Linguistic Inquiry* 21:589-632.

Leben, Will
1978 The representation of tone. In *Tone: A Linguistic Survey*, Victoria Fromkin (ed.), 177-219. New York: Academic Press.

Leslie, Alan
1994 ToMM, ToBy, and agency: Core architecture and domain specificity. In *Mapping the Mind. Domain Specificity and Culture*, Lawrence A. Hirschfeld, and Susan A. Gelman (eds.), 119-148. New York: Cambridge University Press.
Levin, Beth, and Malka Rappaport Hovav
1995 *Unaccusativity: At the Syntax-Lexical Semantics Interface*. Cambridge, Mass.: MIT Press.
1996 From lexical semantics to argument realization. Ms., Northwestern University and Bar Ilan University.
Lewis, David
1981 Mad pain and Martian pain. In *Readings in Philosophy of Psychology*, Ned Block (ed.). Cambridge, Mass.: Harvard University Press.
Lowenstamm, Jean
1996 CV as the only syllable type. In *Current Trends in Phonology*, Jaques Durand, and Bernard Laks (eds.), 419-441. Manchester: ESRI.
2003 À propos des gabarits. *Recherches Linguistiques de Vincennes* 32:7-30.
Löbel, Elisabeth
1990 D und Q als funktionale Kategorien in der Nominalphrase des Deutschen. *Linguistische Berichte* 127:232-264.
Lüdeling, Anke
2001 *Particle Verbs and Similar Constructions in German*. Stanford: CSLI Publications.
Marantz, Alec
1984 *On the Nature of Grammatical Relations*. Cambridge, Mass.: MIT Press.
Marelj, Marjana
2004 Middles and argument structure across languages. Ph.D. diss., LOT, Utrecht University.
May, Robert
1985 *Logical Form. Its Structure and Derivation*. Cambridge, Mass.: MIT Press.
Mc Carthy, John
1979 *Formal Problems in Semitic Phonology and Morphology*: Indiana University Linguistics Club. New York: Garland Press.
1981 A prosodic theory of nonconcatenative morphology. *Linguistic Inquiry* 12:373-418.

Meurers, Walt Detmar
1999 Raising spirits (and assigning them case). *Groninger Arbeiten zur Germanistischen Linguistik* 43:173-226.
Michotte, Albert E.
1963 *The Perception of Causality*. New York: Basic Books.
Miller, George A., and Philip. N. Johnson-Laird
1976 *Language and Perception*. Cambridge, Mass.: Harvard University Press.
Montgomery, Derek E.
1996 The role of action-initiation in young children's causal explanations of action. *Cognitive Development* 11:467-489.
Müller, Stefan
2002 *Complex Predicates: Verbal Complexes, Resultative Constructions, and Particle Verbs in German*. Stanford: CSLI Publications.
Naigles, Letitia R.
2002 Form is easy, meaning is hard: resolving a paradox in early child language. *Cognition* 86:157-199.
Nunberg, Geoffrey, Ivan A. Sag, and Tom Wasow
1994 Idioms. *Language* 70:491-538.
Opfer, John E.
2002 Identifying living and sentient kinds from dynamic information: the case of goal-directed versus aimless autonomous movement in conceptual change. *Cognition* 86:97-122.
Opfer, John E., and Susan A. Gelman
2001 Children's and adults' models for predicting teleological action: the development of a biology-based model. *Child Development* 72:1367-1381.
Parsons, Terence
1990 *Events in the Semantics of English: A Study in Sub-Atomic Semantics*. Cambridge, Mass.: MIT Press.
Perlmutter, David. M., and Paul Postal
1984 The 1-advancement exclusiveness law. In *Studies in Relational Grammar*, David M. Perlmutter, and Carol Rosen (eds.), 81-125. Chikago: University of Chikago Press.
Perner, Josef
1995 The many faces of belief: reflections on Fodor's and the child's theory of mind. *Cognition* 57:241-269.
Perner, Josef, and Graham Davies
1991 Understanding the mind as an active information processor: Do young children have a "copy theory of mind"?. *Cognition* 39:51-69.

Pesetsky, David
1995 *Zero Syntax: Experiencers and Cascades*. Cambridge, Mass.: MIT Press.
Pinker, Stephen
1984 *Language Learnability and Language Development*. Cambridge Mass., London: Harvard University Press.
1999 *Words and Rules: The Ingredients of Language*. New York: Basic Books.
Premack, David, and Ann J. Premack
1997 Infants attribute value ± to the goal-directed actions of self-propelled objects. *Journal of Cognitive Neuroscience* 9:848-856.
Pustejovsky, James
1995 *The Generative Lexicon*. Cambridge, Mass.: MIT Press.
Rapp, Irene
1997 *Partizipien und semantische Struktur: zu passivischen Konstruktionen mit dem 3. Status*. Tübingen: Stauffenberg.
2001 The present participle in German: Restrictions for its predicative use. Ms., Tübingen.
2002 Argumentstruktur und Erstgliedinterpretation bei deverbalen Derivaten - ein semantikbasierter Ansatz. *Folia Linguistica* 35 (3-4):243-284.
Reinhart, Tanya
1983 *Anaphora and semantic interpretation*. London: Croom Helm.
2000 The Theta System: Syntactic Realization of Verbal Concepts. Utrecht: OTS (OTS Working Papers in Linguistics).
2001 A synopsis of "The Theta System". Ms., University of Utrecht and Tel Aviv University.
2002 The Theta System - an overview. *Theoretical Linguistics* 28 (3): 229-290.
Reinhart, Tanya, and Eric Reuland
1993 Reflexivity. *Linguistic Inquiry* 24:657-720.
Reinhart, Tanya, and Tal Siloni
1999 Against the unaccusative analysis of reflexives. Ms. (appeared as Reinhart and Siloni 2004).
2004 Against the unaccusative analysis of reflexives. In *The Unaccusativity Puzzle: Explorations of the Syntax-Lexicon Interface,* Artemis Alexiadou, Elena Anagnostopoulou, and Martin Everaert (eds.), 159-180. Oxford: Oxford University Press.
2005 The Lexicon-Syntax Parameter: reflexivization and other arity operations. *Linguistic Inquiry* 36.

Riemsdijk, Henk C. van
1989 Movement and regeneration. In *Dialectal Variation and the Theory of Grammar*, Paolo Benincà (ed.), 105-136. Dordrecht: Foris.
1998a Trees and scions -- science and trees. In *Chomsky 70th Birthday Celebration Fest-Web-Page* (http://cognet.mit.edu/library/books/chomsky/celebration/essays/riemsdyk.html).
1998b Categorial feature magnetism: The endocentricity and distribution of projections. *Journal of Comparative Germanic Linguistics* 2:1-48.
2002 The unbearable lightness of GOing. The projection parameter as a pure parameter governing the distribution of elliptic motion verbs in Germanic. *Journal of Comparative Germanic Linguistics* 5:143-196.
2005 Graft is the logically missing case of merge. *Visnyk of the Kiev National Linguistic University* 7.

Ritter, Elizabeth, and Sara Thomas Rosen
1996 Strong and weak predicates: reducing the lexicon burden. *Linguistic Analysis* 26:29-62.

Roberts, Ian
1985 The representation of implicit and dethematized subjects. Ph.D. diss., USC.

Rosen, Carol
1984 The interface between semantic roles and initial grammatical relations. In *Studies in Relational Grammar*, Carol Rosen (ed.), 38-77. Chikago: University of Chikago Press.

Rumelhart, David
1975 Notes on a schema for stories. In *Representation and Understanding: Studies in Cognitive Science*, Daniel G. Bobrow, and Allen Collins (eds.), 211-236. New York: Academic Press.

Runner, Jeffrey
2002 *The accusative plus infinitive construction in English*. In *Syncom*, Martin Everart, and Henk C. van Riemsdijk (eds.).

Sæbø, Kjell Johan
2001 An analysis of the anticausative alternation. Ms., Oslo University.

Schiffer, Steven
1987 *Remnants of Meaning*. Cambridge, Massachusetts: MIT Press.

Schumacher, Helmut (ed.)
1986 *Verben in Feldern. Valenzwörterbuch zur Syntax und Semantik deutscher Verben*. Berlin, New York: Walter de Gruyter.

Ségéral, Philippe, and Tobias Scheer

1998 A generalized theory of ablaut: the case of Modern German strong verbs. In *Models of Inflection*, Albert Ortmann, Ray Fabri, and Teresa Parodi (eds.), 28-59. Tübingen: Niemeyer.

Shen, Yeshayahu

1985 The structure of action in the short narrative text, Ph.D. diss., Tel Aviv University.

Siemund, Peter

2000 *Intensifiers in English and German: A Comparison*. London ; New York: Routledge.

Siloni, Tal

1995 On participial relatives and complementizer D^0: A case study in Hebrew and French. *Natural Language and Linguistic Theory* 13:445-487.

2002 Active lexicon. *Theoretical Linguistics* 28:383-400.

Speas, Margaret

1990 *Phrase Structure in Natural Language*. Dordrecht: Kluwer.

Sperber, Dan

1994 The modularity of thought and the epidemiology of representations. In *Mapping the Mind.*, Lawrence A. Hirschfeld, and Susan A. Gelman (eds.), 39-67. Cambridge: Cambridge University Press.

Sportiche, Dominique

1998 *Partitions and Atoms of Clause Structure: Subjects, Agreement, Case, and Clitics*. London, New York: Routledge.

Stechow, Arnim von

1995 Lexical decomposition in syntax. In *Lexical Knowledge in the Organization of Language*, Urs Egli, Peter E. Pause, and Christoph Schwarze (eds.), 81-117. Amsterdam, Philadelphia: Benjamins.

Stiebels, Barbara, and Dieter Wunderlich

1994 Morphology feeds syntax: the case of particle verbs. *Linguistics* 32:913-968.

Stiebels, Barbara

1996 *Lexikalische Argumente und Adjunkte*. Berlin: Akademie Verlag.

Talmy, Leonard

1976 Semantic causative types. In *The Grammar of Causative Constructions*, Masayoshi Shibatani (ed.), 43-116. New York: Academic Press (Syntax and Semantics 6).

1988 Force dynamics in language and thought. *Cognitive Science* 12:49-100.

2000 *Toward a Cognitive Semantics*. Cambridge, Mass.: MIT Press.

Tenny, Carol
1994 *Aspectual Roles and the Syntax-Semantics Interface*. Dordrecht: Kluwer.

Toman, Jindrich
1986 A (word-) syntax for participles. *Linguistische Berichte* 105:367-408.

van Valin, Robert D. Jr.
1990 Semantic parameters of split intransitivity. *Language* 66:221-260.

Wasow, Thomas
1977 Transformations and the lexicon. In *Formal syntax*, Peter W. Culicover, Thomas Wasow, and Adrian Akmajian (eds.), 327-360. New York: Academic Press.

Wegner, Daniel M., and Thalia Wheatley
1999 Apparent mental causation. Sources of the experience of will. *American Psychologist* 54:480-492.

Wexler, Ken
2003 Lenneberg's dream: learning, normal language development and Specific Language Impairment. In *Language Competence Across Populations: Towards a Definition of Specific Language Impairment*, Yonata Levy, and Jeannette Schaeffer (eds.), 11-61. Mahwah, NJ: Erlbaum.

White, Peter. A., and Alan Milne
1997 Phenomenal causality: impressions of pulling in the visual perception of objects in motion. *American Journal of Psychology* 110 (4):573-602.

Williams, Edwin
1981 On the notions "lexically related" and "head of a word". *Linguistic Inquiry* 12:245-474.
1986 A reassignment of the functions of LF. *Linguistic Inquiry* 17:265-299.

Wiltschko, Martina
1998 On the syntax and semantics of (relative) pronouns and determiners. *Journal of Comparative Germanic Linguistics* 2:143-181.

Wunderlich, Dieter
1987 Partizipien im Deutschen. *Linguistische Berichte* 111:345-366.
1997 Cause and the structure of verbs. *Linguistic Inquiry* 28:27-68.

Wurmbrand, Susanne
2001 *Infinitives. Restructuring and Clause Structure*. Berlin: Mouton de Gruyter.

Index